FROM CRITICAL THINKING TO ARGUMENT
A Portable Guide

SYLVAN BARNET
Tufts University

HUGO BEDAU
Tufts University

Bedford/St. Martin's   BOSTON   ◆   NEW YORK

r Bedford/St. Martin's

ecutive Editor: Stephen A. Scipione
evelopmental Editor: John E. Sullivan III
ditorial Assistants: Sarah Whitesel, Amy Hurd
roduction Supervisor: Jessie Markland
roject Management: DeMasi Design and Publishing, Inc.
Marketing Manager: Rachel Falk
Cover Design: Donna Lee Dennison
Composition: Pine Tree Composition, Inc.
Printing and Binding: Haddon Craftsmen, an RR Donnelley & Sons
   Company

President: Joan E. Feinberg
Editorial Director: Denise B. Wydra
Director of Marketing: Karen Melton Soeltz
Director of Editing, Design, and Production: Marcia Cohen
Manager, Publishing Services: Emily Berleth

Library of Congress Control Number: 2004107371

0 9 8 7 6 5
f e d c b a

For information, write: Bedford/St. Martin's, 75 Arlington Street,
Boston, MA 02116   (617-399-4000)

ISBN: 0-312-43626-2
EAN: 978-0-312-43626-1

Acknowledgments

Alan M. Dershowitz. "Why Fear National ID Cards?" Originally
   published in the *New York Times*, September 13, 2001.
   Reprinted by permission of the author.

*Acknowledgments and copyrights are continued at the back of the book
on page 270, which constitutes an extension of the copyright page.*

Preface

This brief book is about reading other people's arguments and writing your own. In a moment we will be more specific, but first we want to mention our chief assumptions about the aims of a course that might use *From Critical Thinking to Argument: A Portable Guide.*

Probably most students and instructors agree that, as critical readers, students should be able to do the following:

- Summarize accurately an argument they have read
- Locate the thesis of an argument
- Locate the assumptions, stated and unstated
- Analyze and evaluate the strength of the evidence and the soundness of the reasoning offered in support of the thesis
- Analyze, evaluate, and account for discrepancies among various readings on a topic (for example, explain why certain facts are used, why others are ignored, or why two sources might interpret the same facts differently)

Probably students and instructors would also agree that, as thoughtful writers, students should be able to do the following:

- Imagine an audience and write effectively for it (for instance, by using the appropriate tone and providing the appropriate amount of detail)
- Present information in an orderly and coherent way

- Be aware of their own assumptions
- Locate sources and incorporate them into their own writing, not simply by quoting extensively or by paraphrasing but also by having digested material so that they can present it in their own words
- Properly document all borrowings — not merely quotations and paraphrases but also borrowed ideas
- Do all these things in the course of developing a thoughtful argument of their own

In writing an essay one is engaging in a serious effort to know what one's own ideas are and, having found them, to contribute to a multi-sided conversation. One is not setting out to trounce an opponent, and that is partly why such terms as marshaling evidence, attacking an opponent, and defending a thesis are misleading. True, in television talk shows we see people who have made up their minds and who are concerned only with pushing their own views and brushing aside all other views. But we learn by listening to others and also by listening to ourselves. We draft a response to something we have read, and in the very act of drafting we may find — if we think critically about the words we are putting down on paper — we are changing (perhaps slightly, perhaps radically) our own position. Even if we do not drastically change our views, we and our readers at least understand why we hold the views we do.

WHAT'S IN THIS BOOK

In Part One, the first four chapters deal with recognizing and evaluating assumptions — in both texts and images — as a way to start annotating, summarizing, and analyzing arguments. Among the topics discussed are critical thinking, analysis, summary and paraphrase, reasoning, and the uses of humor, emotion, and images. Chapter 4, "Visual Rhetoric: Images as Arguments," not only helps students to analyze advertisements but also offers suggestions about using visuals such as maps, graphs, tables, and pie charts in their own arguments.

Chapters 5 and 6 focus principally on writing. Students are expected to apply the critical thinking and reading skills they have learned to writing analytical and argumentative papers. We include two sample student papers as models. Chapter 7, on research, includes information on finding, evaluating, and documenting electronic and other sources and discusses ways to choose topics for research, take notes, avoid plagiarism, integrate quotations, and document sources. Two annotated student papers — one in MLA style and one in APA style — provide models for reading and reference.

Part Two, a kind of appendix, presents alternative perspectives on argument: the Toulmin model, logical reasoning (a detailed discussion of induction, deduction, and fallacies), and a brief description of Rogerian argument (named for the psychologist Carl Rogers).

Students and instructors will find additional material on argument at a companion Web site, **bedfordstmartins.com/barnetbedau**.

We trust that this book is brief enough and affordable enough to be assigned as an accompaniment to a separate anthology of readings or as a supplement to a selection of individual longer works that do not include necessary instruction in critical thinking and argument.

ACKNOWLEDGMENTS

We would like to thank the hundreds of instructors who have taught with *Current Issues and Enduring Questions,* the larger book from which this short book is adapted, through its many editions. Their comments have helped to improve the book you hold. At Bedford/St. Martin's, we thank Joan Feinberg, Denise Wydra, Karen Henry, John Sullivan, and Steve Scipione. They proposed this book and convinced us that it was well worth publishing.

CONTENTS

From Critical Thinking to Argument and Research

1

Critical Thinking

What is the hardest task in the world? To think. — RALPH
WALDO EMERSON

Although Emerson said simply "to think," he pretty clearly was using the
word *think* in the sense of *critical thinking.* By itself, *thinking* can mean
almost any sort of mental activity, from idle daydreaming ("During the
chemistry lecture I kept thinking about how I'd like to go camping") to
careful analysis ("I'm thinking about whether I can afford more than one
week — say two weeks — of camping in the Rockies," or even "I'm thinking about whether Emerson's comment is true").

In short, when we add the adjective *critical* to the noun *thinking,* we
pretty much eliminate reveries, just as we also eliminate snap judg-
ments. We are talking about searching for hidden assumptions, noticing
various facets, unraveling different strands, and evaluating what is most
significant. (The word *critical* comes from a Greek word, *krinein,* meaning "to separate," "to choose"; it implies conscious, deliberate inquiry.)

THINKING ABOUT DRIVERS' LICENSES
AND PHOTOGRAPHIC IDENTIFICATION

By way of illustration, let's think about a case that was in the news in
2003. When Sultaana Freeman, an American Muslim woman in Florida,
first applied for a driver's license, she refused on religious grounds to
unveil her face for the photograph that Florida requires. She was allowed to remain veiled for the photo, with only her eyes showing.
Probably in a response to the terrorist attacks of September 11, 2001,
she was informed in 2002 that her license would be revoked if she

"It sort of makes you stop and think, doesn't it."

refused to allow the Department of Motor Vehicles to photograph her face. She sued the state of Florida, saying that unveiling would violate her Islamic beliefs. "I'm fighting for the principle and the religious freedom of all people in the country," she said. "It's not about me."

Well, let's think about this—let's think critically, and to do this, we will use a simple aid that is equal to the best word processor, a pencil. Your own experience has already taught you that thinking is largely a matter of association; one thought leads to another, as when you jot down "peanut butter" on a shopping list and then add "bread," and "bread" somehow reminds you—you don't know why—that you also need paper napkins. As the humorist Finley Peter Dunne observed, philosophers and cows have the gift of meditation, but "others don't begin to think till they begin to talk or write." So what are some thoughts that come to mind when we begin to talk or write about this Florida case? Here is what we came up with in a few minutes, using a process called *clustering*. (We illustrate clustering again on p. 115.)

In the center of a sheet of paper, we jotted down a phrase summarizing the basic issue, and then we began jotting down what must be the

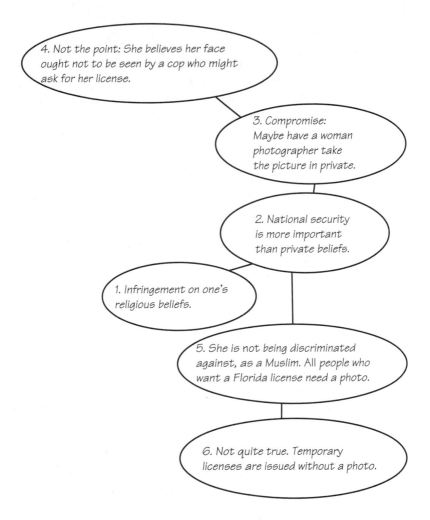

4. Not the point: She believes her face ought not to be seen by a cop who might ask for her license.

3. Compromise: Maybe have a woman photographer take the picture in private.

2. National security is more important than private beliefs.

1. Infringement on one's religious beliefs.

5. She is not being discriminated against, as a Muslim. All people who want a Florida license need a photo.

6. Not quite true. Temporary licenses are issued without a photo.

most obvious justification for demanding the picture—national safety. (We might equally well have begun with the most obvious justifications for refusing to be photographed—religious belief and perhaps privacy, to think of arguments that Sultaana Freeman—or, more likely, her lawyer—might set forth.) Then we let our minds work, and one thought led to another. Sometimes almost as soon as we jotted down an idea we saw that it wasn't very good, but we made considerable progress. In the illustration, we have added numbers to the ideas, simply so that you can see how our

4. Not the point: She believes her face ought not to be seen by a cop who might ask for her license.

3. Compromise: Maybe have a woman photographer take the picture in private.

7. Maybe infringement. But the gov't sometimes prohibits beliefs it considers harmful to society. It does not permit the use of drugs in religious ceremonies, or sacrifice.

2. National security is more important than private beliefs.

1. Infringement on one's religious beliefs.

9. But those things are harmful actions that the believer engages in. In the case at issue, the believer is not engaging in harmful action. It's the gov't that is doing the acting — taking a picture.

5. She is not being discriminated against, as a Muslim. All people who want a Florida license need a photo.

6. Not quite true. Temporary licenses are issued without a photo.

8. Some states do not require pictures on licenses.

10. Florida itself issues temporary licenses without photos.

minds worked, which is to say how we jumped around. Notice, for instance, that our fifth point—our fifth idea—is connected to our second point. When we were rereading our first four jottings, the fifth idea—that she is not being discriminated against as a Muslim—came to mind, and we saw that it should be linked with the second point. Our sixth point—a modification of our fifth, occurred to us even before we finished writing the fifth. The sixth point, that temporary licenses in Florida are issued without photographs, prompted us to start thinking more vigorously about the arguments that Ms. Freeman, or her lawyer, might offer.

A very brief digression: A legal case is pretty much a matter of guilty or not guilty, right or wrong, yes or no. Of course in some trials a defendant can be found guilty of certain charges and innocent of others, but, again, it is usually an either/or situation: The prosecution wins, or the defense wins. But in many other aspects of life, there is room for compromise, and it may well be that *both* sides win—by seeing what ground they share and by developing additional common ground. We go into this topic at greater length on page 264, where we discuss Rogerian argument (named for Carl Rogers, a psychotherapist). Now back to the *State of Florida v. Sultaana Freeman,* where we began by trying to list arguments on one side versus arguments on the other.

Plaintiff in Sultaana Freeman v. State of Florida, Department of Highway Safety and Motor Vehicles. *(Peter Cosgrove/(c) AP/Worldwide Photos.)*

Back to our topic: After making our seventh note, which goes directly back to the central issue (hence we connected it with a line) and which turned out to be an argument that the government rather than the plaintiff might make, we decided to keep thinking about government positions, and wrote the eighth note—that some states do not require pictures on drivers' licenses. The ninth note—that the government is prohibiting a belief, not a harmful action—is a sort of refutation of our seventh note, so we connected it to the seventh. Again, if you think with a pencil and a sheet of paper and let your mind make associations, you will find, perhaps to your surprise, that you have plenty of interesting ideas. Doubtless you will also have some not-so-interesting ones. We confess that we have slightly edited our notes; originally they included two points that we are ashamed we thought of:

- "What is she complaining about? In some strict Islamic countries they don't even let women drive, period."
- "Being deprived of a license isn't a big deal. She can take the bus."

It will take only a moment of reflection to decide that these thoughts can scarcely be offered as serious arguments: What people do in strict Islamic countries has nothing to do with what we should do in ours, and that bus service is available is utterly irrelevant to the issue of whether this woman's rights are being infringed. Still, if a fear of making fools of ourselves had prevented us from jotting down ideas, we would not have jotted down any decent ideas, and the page would not have gotten written.

> *A Rule for Writers:* One good way to start writing an
> essay is to start generating ideas—and at this point
> don't worry that some of them may be nonsense. Just
> get ideas down on paper, and evaluate them later.

The outcome of the driver's license photo case? Judge Janet C. Thorpe ruled against the plaintiff, explaining that "The State has always had a compelling interest in promoting public safety. That interest is served by having the means to accurately and swiftly determine identities in given circumstances." (You can read Judge Thorpe's entire decision online—sixteen highly readable double-spaced pages—by going to *www.findlaw.com*, clicking on *U.S. Federal Law: Circuit Court Opinions,* clicking on *Sultaana Freeman,* and then clicking on *Sultaana Lakiana Kyke Freeman v. State of Florida.*)

Topics for Critical Thinking and Writing

1. Think about Judge Thorpe's comment, quoted in the preceding paragraph. Even if we agree that a photograph establishes identity—itself a debatable point—one might raise a question: Given the fact that Florida has not passed a law requiring a photo ID, why should it say that the driver of a vehicle must provide a photo ID? Isn't a driver's license a mere certification of permission to drive?

2. In her decision, Judge Thorpe wrote the following as part of her explanation for her decision:

   > Although the Court acknowledges that Plaintiff herself most likely poses no threat to national security, there likely are people who would be willing to use a ruling permitting the wearing of fullface cloaks in driver's license photos by pretending to ascribe to religious beliefs in order to carry out activities that would threaten lives.

   Is the judge in effect saying that we should infringe on Sultaana Freeman's religious beliefs because someone else might do something wicked?

THINKING ABOUT ANOTHER ISSUE CONCERNING DRIVERS' LICENSES: IMAGINATION, ANALYSIS, EVALUATION

Let's think critically about a law passed in West Virginia in 1989. The law provides that although students may drop out of school at the age of sixteen, no dropout younger than eighteen can hold a driver's license. (Eighteen states now have comparable laws.)

What ought we to think of such a law?

- Is it fair?
- What is its purpose?
- Is it likely to accomplish its purpose?
- Might it unintentionally do some harm?
- If so, can we weigh the potential harm against the potential good?

Suppose you had been a member of the West Virginia state legislature in 1989: How would you have voted?

In thinking critically about a topic, we try to see it from all sides before we come to our conclusion. We conduct an argument with ourselves, advancing and then questioning opinions:

- What can be said *for* the proposition, and
- What can be said *against* it?

Our first reaction may be quite uncritical, quite unthinking: "What a good idea!" or "That's outrageous!" But critical thinking requires us to reflect further, trying to support our position *and also* trying to see the other side. One can almost say that the heart of critical thinking is a *willingness to face objections to one's own beliefs,* a willingness to adopt a skeptical attitude not only toward authority and toward views opposed to our own but also toward common sense—that is, toward the views that seem obviously right to us. If we assume we have a monopoly on the truth and we dismiss as bigots those who oppose us, or if we say our opponents are acting merely out of self-interest and we do not in fact analyze their views, we are being critical but we are not engaged in critical thinking.

> *A Rule for Writers:* Early in the process of jotting
> down your ideas on a topic, stop to ask yourself,
> "What might reasonably be offered as an objection to
> my view?"

Critical thinking requires us to use our *imagination,* seeing things from perspectives other than our own and envisioning the likely consequences of our position. (This sort of imaginative thinking—grasping a perspective other than our own and considering the possible consequences of positions—is, as we have said, very different from daydreaming, an activity of unchecked fantasy.)

Thinking critically involves, along with imagination (so that we can see our own beliefs from another point of view), a twofold activity:

analysis, finding the parts of the problem and then separating them, trying to see how things fit together; and

evaluation, judging the merit of our claims and assumptions and the weight of the evidence in their favor.

If we engage in imaginative, analytic, and evaluative thought, we will have second and third ideas; almost to our surprise we may find ourselves adopting a position that we initially couldn't imagine we would hold. As we think about the West Virginia law, we might find ourselves coming up with a fairly wide variety of ideas, each triggered by the preceding idea but not necessarily carrying it a step further. For instance, we may think *X* and then immediately think, "No, that's not quite right. In fact, come to think of it, the opposite of *X* is probably true." We haven't carried *X* further, but we have progressed in our thinking.

WRITING AS A WAY OF THINKING

"To learn to write," Robert Frost said, "is to learn to have ideas." But how do we get ideas? One way, practiced by the ancient Greeks and Romans and still regarded as among the best ways, is to consider what the ancients called **topics,** from the Greek word *topos,* meaning "place," as in our word *topography* (a description or representation of a place). For the ancients, certain topics, put into the form of questions, were in effect places where one went to find ideas. Among the classical *topics* were

- Definition (What is it?);
- Comparison (What is it like or unlike?);
- Relationship (What caused it, and what will it cause?);
- Testimony (What is said about it, for instance by experts?).

All of these topics or idea-generating places will be treated in detail in later chapters, but here we can touch briefly on a few of them.

If we are talking about the West Virginia law, it's true that we won't get ideas by asking questions concerning definition, but we may generate ideas by asking ourselves if this law is like any other (and, if so, how well did the corresponding law work) and by asking what caused this law and what it may in turn cause. Similarly, if we go to the topic of testimony, we may want to find out what some students, teachers, parents, police officers, and lawmakers have to say.

If you think you are at a loss for ideas when confronted with an issue (and when confronted with an assignment to write about it), you probably will find ideas coming to you if you turn to the relevant classical topics and begin jotting down your responses. (In classical terminology, you are engaged in the process of **invention,** from the Latin *invenire,* "to come upon," "to find.") Seeing your ideas on paper—even in the briefest form—will help bring other ideas to mind and will also help you to evaluate them. For instance, after jotting down ideas as they come and responses to them,

1. You might go on to organize them into two lists, pro and con;
2. Next, you might delete ideas that, when you come to think about them, strike you as simply wrong or irrelevant; and
3. Then you might develop those ideas that strike you as pretty good.

You probably won't know where you stand until you have gone through some such process. It would be nice if we could make a quick decision, immediately justify it with three excellent reasons, and then give three further reasons showing why the opposing view is inadequate. In fact, however, we almost never can come to a reasoned decision without a good deal of preliminary thinking.

Consider again the West Virginia law. Here is a kind of inner dialogue that you might engage in as you think critically about it:

> The purpose is to give students an incentive to stay in school by making them pay a price if they choose to drop out.
>
> Adolescents will get the message that education really is important.
>
> But come to think of it, *will* they? Maybe they will see this as just another example of adults bullying young people.
>
> According to a newspaper article, the dropout rate in West Virginia decreased by 30 percent in the year after the bill was passed.
>
> Well, that sounds good, but is there any reason to think that kids who are pressured into staying really learn anything? The *assumption* behind the bill is that if would-be dropouts stay in school, they—and society—will gain. But is the assumption sound? Maybe such students will become resentful, will not learn anything, and may even be so disruptive that they will interfere with the learning of other students.

Notice how part of the job is *analytic*, recognizing the elements or complexities of the whole, and part is *evaluative*, judging the adequacy of all of these ideas, one by one. Both tasks require *imagination*.

So far we have jotted down a few thoughts and then immediately given some second thoughts contrary to the first. Of course, the counterthoughts might not immediately come to mind. For instance, they might not occur until we reread the jottings, or try to explain the law to a friend, or until we sit down and begin drafting an essay aimed at supporting or undermining the law. Most likely, in fact, some good ideas won't occur until a second or third or fourth draft.

Here are some further thoughts on the West Virginia law. We list them more or less as they arose and as we typed them into a word processor—not sorted out neatly into two groups, pro and con, or evaluated as you would want to do in further critical thinking of your own. And of course, a later step would be to organize the material into some useful pattern. As you read, you might jot down your own responses in the margin.

Education is not optional, something left for the individual to take or not to take—like going to a concert, jogging, getting annual health checkups, or getting eight hours of sleep each night. Society has determined that it is for the public good that citizens have a substantial education, so we require education up to a certain age.

Come to think about it, maybe the criterion of age doesn't make much sense. If we want an educated citizenry, it would make more sense to require people to attend school until they demonstrated competence in certain matters rather than until they reached a certain age. Exceptions, of course, would be made for mentally retarded persons and perhaps for certain other groups.

What is needed is not legal pressure to keep teenagers in school but schools that hold the interest of teenagers.

A sixteen-year-old usually is not mature enough to make a decision of this importance.

Still, a sixteen-year-old who finds school unsatisfying and who therefore drops out may become a perfectly useful citizen.

Denying a sixteen-year-old a driver's license may work in West Virginia, but it would scarcely work in a state with great urban areas, where most high school students rely on public transportation.

We earn a driver's license by demonstrating certain skills. The state has no right to take away such a license unless we have demonstrated that we are unsafe drivers.

To prevent a person of sixteen from having a driver's license prevents that person from holding certain kinds of jobs, and that's unfair.

A law of this sort deceives adults into thinking that they have really done something constructive for teen-age education, but it may work against improving the schools. If we are really serious about educating youngsters, we have to examine the curriculum and the quality of our teachers.

Doubtless there is much that we haven't said, on both sides, but we hope you will agree that the issue deserves thought. In fact, eighteen states now revoke the driver's license of a teenager who drops out of school, and four of these states go even further and revoke the licenses of students whose academic work does not reach a given standard. On the other hand, Louisiana, which for a while had a law like West Virginia's, dropped it in 1997.

If you were a member of a state legislature voting on this proposal, you would *have* to think about the issue. But just as a thought experiment, try to put into writing your tentative views.

One other point about this issue. If you had to think about the matter *today*, you might also want to know whether the West Virginia legislation of 1989 is considered a success and on what basis. That is, you would want to get answers to such questions as the following:

- What sort of evidence tends to support the law or tends to suggest that the law is a poor idea?
- Did the reduction in the dropout rate continue, or did the reduction occur only in the first year following the passage of the law?
- If indeed students who wanted to drop out did not, was their presence in school a good thing, both for them and for their classmates?
- Have some people emerged as authorities on this topic? What makes them authorities, and what do they have to say?
- Has the constitutionality of the bill been tested? With what results?

Some of these questions require you to do **research** on the topic. The questions raise issues of fact, and some relevant evidence probably is available. If you are to arrive at a conclusion in which you can have confidence, you will have to do some research to find out what the facts are.

Even without doing any research, however, you might want to look over the ideas, pro and con, perhaps adding some totally new thoughts or perhaps modifying or even rejecting (for reasons that you can specify) some of those already given. If you do think a bit further about this

A CHECKLIST FOR CRITICAL THINKING

Attitudes

☐ Does my thinking show imaginative open-mindedness and intellectual curiosity?

  ☐ Am I willing to examine my assumptions?

  ☐ Am I willing to entertain new ideas—both those that I encounter while reading and those that come to mind while writing?

  ☐ Am I willing to exert myself—for instance, to do research—to acquire information and to evaluate evidence?

Skills

☐ Can I summarize an argument accurately?

☐ Can I evaluate assumptions, evidence, and inferences?

☐ Can I present my ideas effectively—for instance, by organizing and by writing in a manner appropriate to my imagined audience?

issue, and we hope that you will, notice an interesting point about *your own* thinking: It probably is not *linear* (moving in a straight line from A to B to C) but *recursive*, moving from A to C and back to B or starting over at C and then back to A and B. By zigging and zagging almost despite yourself, you'll get to a conclusion that may finally seem correct. In retrospect it seems obvious; *now* you can chart a nice line from A to B to C—but that was not at all evident to you at the start.

A SHORT ESSAY ILLUSTRATING CRITICAL THINKING

When we read an essay, we expect the writer to have thought things through, at least to a considerable degree. We do not want to read every false start, every fuzzy thought, every ill-organized paragraph that the writer knocked off. Yes, writers make false starts, put down fuzzy thoughts, write ill-organized paragraphs, but then they revise and revise yet again, and they end by giving us a readable essay that seems effortlessly written. Still—and here we get to our real point—in argumentative essays, writers need to show their readers that they have made some effort; they need to show us *how* they got to their final (for the moment) views. It is not enough for the writer to say, "I believe *X*"; rather, the writer must in effect say, "I believe *X*—and I hope you will believe it also—because *Y* and *Z*, though attractive, just don't stand up to inquiry as well as *X* does. *Y* is superficially plausible, but . . . , and *Z*, which is an attractive alternative to *Y*, nevertheless fails because. . . ."

Notice in the following short essay that Alan Dershowitz frequently brings up objections to his own position; i.e., he shows his awareness of other views, and then tries to show why he thinks his position is preferable. In the very first paragraph he speaks of "a tradeoff between privacy and convenience." That is, he sees that the course he is advocating ("convenience") has its cost, its downside. And in the third paragraph he says, "As a civil libertarian, I am instinctively skeptical of such tradeoffs. But. . . ." In the fourth paragraph he says, "I can hear the objections." He may not convince you, but we think you will probably grant that he does a pretty good job (though maybe not a perfect job) of scrutinizing his own thoughts.

ALAN DERSHOWITZ

Alan Dershowitz, educated at Brooklyn College and Yale Law School, is a professor at the Harvard Law School. Among his books are Why Terrorism Works *(2002) and* Shouting Fire: Civil Liberties in a Turbulent Era *(2002). The following essay was published in the* New York Times *on September 13, 2001—two days after the destruction of the Twin Towers at the World Trade Center.*

Why Fear National ID Cards?

At many bridges and tunnels across the country, drivers avoid long delays at the toll booths with an unobtrusive device that fits on a car's dashboard. Instead of fumbling for change, they drive right through; the device sends a radio signal that records their passage. They are billed later. It's a tradeoff between privacy and convenience: the toll-takers know more about you—when you entered and left Manhattan for instance—but you save time and money.

An optional national identity card could be used in a similar way, offering a similar kind of tradeoff: a little less anonymity for a lot more security. Anyone who had the card could be allowed to pass through airports or building security more expeditiously, and anyone who opted out could be examined much more closely.

As a civil libertarian, I am instinctively skeptical of such tradeoffs. But I support a national identity card with a chip that can match the holder's fingerprint. It could be an effective tool for preventing terrorism, reducing the need for other law-enforcement mechanisms—especially racial and ethnic profiling—that pose even greater dangers to civil liberties.

I can hear the objections: What about the specter of Big Brother? What about fears of identity cards leading to more intrusive measures? (The National Rifle Association, for example, worries that a government that registered people might also decide to register guns.) What about fears that such cards would lead to increased deportation of illegal immigrants?

First, we already require photo IDs for many activities, including   5 flying, driving, drinking and check-cashing. And fingerprints differ from photographs only in that they are harder to fake. The vast majority of Americans routinely carry photo IDs in their wallets and pocketbooks. These IDs are issued by state motor vehicle bureaus and other public and private entities. A national card would be uniform and difficult to forge or alter. It would reduce the likelihood that someone could, intentionally or not, get lost in the cracks of multiple bureaucracies.

The fear of an intrusive government can be addressed by setting criteria for any official who demands to see the card. Even without a national card, people are always being asked to show identification. The existence of a national card need not change the rules about when ID can properly be demanded. It is true that the card would facilitate the deportation of illegal immigrants. But President Bush has proposed giving legal status to many of the illegal immigrants now in this country. And legal immigrants would actually benefit from a national ID card that could demonstrate their status to government officials.

Finally, there is the question of the right to anonymity. I don't believe we can afford to recognize such a right in this age of terrorism. No such right is hinted at in the Constitution. And though the Supreme Court has identified a right to privacy, privacy and anonymity are not the same. American taxpayers, voters and drivers long ago gave up any right of anonymity without loss of our right to engage in lawful conduct within zones of privacy. Rights are a function of experience, and our recent experiences teach that it is far too easy to be anonymous—even to create a false identity—in this large and decentralized country. A national ID card would not prevent all threats of terrorism, but it would make it more difficult for potential terrorists to hide in open view, as many of the Sept. 11 hijackers apparently managed to do.

A national ID card could actually enhance civil liberties by reducing the need for racial and ethnic stereotyping. There would be no excuse for hassling someone merely because he belongs to a particular racial or ethnic group if he presented a card that matched his print and that permitted his name to be checked instantly against the kind of computerized criminal-history retrieval systems that are already in use. (If there is too much personal information in the system, or if the information is being used improperly, that is a separate issue. The only information the card need contain is name, address, photo and print.)

From a civil liberties perspective, I prefer a system that takes a little bit of freedom from all to one that takes a great deal of freedom and dignity from the few—especially since those few are usually from a racially or ethnically disfavored group. A national ID card would be much more effective in preventing terrorism than profiling millions of men simply because of their appearance.

Topics for Critical Thinking and Writing

1. Might one say that Dershowitz doesn't recognize that an ID might serve not simply to *identify* but to *authorize?* That is, some people fear that if the government issues national identity cards, the government would soon be regulating whether or not we can buy knives or fertilizer or any other substance that the government considers dangerous, whether or not we can take flying lessons, and whether or not we can travel to certain destinations. Does Dershowitz take account of this objection—or is the objection so far-fetched that there is no reason for him to face it?

2. To the best of your knowledge, would an ID card such as Dershowitz advocates have helped to avert the disaster of September 11, 2001? If not, does his argument lose all force? Explain.

3. Dershowitz admits (para. 4) that one might argue against a national identity card on the grounds that it raises "the specter of Big Brother." What is Dershowitz's reply to this objection, and how convincing do you find it? By the way, where does the expression "Big Brother" come from?

4. Dershowitz mentions the "right to anonymity" (para. 7). Do we really have such a right? If so, can other morally important considerations conflict with this right? If they can, which should prevail and why? Explain in an essay of 500 words.

5. Dershowitz says that the kind of national ID card he favors would have on it only the bearer's "name, address, photo and [finger] print" (para. 8). Do you think the bearer's social security card number should be on it as well? Explain in an essay of 100 words.

6. Dershowitz's essay was first published as an op-ed piece in a newspaper. Write a letter to the editor explaining why you disagree with some or all

of his points, or explaining why, although you accept some or all of his points, you think he has neglected others.

EXAMINING ASSUMPTIONS

In Chapter 3 we will discuss **assumptions** in some detail, but here we want to introduce the topic by emphasizing the importance of *identifying* and *examining* assumptions—the assumptions you will encounter in the writings of others and the assumptions you will rely on in your own essays.

With this in mind, let's return to considering the West Virginia driver's license law. What assumptions did the legislature make in enacting this statute? We earlier mentioned one such assumption: If the law helped to keep teenagers from dropping out of school, then that was a good thing for them and for society in general. For all we know, the advocates of this legislation may have made this assumption *explicit* in the course of their argument in favor of the statute. Perhaps they left this assumption *tacit*, believing that the point was obvious and that everyone shared this assumption. The assumption may be obvious, but it was not universally shared; the many teenagers who wanted to drop out of school at sixteen and keep their drivers' licenses did not share it. Another assumption that the advocates of this legislation may have made is this: The provisions of this statute are the most efficient way to keep teenagers in high school. Defending such an assumption is no easy task because it requires identifying other possible legislative strategies and evaluating their merits against those of the proposed legislation.

Consider now two of the assumptions involved in the Sultaana Freeman case. Thanks to the "clustering" exercise (p. 4), these and other assumptions are already on display. Perhaps the most important and fundamental assumption Ms. Freeman made is this: Where private religious beliefs conflict with duly enacted laws, the former should prevail—an assumption widely shared in our society and by no means unique to Muslim women seeking a driver's license in Florida after September 11, 2001. Freeman's opponents probably assumed a very different but equally fundamental proposition: Private religious practices and beliefs must yield to the demands of national security. Obviously these two assumptions were on a collision course and neither side could hope to prevail so long as the key assumptions of the other side were ignored.

Finally, let us examine Alan Dershowitz's essay defending a national ID card with an eye to identifying some of the assumptions made in the course of his argument. In his second paragraph, he asserts that "a lot more security" than we have at present is available to us through a national ID card. This assertion verges on being only an assumption, since it really isn't argued for. In paragraph 3, Dershowitz assumes that the invasion of privacy such a card would allow would make unnecessary "other law enforcement mechanisms" that are far more invasive (though he gives no examples). Finally, he assumes that it is better to take "a little bit of freedom from all" rather than "a great deal of freedom and dignity from the few."

Remember, also, to ask these questions (except the last two) when you are reading your own drafts. And remember to ask yourself why some people may *not* grant your assumptions.

A CHECKLIST FOR EXAMINING ASSUMPTIONS

- ☐ What assumptions does the writer's argument presuppose?
- ☐ Are these assumptions explicit or implicit?
- ☐ Are these assumptions important to the author's argument or only incidental?
- ☐ Does the author give any evidence of being aware of the hidden assumptions in her or his argument?
- ☐ Would a critic be likely to share these assumptions, or are they exactly what a critic would challenge?
- ☐ What sort of evidence would be relevant to supporting or rejecting these assumptions?
- ☐ Are you willing to grant the author's assumptions?
  - ☐ If not, why not?

Exercises

1. Think further about the 1989 West Virginia law that prohibits high school dropouts younger than eighteen from holding a driver's license. Jot down pros and cons, and then write a balanced dialogue between two imagined speakers who hold opposing views on the merits of the law. You'll doubtless have to revise your dialogue several times, and in revising your drafts you will find that further ideas come to you. Present *both* sides as strongly as possible. (You may want to give the two speakers distinct characters; for instance, one may be a student who has dropped out and the other a concerned teacher, or one a parent—who perhaps argues that he or she needs the youngster to work full-time driving a delivery truck—and one a legislator. But do not write as if the speakers must present the arguments they might be expected to hold. A student might argue *for* the law, and a teacher *against* it.)

2. Take one of the following topics and jot down all the pro and con arguments you can think of in, say, ten minutes. Then, at least an hour or two later, return to your jottings and see whether you can add to them. Finally, as in Exercise 1, write a balanced dialogue, presenting each idea as strongly as possible. (If none of these topics interests you, talk with your instructor about the possibility of choosing a topic of your own.) Suggested topics:

   a. Colleges should not award athletic scholarships.
   b. Bicyclists and motorcyclists should be required by law to wear helmets.
   c. High school teachers should have the right to search students for drugs on school grounds.
   d. Smoking should be prohibited in all parts of all college buildings.
   e. College administrators should take no punitive action against students who use racist language or language that offends any minority.
   f. Students should have the right to drop out of school at any age.
   g. In rape trials, the names of the alleged victims should not be released to the public.
   h. The United States ought to require a national identity card.

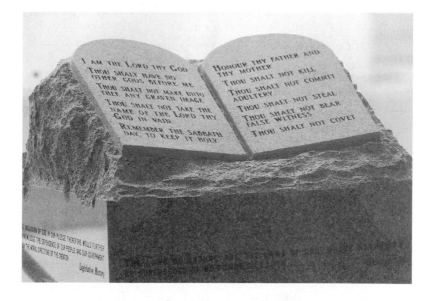

3. On the evening of July 31, 2001, after court employees had left the Alabama Judicial Building in Montgomery, Chief Justice Roy S. Moore of the Alabama Supreme Court and his supporters installed in the lobby of the courthouse a four-foot high, 5,200 pound granite block bearing

the text of the Ten Commandments. Moore had not discussed his plan with other justices. Civil liberties groups complained that the monument was an unconstitutional attempt to endorse a specific religion (the First Amendment to the U.S. Constitution says, "Congress shall make no law respecting an establishment of religion"), and in 2002 a federal judge ordered Moore to remove the monument. He refused, saying that the monument is a symbol of the roots of American law. He also said, "To do my duty, I must obey God." His supporters have offered several arguments on his behalf, notably that (a) the Founding Fathers often spoke of God; (b) every courtroom has a Bible to swear in witnesses and jurors; (c) the U.S. Supreme Court has a frieze of lawgivers, including Moses with the Ten Commandments, Hammurabi, Confucius, and Muhammad. In August 2003, Moore was suspended from his position on the court, and the monument was removed from view. Your views?

2

Critical Reading: Getting Started

Some books are to be tasted, others to be chewed, and some few to be chewed and digested. — FRANCIS BACON

ACTIVE READING

In the passage that we quote at the top of this page, Bacon makes at least two good points. One is that books are of varying worth; the second is that a taste of some books may be enough.

But even a book (or an essay) that you will chew and digest is one that you first may want to taste. How can you get a taste—that is, how can you get some sense of a piece of writing *before* you sit down to read it carefully?

Previewing

Even before you read a work, you may have some ideas about it, perhaps because you already know something about the **author.** You know, for example, that a work by Martin Luther King Jr. will probably deal with civil rights. You know, too, that it will be serious and eloquent. On the other hand, if you pick up an essay by Woody Allen, you will probably expect it to be amusing. It may be serious—Allen has written earnestly about many topics, especially those concerned with the media—but it's your hunch that the essay will be at least somewhat entertaining and probably will not be terribly difficult to understand. In short, a reader who has some knowledge of the author probably has some idea of what the writing will be like, and so the reader reads it in a certain mood. Admittedly, most of the authors represented in this book are not widely known, but we give biographical notes that may provide you with some sense of what to expect.

The **place of publication** may also tell you something about the essay. For instance, the *National Review* is a conservative journal. If you notice that an essay on affirmative action was published in the *National Review*, you are probably safe in tentatively assuming that the essay will not endorse affirmative action. On the other hand, *Ms. Magazine* is a liberal publication, and an essay on affirmative action published in *Ms.* will probably be an endorsement.

The **title** of an essay, too, may give you an idea of what to expect. Of course, a title may announce only the subject and not the author's thesis or point of view ("On Gun Control," "Should Drugs Be Legal?"), but fairly often it will indicate the thesis too, as in "Give Children the Vote" and "Gay Marriages: Make Them Legal." Knowing more or less what to expect, you can probably take in some of the major points even on a quick reading.

Skimming: Finding the Thesis

Although most of the material in this book is too closely argued to be fully understood by merely skimming, still, skimming can tell you a good deal. Read the first paragraph of an essay carefully because it may announce the author's **thesis** (chief point, major claim), and it may give you some sense of how the argument for that thesis will be conducted. (What we call the *thesis* can also be called the *main idea*, the *point*, or even the *argument*, but in this book we use *argument* to refer not only to the thesis statement but also to the entire development of the thesis in the essay.) Run your eye over the rest, looking for key expressions that indicate the author's conclusions, such as "It follows, then, that . . ." Passages of this sort often occur as the first or last sentence in a paragraph. And of course, pay attention to any headings within the text. Finally, pay special attention to the last paragraph because it probably will offer a summary and a brief restatement of the writer's thesis.

Having skimmed the work, you probably know the author's thesis, and you may detect the author's methods—for instance, whether the author supports the thesis chiefly by personal experience, by statistics, or by ridiculing the opposition. You also have a clear idea of the length and some idea of the difficulty of the piece. You know, then, whether you can read it carefully now before dinner or whether you had better put off a careful reading until you have more time.

Reading with a Pencil: Underlining, Highlighting, Annotating

Once you have a general idea of the work—not only an idea of its topic and thesis but also a sense of the way in which the thesis is argued—you can then go back and start reading it carefully.

As you read, **underline** or **highlight** key passages, and make **annotations** in the margins (but not in library books, please). Because you are reading actively, or interacting with the text, you will not simply let your eye rove across the page. You will underline or highlight what seem to be the chief points, so that later when you review the essay you can easily locate the main passages. But don't overdo a good thing. If you find yourself underlining or highlighting most of a page, you are probably not thinking carefully enough about what the key points are. Similarly, your marginal annotations should be brief and selective. Probably they will consist of hints or clues, things like "really?," "doesn't follow," "!!!," "???," "good," "compare with Jones," and "check this." In short, in a paragraph you might underline or highlight a key definition, and in the margin you might write "good" or, on the other hand, "?," if you think the definition is fuzzy or wrong. You are interacting with the text and laying the groundwork for eventually writing your own essay on what you have read.

What you annotate will depend largely on your **purpose.** If you are reading an essay in order to see the ways in which the writer organizes an argument, you will annotate one sort of thing. If you are reading in order to challenge the thesis, you will annotate other things. Here is a passage from an essay entitled "On Racist Speech," with a student's rather skeptical, even aggressive annotations. But notice that at least one of the annotations—"Definition of 'fighting words'"—apparently was made chiefly in order to remind the reader of where an important term appears in the essay. The essay is by Charles R. Lawrence III, a professor of law at Stanford University. It originally appeared in the *Chronicle of Higher Education* (October 25, 1989), a publication read chiefly by college and university faculty members and administrators.

Example of such a policy?
University officials who have formulated <u>policies</u> to respond to incidents of racial harassment have been characterized in the press as "thought police," but such policies generally do nothing more than impose sanctions against intentional face-to-face insults. When <u>racist speech takes</u> the form of <u>face-to-face insults</u>, *What about* catcalls, or other assaultive speech aimed at an individual or *sexist speech?* small group of persons, it falls directly within the "<u>fighting</u>

?

Example? words" exception to First Amendment protection. The Supreme Definition of "fighting words" Court has held that <u>words which "by their very utterance inflict injury</u> or tend to incite an immediate breach of the peace" are not protected by the First Amendment.

    If the purpose of the First Amendment is to foster the greatest amount of speech, racial insults disserve that purpose. Assaultive racist speech functions as a preemptive strike. The invective is experienced as a blow, not as a proffered idea, and Really? Probably depends on the individual. once the blow is struck, it is unlikely that a dialogue will follow. Racial insults are particularly undeserving of First Amendment Why must speech always seek "to discover truth"? protection because the perpetrator's <u>intention is not to discover truth</u> or initiate dialogue but to injure the victim. <u>In most situa-</u> How does he know? tions, members of minority groups realize that they are likely to lose if they respond to epithets by fighting and are forced to remain silent and submissive.

"This; Therefore, That"

    To arrive at a coherent thought or a coherent series of thoughts that will lead to a reasonable conclusion, a writer has to go through a good deal of preliminary effort. And if the writer is to convince the reader that the conclusion is sound, the reasoning that led to the conclusion must be set forth in detail, with a good deal of "This; therefore, that"; If this, then that"; and "It might be objected at this point that. . . ." The arguments in this book require more comment than President Calvin Coolidge provided when his wife, who hadn't been able to go to church on a Sunday, asked him what the preacher's sermon was about. "Sin," he said. His wife persisted: "What did the preacher say about it?" Coolidge's response: "He was against it."

    But, again, when we say that most of the arguments in this book are presented at length and require careful reading, we do not mean that they are obscure; we mean, rather, that the reader has to take the sentences thoughtfully, one by one. And speaking of one by one, we are reminded of an episode in Lewis Carroll's *Through the Looking-Glass:*

    "Can you do Addition?" the White Queen asked. "What's one and one and one and one and one and one and one and one and one and one?"
    "I don't know," said Alice. "I lost count."
    "She can't do Addition," the Red Queen said.

It's easy enough to add one and one and one and so on, and Alice can, of course, do addition, but not at the pace that the White Queen sets.

Fortunately, you can set your own pace in reading the cumulative thinking set forth in the essays we reprint. Skimming won't work, but slow reading—and thinking about what you are reading—will.

When you first pick up an essay, you may indeed want to skim it, for some of the reasons mentioned on page 24, but sooner or later you have to settle down to read it and to think about it. The effort will be worthwhile. John Locke, the seventeenth-century English philosopher, said,

> *Reading* furnishes the mind with materials of knowledge; it is *thinking* [that] makes what we read ours. We are of the ruminating kind, and it is not enough to cram ourselves with a great load of collections; unless we chew them over again they will not give us strength and nourishment.

First, Second, and Third Thoughts

Suppose you are reading an argument about pornographic pictures. For the present purpose, it doesn't matter whether the argument favors or opposes censorship. As you read the argument, ask yourself whether *pornography* has been adequately defined. Has the writer taken the trouble to make sure that the reader and the writer are thinking about the same thing? If not, the very topic under discussion has not been adequately fixed; and therefore further debate over the issue may well be so unclear as to be futile. How, then, ought a topic such as this be for effective critical thinking?

It goes without saying that pornography can't be defined simply as pictures of nude figures or even of nude figures copulating, for such a definition would include not only photographs taken for medical, sociological, and scientific purposes but also some of the world's great art. Nobody seriously thinks that such images should be called pornography.

Is it enough, then, to say that pornography "stirs lustful thoughts" or "appeals to prurient interests"? No, because pictures of shoes probably stir lustful thoughts in shoe fetishists, and pictures of children in ads for underwear probably stir lustful thoughts in pedophiles. Perhaps, then, the definition must be amended to "material that stirs lustful thoughts in the average person." But will this restatement do? First, it may be hard to agree on the characteristics of "the average person." In other matters, the law often does assume that there is such a creature as "the reasonable person," and most people would agree that in a given situation there might be a reasonable response—for almost everyone. But we cannot be so sure that the same is true about the emotional responses of this "average person." In any case, far from stimulating sexual impulses, sadomasochistic pictures of booted men wielding whips on naked women probably turn off "the average person," yet this is the sort of material that most people would agree is pornographic.

Something must be wrong, then, with the definition that pornography is material that "stirs lustful thoughts in the average person." We began with a definition that was too broad ("pictures of nude figures"), but now we have a definition that is too narrow. We must go back to the drawing board. This is not nitpicking. The label "average person" was found to be inadequate in a pornography case argued before the Supreme Court; because the materials in question were aimed at a homosexual audience, it was agreed that the average person would not find them sexually stimulating.

One difficulty has been that pornography is often defined according to its effect on the viewer ("genital commotion," Father Harold Gardiner, S.J., called it, in *Catholic Viewpoint on Censorship*), but different people, we know, may respond differently. In the first half of the twentieth century, in an effort to distinguish between pornography and art — after all, most people don't want to regard Botticelli's *Venus* or Michelangelo's *David* as "dirty" — it was commonly said that a true work of art does not stimulate in the spectator ideas or desires that the real object might stimulate. But in 1956, Kenneth Clark, probably the most influential English-speaking art critic of the twentieth century, changed all that; in a book called *The Nude* he announced that "no nude, however abstract, should fail to arouse in the spectator some vestige of erotic feeling."

SUMMARIZING AND PARAPHRASING

Perhaps the best approach to a fairly difficult essay is, after first reading, to reread it and simultaneously to take notes on a sheet of paper, perhaps summarizing each paragraph in a sentence or two. Writing a summary will help you to

- Understand the contents and
- See the strengths and weaknesses of the piece.

Don't confuse a summary with a paraphrase. A **paraphrase** is a word-by-word or phrase-by-phrase rewording of a text, a sort of translation of the author's language into your own. A paraphrase is therefore as long as the original or even longer; a **summary** is much shorter. A book may be summarized in a page, or even in a paragraph or a sentence.

Obviously the summary will leave out all detail, but—if the summary is a true summary—it accurately states the gist, the essential thesis or claim or point of the original.

Why would anyone ever summarize, and why would anyone ever paraphrase? Because, as we have already said, these two activities—in different ways—help readers follow the original author's ideas. But, again, summarizing and paraphrasing are not the same. When you summarize, you are standing back, saying very briefly what the whole adds up to; you are seeing the forest, not the individual trees. When you paraphrase, you are inching through the forest, scrutinizing each tree, i.e., finding a synonym for almost every word in the original, in an effort to make sure that you know exactly what you are dealing with. (Caution: Do *not* incorporate a summary or a paraphrase into your own essay without acknowledging your source and stating that you are summarizing or paraphrasing.)

Let's examine the distinction between summary and paraphrase in connection with the first two paragraphs of Paul Goodman's essay, "A Proposal to Abolish Grading." The two paragraphs run thus:

> Let half a dozen of the prestigious Universities—Chicago, Stanford, the Ivy League—abolish grading, and use testing only and entirely for pedagogic purposes as teachers see fit.
>
> Anyone who knows the frantic temper of the present schools will understand the transvaluation of values that would be effected by this modest innovation. For most of the students, the competitive grade has come to be the essence. The naive teacher points to the beauty of the subject and the ingenuity of the research; the shrewd student asks if he is responsible for that on the final exam.

A *summary* of these two paragraphs might run thus:

> If some top universities used tests only to help students to learn, students would stop worrying about grades and might share the teacher's interest in the beauty of the subject.

We hope we have accurately summarized Goodman's point, though we know we have lost his flavor, his style—for instance, the wry tone in his pointed contrast between "the naive teacher" and "the shrewd student."

Now for a paraphrase. Suppose you are not quite sure what Goodman is getting at, maybe because you are uncertain about the meanings of some words (perhaps *pedagogic* and *transvaluation*?), or maybe just because the whole passage is making such a startling point that you want to make sure that you have understood it. In such a case, you may want to move slowly through the sentences, translating them (so to speak) into your own English. For instance, you might turn Goodman's "pedagogic purposes" into "goals in teaching" or "attempts to help students to learn," or some such thing. Here is a paraphrase—not an abridgment but a rewording—of Goodman's paragraphs:

> Suppose some of the top universities—such as Chicago, Stanford, Harvard, and Yale, and whatever other schools are in the Ivy League—stopped using grades and used tests only in order to help students to learn.
> Everyone who is aware of the hysterical mood in schools today will understand the enormous change in views of what is good and bad that would come about by this small change. At present, instructors, unworldly folk, talk about how beautiful their subjects are, but smart students know that grades are what count, so they listen to instructors only if they know that the material the instructor is talking about will be on the exam.

In short, you may want to paraphrase an important text that your imagined reader may find obscure because it is written in specialized, technical language, for instance the language of psychiatry or of sociology. You want the reader to see the passage itself—you don't want to give just the gist, just a summary—but you know that the full passage will puzzle the reader, so you offer help, giving a paraphrase before going on to make your own point about the author's point.

Note: Be sure to tell the reader, explicitly, that you are offering a paraphrase. If you do not say that the material is a paraphrase, you are plagiarizing, even if you say that you have used so-and-so as a source, because you are using not only the source's ideas but even the sequence (though not the same words) in which the ideas were first presented. (For a further comment on plagiarism, see p. 161.)

A second good reason to offer a paraphrase is if there is substantial disagreement about what the text says. The Second Amendment to the U.S. Constitution is a good example of this sort of text:

> A well regulated Militia being necessary to the security of a free State, the right of the people to keep and bear Arms shall not be infringed.

Exactly what, one might ask, is a "Militia"? And what does it mean for a militia to be "well regulated"? And does "the people" mean each individual, or does it mean—something very different—the citizenry as some sort of unified group? After all, elsewhere in the document, when the

Constitution speaks of individuals, it speaks of a "man" and a "person," not "the people." To speak of "the people" is to use a term (some argue) that sounds like a reference to a unified group—perhaps the citizens of each of the thirteen states?—rather than a reference to individuals. On the other hand, if Congress did mean a unified group rather than individuals, why didn't it say "Congress shall not prohibit the states from organizing militias"?

In fact, thousands of pages have been written about this sentence, and if you are going to talk about it, you certainly have to let your reader know exactly what you make out of each word. In short, you almost surely will paraphrase it. Here is one paraphrase:

> Because an independent society needs the protection of an armed force if it is to remain free, the government may not limit the right of the individuals (who may some day form the militia needed to keep the society free) to possess weapons.

In this interpretation, the Constitution grants individuals the right to possess weapons, and that is that. Other students of the Constitution, however, offer very different paraphrases, usually along these lines:

> Because each state that is now part of the United States may need to protect its freedom [from the new national government], the national government may not infringe on the right of each state to form its own disciplined militia.

This second paraphrase says that the federal government may not prevent each state from having a militia; it says nothing about every individual person having a right to possess weapons. The first of these two paraphrases, or something like it, is one that might be offered by the National Rifle Association or any other group that interprets the Constitution as guaranteeing individuals the right to own guns. The second paraphrase, or something like it, might be offered by groups that seek to limit the ownership of guns.

Because literary texts, especially poems, often are densely packed with meaning, paraphrase is common in essays that analyze literature. Literature is often metaphoric ("a sea of troubles," "a sunny disposition"), so the essayist tries to help the reader see what is in the text, to grasp (so to speak) the literal or the prose meaning (troubles that are unimaginably vast, apparently endless and overwelming) before going on to argue that, say, the poem is good or bad, or witty or dull, or confused. Suppose you are writing an argument about one of Shakespeare's sonnets, Sonnet 130, a light-hearted poem (we are already interpreting!)

in which Shakespeare says that the woman he loves is nothing like the women loved by other poets, who praise their women by saying that their eyes are brighter than the sun, their lips are redder than coral, and so forth. Here is how Shakespeare begins his fourteen-line poem:

> My mistress' eyes are nothing like the sun;
> Coral is far more red than her lips' red.

These lines are pretty clear, and they probably do not need to be paraphrased, but now look at the last two lines of the poem:

> And yet, by heaven, I think my love as rare
> As any she belied with false compare.

As a writer about to discuss the poem, you may have a hunch that your reader can use a little help with these lines. "Any she" is an odd expression. What does it mean? And what does "belied" mean? And, come to think of it, in the first of these two final lines, exactly what or who is "my love"? Does it mean "the love I feel," or does it mean something else, perhaps "the woman whom I love"? Because you know that it is your job, as a writer, to be aware of the needs of your audience, you decide that your reader will be grateful for a paraphrase, and in your essay you write something like this:

> A paraphrase of the final two lines, which offer a sort of reversal of the earlier lines that seem to disparage the woman, may clarify some obscurities. The last two lines mean something like this: "And nevertheless, by all that is holy, I think the woman whom I love is as precious ("rare") as any woman ("any she") who is described untruthfully ("belied") with erroneous comparisons.

We think that if we were writing an essay on this sonnet, we probably would include a paraphrase of these lines for the sake of the reader. On the other hand, if we were writing an essay on Robert Frost's "Stopping by Woods on a Snowy Evening," we probably would not paraphrase the poem because, in our view, it does not include difficulties of this sort. After all, what difficulty is offered by "Whose woods these are I think I know, / His house is in the village though"? Would any reader be helped if we said, "These lines may be paraphrased thus: 'I believe I am aware of who is the owner of this wooded tract, although he lives in one of the dwellings in a small rural area'"?

There really are only two reasons why you might paraphrase a passage:

- To help yourself to understand it—and in this case it will not appear in your paper,
- To help your reader to understand a passage that is especially important but that for one reason or another is not immediately clear. In this case, you paraphrase it to let the reader know exactly what the passage means, and of course the paraphrase appears in your essay.

> *A Rule for Writers:* Your essay is likely to include brief summaries of points of view that you are agreeing or disagreeing with, but it will rarely include a paraphrase unless the original is obscure and you think you need to present a passage at length but in words that are clearer than those of the original. If you do paraphrase, explictly identify the material as a paraphrase.

Summarizing each paragraph or each group of closely related paragraphs will help you to follow the thread of the discourse and, when you are finished, will provide you with a useful map of the essay. Then, when you reread the essay yet again, you may want to underline passages that you now understand are the author's key ideas—for instance, definitions, generalizations, summaries—and you may want to jot notes in the margins, questioning the logic, expressing your uncertainty, or calling attention to other writers who see the matter differently.

Here is a paragraph from a 1973 decision of the U.S. Supreme Court, written by Chief Justice Warren Burger, setting forth reasons that the government may censor obscene material. We follow it with a sample summary.

If we accept the unprovable assumption that a complete education requires the reading of certain books, and the well-nigh universal belief that good books, plays, and art lift the spirit, improve the mind, enrich the human personality, and develop character, can we then say that a state legislature may not act on the corollary assumption that commerce in obscene books, or public exhibitions focused on obscene conduct, have a tendency to exert a corrupting and debasing impact leading to antisocial behavior? The sum of experience, including that of the past two decades, affords an ample basis for legislatures to conclude that a sensitive, key relationship of human existence, central to family life, community welfare, and the development of human personality, can be debased and distorted by crass commercial exploitation of sex. Nothing in the Constitution prohibits a State from reaching such a conclusion and acting on it legislatively simply because there is no conclusive empirical data.

Now for a student's summary. Notice that the summary does *not* include the reader's evaluation or any other sort of comment on the original; it is simply an attempt to condense the original. Notice too that, because its purpose is merely to assist the reader to grasp the ideas of the original by focusing on them, it is written in a sort of shorthand (not every sentence is a complete sentence), though, of course, if this summary were being presented in an essay, it would have to be grammatical.

> Unprovable but acceptable assumption that good books etc. shape character, so that legislature can assume obscene works debase character. Experience lets one conclude that exploitation of sex debases the individual, family, and community. Though no conclusive evidence for this view, Constitution lets states act on it legislatively.

The first sentence of the original, some eighty words, is reduced in the summary to nineteen words. Of course the summary loses much of the detail and flavor of the original: "Good books etc." is not the same as "good books, plays, and art"; and "shape character" is not the same as "lift the spirit, improve the mind, enrich the human personality, and develop character." But the statement in the summary will do as a rough approximation, useful for a quick review. More important, the act of writing a summary forces the reader to go slowly and to think about each sentence of the original. Such thinking may help the reader-writer to see the complexity—or the hollowness—of the original.

The sample summary in the preceding paragraph was just that, a summary; but when writing your own summaries, you will often find it useful to inject your own thoughts ("seems far-fetched," "strong point," "I don't get it"), enclosing them within square brackets, [ ], or in some other way keeping these responses distinct from your summary of the writer's argument. Remember, however, that if your instructor asks you to hand in a summary,

- It should not contain ideas other than those found in the original piece.
- You can rearrange these, add transitions as needed, and so forth, but
- The summary should give the reader nothing but a sense of the original piece.

We don't want to nag you, but we do want to emphasize the need to read with a pencil in hand. If you read slowly and take notes, you will find that what you read will give you the strength and nourishment that Locke spoke of.

Having insisted that although skimming is a useful early step and that the essays in this book need to be read slowly because the writers build one reason on another, we will now seem to contradict ourselves by presenting an essay that can *almost* be skimmed. Susan Jacoby's essay originally appeared in the *New York Times*, a thoroughly respectable newspaper but not one that requires its readers to linger over every sentence. Still, compared with most of the news accounts, Jacoby's essay requires close reading. When you read the essay, you will notice that it zigs and zags, not because Jacoby is careless or wants to befuddle her readers but because she wants to build a strong case to support her point of view and must therefore look at some widely held views that she does *not* accept; she must set these forth and then give her reasons for rejecting them.

SUSAN JACOBY

Susan Jacoby (b. 1946), a journalist since the age of seventeen, is well known for her feminist writings. "A First Amendment Junkie" (our title) appeared in a "Hers" column in the New York Times *in 1978.*

A First Amendment Junkie

It is no news that many women are defecting from the ranks of civil libertarians on the issue of obscenity. The conviction of Larry Flynt, publisher of *Hustler* magazine—before his metamorphosis into a born-again Christian—was greeted with unabashed feminist approval. Harry Reems, the unknown actor who was convicted by a Memphis jury for conspiring to distribute the movie *Deep Throat*, has carried on his legal battles with almost no support from women who ordinarily regard themselves as supporters of the First Amendment. Feminist writers and scholars have even discussed the possibility of making common cause against pornography with adversaries of the women's movement—including opponents of the equal rights amendment and "right-to-life" forces.

All of this is deeply disturbing to a woman writer who believes, as I always have and still do, in an absolute interpretation of the First Amendment. Nothing in Larry Flynt's garbage convinces me that the late Justice Hugo L. Black was wrong in his opinion that "the Federal Government is without any power whatsoever under the Constitution to put any type of burden on free speech and expression of ideas of any kind (as distinguished from conduct)." Many women I like and respect tell me I am wrong; I cannot remember having become involved in so many heated discussions of a public issue since the end of the Vietnam War. A feminist writer described my views as those of a "First Amendment junkie."

Many feminist arguments for controls on pornography carry the implicit conviction that porn books, magazines, and movies pose a greater threat to women than similarly repulsive exercises of free speech pose to other offended groups. This conviction has, of course, been shared by everyone—regardless of race, creed, or sex—who has ever argued in favor of abridging the First Amendment. It is the argument used by some Jews who have withdrawn their support from the American Civil Liberties Union because it has defended the right of American Nazis to march through a community inhabited by survivors of Hitler's concentration camps.

If feminists want to argue that the protection of the Constitution should not be extended to *any* particularly odious or threatening form of speech, they have a reasonable argument (although I don't agree with it). But it is ridiculous to suggest that the porn shops on 42nd Street are more disgusting to women than a march of neo-Nazis is to survivors of the extermination camps.

The arguments over pornography also blur the vital distinction be-   5
tween expression of ideas and conduct. When I say I believe unreservedly in the First Amendment, someone always comes back at me with the issue of "kiddie porn." But kiddie porn is not a First Amendment issue. It is an issue of the abuse of power—the power adults have over children—and not of obscenity. Parents and promoters have no more right to use their children to make porn movies than they do to send them to work in coal mines. The responsible adults should be

prosecuted, just as adults who use children for back-breaking farm labor should be prosecuted.

Susan Brownmiller, in *Against Our Will: Men, Women and Rape*, has described pornography as "the undiluted essence of antifemale propaganda." I think this is a fair description of some types of pornography, especially of the brutish subspecies that equates sex with death and portrays women primarily as objects of violence.

The equation of sex and violence, personified by some glossy rock record album covers as well as by *Hustler*, has fed the illusion that censorship of pornography can be conducted on a more rational basis than other types of censorship. Are all pictures of naked women obscene? Clearly not, says a friend. A Renoir nude is art, she says, and *Hustler* is trash. "Any reasonable person" knows that.

But what about something between art and trash—something, say, along the lines of *Playboy* or *Penthouse* magazines? I asked five women for their reactions to one picture in *Penthouse* and got responses that ranged from "lovely" and "sensuous" to "revolting" and "demeaning." Feminists, like everyone else, seldom have rational reasons for their preferences in erotica. Like members of juries, they tend to disagree when confronted with something that falls short of 100 percent vulgarity.

In any case, feminists will not be the arbiters of good taste if it becomes easier to harass, prosecute, and convict people on obscenity charges. Most of the people who want to censor girlie magazines are equally opposed to open discussion of issues that are of vital concern to women: rape, abortion, menstruation, contraception, lesbianism— in fact, the entire range of sexual experience from a women's viewpoint.

Feminist writers and editors and filmmakers have limited financial 10 resources: Confronted by a determined prosecutor, Hugh Hefner[1] will fare better than Susan Brownmiller. Would the Memphis jurors who convicted Harry Reems for his role in *Deep Throat* be inclined to take a more positive view of paintings of the female genitalia done by sensitive feminist artists? *Ms.* magazine has printed color reproductions of some of those art works; *Ms.* is already banned from a number of high school libraries because someone considers it threatening and/or obscene.

Feminists who want to censor what they regard as harmful pornography have essentially the same motivation as other would-be censors: They want to use the power of the state to accomplish what they have been unable to achieve in the marketplace of ideas and images. The impulse to censor places no faith in the possibilities of democratic persuasion.

[1]**Hugh Hefner** Founder and longtime publisher of *Playboy* magazine. [—Ed.]

It isn't easy to persuade certain men that they have better uses for $1.95 each month than to spend it on a copy of *Hustler?* Well, then, give the men no choice in the matter.

I believe there is also a connection between the impulse toward censorship on the part of people who used to consider themselves civil libertarians and a more general desire to shift responsibility from individuals to institutions. When I saw the movie *Looking for Mr. Goodbar,* I was stunned by its series of visual images equating sex and violence, coupled with what seems to me the mindless message (a distortion of the fine Judith Rossner novel) that casual sex equals death. When I came out of the movie, I was even more shocked to see parents standing in line with children between the ages of ten and fourteen.

I simply don't know why a parent would take a child to see such a movie, any more than I understand why people feel they can't turn off a television set their child is watching. Whenever I say that, my friends tell me I don't know how it is because I don't have children. True, but I do have parents. When I was a child, they did turn off the TV. They didn't expect the Federal Communications Commission to do their job for them.

I am a First Amendment junkie. You can't OD on the First   15 Amendment, because free speech is its own best antidote.

Suppose we want to make a rough summary, more or less paragraph by paragraph, of Jacoby's essay. Such a summary might look something like this (the numbers refer to Jacoby's paragraphs):

1. Although feminists usually support the First Amendment, when it comes to pornography, many feminists take pretty much the position of those who oppose ERA and abortion and other causes of the women's movement.

2. Larry Flynt produces garbage, but I think his conviction represents an unconstitutional limitation of freedom of speech.

3, 4. Feminists who want to control (censor) pornography argue that it poses a greater threat to women than similar repulsive speech poses to other groups. If feminists want to say that all offensive speech should be restricted, they can make a case, but it is absurd to say that pornography is a "greater threat" to women than a march of neo-Nazis is to survivors of concentration camps.

5. Trust in the First Amendment is not refuted by kiddie porn; kiddie porn is not a First Amendment issue but an issue of child abuse.

6, 7, 8. Some feminists think censorship of pornography can be more "rational" than other kinds of censorship, but a picture of a nude woman strikes some women as base and others as "lovely." There is no unanimity.

9, 10. If feminists censor girlie magazines, they will find that they are unwittingly helping opponents of the women's movement to censor discussions of rape, abortion, and so on. Some of the art in the feminist magazine Ms. would doubtless be censored.

11, 12. Like other would-be censors, feminists want to use the power of the state to achieve what they have not achieved in "the marketplace of ideas." They display a lack of faith in "democratic persuasion."

13, 14. This attempt at censorship reveals a desire to "shift responsibility from individuals to institutions." The responsibility — for instance, to keep young people from equating sex with violence — is properly the parents'.

15. We can't have too much of the First Amendment.

Jacoby's **thesis,** or major claim, or chief proposition — that any form of censorship of pornography is wrong — is clear enough, even as early as the end of her first paragraph, but it gets its life or its force from the **reasons** offered throughout the essay. If we want to reduce our summary even further, we might say that Jacoby supports her thesis by arguing several subsidiary points. We will merely assert them briefly, but Jacoby **argues** them — that is, she gives reasons:

a. Pornography can scarcely be thought of as more offensive than Nazism.

b. Women disagree about which pictures are pornographic.

c. Feminists who want to censor pornography will find that they help antifeminists to censor discussions of issues advocated by the women's movement.

d. Feminist who favor censorship are in effect turning to the government to achieve what they haven't achieved in the free marketplace.

e. One sees this abdication of responsibility in the fact that parents allow their children to watch unsuitable movies and television programs.

If we want to present a brief summary in the form of one coherent paragraph — perhaps as part of our own essay to show the view we are arguing in behalf of or against — we might write something like this summary. (The summary would, of course, be prefaced by a **lead-in** along these lines: "Susan Jacoby, writing in the *New York Times*, offers a forceful argument against censorship of pornography. Jacoby's view, briefly, is . . .".)

When it comes to censorship of pornography, some feminists take a position shared by opponents of the feminist movement. They argue that pornography poses a greater threat to women than other forms of offensive speech offer to other groups, but this interpretation is simply a mistake. Pointing to kiddie porn is also a mistake, for kiddie porn is an issue involving not the First Amendment but child abuse. Feminists who support censorship of pornography will inadvertently aid those who wish to censor discussions of abortion and rape or censor art that is published in magazines such as <u>Ms.</u> The solution is not for individuals to turn to institutions (that is, for the government to limit the First Amendment) but for individuals to accept the responsibility for teaching young people not to equate sex with violence.

Whether we agree or disagree with Jacoby's thesis, we must admit that the reasons she sets forth to support it are worth thinking about. Only a reader who closely follows the reasoning with which Jacoby buttresses her thesis is in a position to accept or reject it.

Topics for Critical Thinking and Writing

1. What does Jacoby mean when she says she is a "First Amendment junkie"?
2. The essay is primarily an argument against the desire of some feminists to try to censor pornography of the sort that appeals to some heterosexual adult males, but the next-to-last paragraph is about television and

children. Is the paragraph connected to Jacoby's overall argument? If so, how?

3. Evaluate the final paragraph as a final paragraph. (Effective final paragraphs are not, of course, all of one sort. Some, for example, round off the essay by echoing something from the opening; others suggest that the reader, having now seen the problem, should think further about it or even act on it. But a good final paragraph, whatever else it does, should make the reader feel that the essay has come to an end, not just broken off.)

4. This essay originally appeared in the *New York Times*. If you are unfamiliar with this newspaper, consult an issue or two in your library. Next, in a paragraph, try to characterize the readers of the paper—that is, Jacoby's audience.

5. Jacoby claims in paragraph 2 that she "believes . . . in an absolute interpretation of the First Amendment." What does such an interpretation involve? Would it permit shouting "Fire!" in a crowded theater even though the shouter knows there is no fire? Would it permit shouting racist insults at blacks or immigrant Vietnamese? Spreading untruths about someone's past? If the "absolutist" interpretation of the First Amendment does permit these statements, does that argument show that nothing is morally wrong with uttering them? (*Does* the First Amendment, as actually interpreted by the Supreme Court today, permit any or all of these claims? Consult your reference librarian for help in answering this question.)

6. Jacoby implies that permitting prosecution of persons on obscenity charges will lead eventually to censorship of "open discussion" of important issues such as "rape, abortion, menstruation, contraception, lesbianism" (para. 9). Do you find her fears convincing? Does she give any evidence to support her claim?

A CHECKLIST FOR GETTING STARTED

- ☐ Have I adequately previewed the work?
- ☐ Can I state the thesis?
- ☐ If I have jotted down a summary,
  - ☐ Is the summary accurate?
  - ☐ Does the summary mention all the chief points?
  - ☐ If there are inconsistencies, are they in the summary or the original selection?
  - ☐ Will the summary be clear and helpful?

3

Critical Reading:
Getting Deeper
into Arguments

He that wrestles with us strengthens our nerves, and sharpens our skill. Our antagonist is our helper. — EDMUND BURKE

PERSUASION, ARGUMENT, DISPUTE

When we think seriously about an argument (not name calling or mere rationalization), not only do we hear ideas that may be unfamiliar, but we are also forced to examine closely our own cherished opinions, and perhaps for the first time really come to see the strengths and weaknesses of what we believe. As John Stuart Mill put it, "He who knows only his own side of the case knows little."

It is customary, and useful, to distinguish between persuasion and argument. **Persuasion** has the broader meaning. To persuade is to win over — whether by giving reasons (that is, by argument), by appealing to the emotions, or, for that matter, by using torture. **Argument,** one form of persuasion, relies on reason; it offers statements as reasons for other statements. Rhetoricians often use the Greek word **logos,** which merely means "word" or "reason," to denote this aspect of persuasive writing — the appeal to reason. (The appeal to the emotions is known as **pathos.** Strictly speaking, *pathos* is Greek for "feeling," and especially for "suffering," but it now covers all sorts of emotional appeal — for instance, to one's sense of pity or sympathy (Greek for "feeling with") or one's sense of patriotism.)

Notice that an argument, in the sense of statements that are offered as reasons for other statements, does not require two speakers or writers who represent opposed positions. The Declaration of Independence is an argument, setting forth the colonists' reasons for declaring their independence. In practice, of course, someone's argument usually advances

42

reasons for a claim in opposition to someone else's position or belief. But even if one is writing only for oneself, trying to clarify one's thinking by setting forth reasons, the result is an argument. **Dispute,** however, is a special kind of argument in which two or more people express views that are at odds.

Most of this book is about argument in the sense of the presentation of reasons in support of claims, but of course, reason is not the whole story. If an argument is to be effective, it must be presented persuasively. For instance, the writer's **tone** (attitude toward self, topic, and audience) must be appropriate if the discourse is to persuade the reader. The careful presentation of the self is not something disreputable, nor is it something that publicity agents or advertising agencies invented. Aristotle (384–22 B.C.) emphasized the importance of impressing on the audience that the speaker is a person of good sense and high moral character. (He called this aspect of persuasion **ethos,** the Greek word for "character," as opposed to *logos,* which we have noted is the word for persuasion by appealing to reason.) We talk at length about tone, along with other matters such as the organization of an argument, in Chapter 5, but here we deal with some of the chief devices used in reasoning, and we glance at emotional appeals.

We should note at once, however, that an argument presupposes a fixed **topic.** Suppose we are arguing about Jefferson's assertion, in the Declaration of Independence, that "all men are created equal." Jones subscribes to this statement, but Smith says it is nonsense and argues that one has only to look around to see that some people are brighter than others, or healthier, or better coordinated, or whatever. Jones and Smith, if they intend to argue the point, will do well to examine what Jefferson actually wrote:

> We hold these truths to be self-evident, that all men are created equal: that they are endowed by their Creator with certain unalienable rights; and that among these are life, liberty, and the pursuit of happiness.

There is room for debate over what Jefferson really meant and about whether he is right, but clearly he was talking about *equality of rights.* If Smith and Jones wish to argue about Jefferson's view of equality—that is, if they wish to offer their reasons for accepting, rejecting, or modifying it—they will do well first to agree on what Jefferson said or what he probably meant to say. Jones and Smith may still hold different views; they may continue to disagree on whether Jefferson was right and proceed to offer arguments and counterarguments to settle the point. But only if they can agree on *what* they disagree about will their dispute get somewhere.

REASON VERSUS RATIONALIZATION

Reason may not be our only way of finding the truth, but it is a way we often rely on. The subway ran yesterday at 6:00 A.M. and the day before at 6:00 A.M. and the day before, and so I infer from this evidence that it will also run today at 6:00 A.M. (a form of reasoning known as **induction**). Bus drivers require would-be passengers to present the exact change; I do not have the exact change; therefore, I infer I cannot ride on the bus (**deduction**). (The terms *deduction* and *induction* are discussed on pages 51–56 and 56–57.)

We also know that, if we set our minds to a problem, we can often find reasons (not necessarily sound ones but reasons nevertheless) for almost anything we want to justify. Here is an entertaining example from Benjamin Franklin's *Autobiography:*

> I believe I have omitted mentioning that in my first voyage from Boston, being becalmed off Block Island, our people set about catching cod and hauled up a great many. Hitherto I had stuck to my resolution of not eating animal food, and on this occasion, I considered with my master Tryon the taking of every fish as a kind of unprovoked murder, since none of them had or ever could do us any injury that might justify the slaughter. All this seemed very reasonable. But I had formerly been a great lover of fish, and when this came hot out of the frying pan, it smelt admirably well. I balanced some time between principle and inclination, till I recollected that when the fish were opened I saw smaller fish taken out of their stomachs. Then thought I, if you eat one another, I don't see why we mayn't eat you. So I dined upon cod very heartily and continued to eat with other people, returning only now and then occasionally to a vegetable diet. So convenient a thing it is to be a reasonable creature, since it enables one to find or make a reason for everything one has a mind to do.

Franklin is being playful; he is *not* engaging in critical thinking. He tells us that he loved fish, that this fish "smelt admirably well," and so we are prepared for him to find a reason (here one as weak as "Fish eat fish, so people may eat fish") to abandon his vegetarianism. (But think: Fish also eat their own young. May we therefore eat ours?) Still, Franklin touches on a truth: If necessary, we can find reasons to justify whatever we want. That is, instead of reasoning we may *rationalize* (devise a self-serving but dishonest reason), like the fox in Aesop's fables who, finding the grapes he desired were out of his reach, consoled himself with the thought they were probably sour.

Perhaps we can never be certain that we are not rationalizing, except when, like Franklin, we are being playful — but we can seek to think critically about our own beliefs, scrutinizing our assumptions, looking for counterevidence, and wondering if different conclusions can reasonably be drawn.

SOME PROCEDURES IN ARGUMENT

Definition

Definition, we mentioned in our first chapter, is one of the classical topics, a "place" to which one goes with questions; in answering the questions, one finds ideas. When we define, we are answering the question "What is it?" and in answering this question as precisely as we can, we will find, clarify, and develop ideas.

We have already glanced at an argument over the proposition that "all men are created equal," and we saw that the words needed clarification. *Equal* meant, in the context, not physically or mentally equal but something like "equal in rights," equal politically and legally. (And of course, "men" meant "white men and women.") Words do not always mean exactly what they seem to: There is no lead in a lead pencil, and a standard 2-by-4 is currently 1⅝ inches in thickness and 3⅝ inches in width.

Definition by Synonym   Let's return, for a moment, to *pornography,* a word that, we saw, is not easily defined. One way to define a word is to offer a **synonym.** Thus, pornography can be defined, at least roughly, as "obscenity" (something indecent). But definition by synonym is usually only a start because we find that we will have to define the synonym and, besides, that very few words have exact synonyms. (In fact, *pornography* and *obscenity* are not exact synonyms.)

Definition by Example   A second way to define something is to point to an example (this is often called **ostensive definition,** from the Latin *ostendere,* "to show"). This method can be very helpful, ensuring that both writer and reader are talking about the same thing, but it also has its limitations. A few decades ago many people pointed to James Joyce's *Ulysses* and D. H. Lawrence's *Lady Chatterley's Lover* as examples of obscene novels, but today these books are regarded as literary masterpieces. Possibly they can be obscene and also be literary masterpieces. (Joyce's wife is reported to have said of her husband, "He may have been a great writer, but . . . he had a very dirty mind.")

One of the difficulties of using an example, however, is that the example is richer and more complex than the term it is being used to define, and this richness and complexity get in the way of achieving a clear definition. Thus, if one cites Lawrence's *Lady Chatterley's Lover* as an example of pornography, a listener may erroneously think that pornography has something to do with British novels or with heterosexual relationships outside of marriage. Yet neither of these ideas is part of the concept of pornography.

We are not trying here to formulate a satisfactory definition of *pornography;* our object is to show that an argument will be most fruitful if the participants first agree on what they are talking about and that one way to secure such agreement is to define the topic ostensively. Choosing the right example, one that has all the central or typical characteristics, can make a topic not only clear but vivid.

Definition by Stipulation   In arguing, you can legitimately offer a **stipulative definition,** saying, perhaps, that by *Native American* you mean any person with any Native American blood; or you might say, "For the purpose of the present discussion, I mean by a *Native American* any person who has at least one grandparent of pure Native American blood." A stipulative definition is appropriate where

- No fixed or standard definition is available, and
- Some arbitrary specification is necessary to fix the meaning of a key term in the argument.

Not everyone may be willing to accept your stipulative definition, and alternatives can probably be defended. In any case, when you stipulate a definition, your audience knows what *you* mean by the term thus defined.

It would *not* be reasonable, of course, to stipulate that by *Native American* you mean anyone with a deep interest in North American aborigines. That's just too idiosyncratic to be useful. Similarly, an essay on Jews in America will have to rely on some definition of the key idea. Perhaps the writer will stipulate the definition used in Israel: A Jew is a person who has a Jewish mother or, if not born of a Jewish mother, a person who has formally adopted the Jewish faith. Or perhaps the writer will stipulate another meaning: Jews are people who consider themselves to be Jews. Some sort of reasonable definition must be offered.

To stipulate, however, that by *Jews* you mean "persons who believe that the area formerly called Palestine rightfully belongs to the Jews" would hopelessly confuse matters. Remember the old riddle and the answer: If you call a dog's tail a leg, how many legs does a dog have? Answer: Four. Calling a tail a leg doesn't make it a leg.

Suppose someone says she means by a *Communist* "anyone who opposes the president, does not go to church, and favors a more nearly equal distribution of wealth and property." A dictionary or encyclopedia will tell us that a person is a Communist who accepts the main doctrines of Karl Marx (or perhaps of Marxism-Leninism). For many purposes, we may think of Communists as persons who belong to some Communist political party, by analogy with Democrats and Republicans. Or we may even think of a Communist as someone who supports what is common to the constitutions and governments currently in power in China and Cuba. But what is the point of the misleading stipulative definition of *Communist* given at the beginning of this paragraph, except to cast disapproval on everyone whose views bring them within the definition?

There is no good reason for offering this definition, and there are two goods reasons against it. The first is that we already have perfectly adequate definitions of the term *Communist,* and one should learn them and rely on them until the need to revise and improve them occurs. The second reason for refraining from using a misleading stipulative definition of the term *Communist* is that it is unfair to tar with a dirty and sticky brush nonchurchgoers and the rest by calling them derogatory names they do not deserve. Even if it is true that Communists favor a more egalitarian distribution of wealth and property, the converse is *not* true: Not all egalitarians are Communists. Furthermore, if something is economically unsound or morally objectionable about such egalitarianism, the only responsible way to make that point is to argue for it.

A stipulation may be helpful and legitimate. Here is the opening paragraph of an essay by Richard B. Brandt titled "The Morality and Rationality of Suicide" (from *A Handbook for the Study of Suicide,* edited by Seymour Perlin). Notice that

- The author first stipulates a definition, and
- Then, aware that the definition may strike some readers as too broad and therefore unreasonable or odd, he offers a reason on behalf of his definition:

"Suicide" is conveniently defined, for our purposes, as doing something which results in one's death, either from the intention of ending one's life or the intention to bring about some other state of affairs (such as relief from pain) which one thinks it certain or highly probable can be achieved only by means of death or will produce death. It may seem odd to classify an act of heroic selfsacrifice on the part of a soldier as suicide. It is simpler, however, not to try to define "suicide" so that an act of suicide is always irrational or immoral in some way; if we adopt a neutral definition like the above we can still proceed to ask when an act of suicide in that sense is rational, morally justifiable, and so on, so that all evaluations anyone might wish to make can still be made.

Sometimes a definition that at first seems extremely odd can be made acceptable, if strong reasons are offered in its support. Sometimes, in fact, an odd definition marks a great intellectual step forward. For instance, in 1990 the U.S. Supreme Court recognized that *speech* includes symbolic nonverbal expression such as protesting against a war by wearing armbands or by flying the American flag upside down. Such actions, because they express ideas or emotions, are now protected by the First Amendment. Few people today would disagree that *speech* should include symbolic gestures.

A definition that seems notably eccentric to many readers and thus far has not gained much support is from page 94 of Peter Singer's *Practical Ethics*, in which the author suggests that a nonhuman being can be a *person*. He admits that "it sounds odd to call an animal a person" but says that it seems so only because of our bad habit of sharply separating ourselves from other species. For Singer, *persons* are "rational and self-conscious beings, aware of themselves as distinct entities with a past and a future." Thus, although a newborn infant is a human being, it is not a person; on the other hand, an adult chimpanzee is not a human being but probably is a person. You don't have to agree with Singer to know exactly what he means and where he stands. Moreover, if you read his essay, you may even find that his reasons are plausible and that by means of his unusual definition he has enlarged your thinking.

The Importance of Definitions   Trying to decide on the best way to define a key idea or a central concept is often difficult as well as controversial. *Death*, for example, has been redefined in recent years. Traditionally, a person was dead when there was no longer any heartbeat. But with advancing medical technology, the medical profession has persuaded legislatures to redefine *death* as cessation of cerebral and cortical functions—so-called brain death. Some scholars have hoped to bring clarity into the abortion debate by redefining *life*.

Traditionally, human life begins at birth or perhaps at viability (the capacity of a fetus to live independently of the uterine environment). However, some have proposed a "brain birth" definition, in the hope of resolving the abortion controversy. A *New York Times* story of November 8, 1990, reported that these thinkers want abortion to be prohibited by law at the point where "integrated brain functioning begins to emerge—about seventy days after conception." Whatever the merits of such a redefinition, the debate is convincing evidence of just how important the definition of certain terms can be.

Last Words about Definition   Since Plato's time, in the fourth century B.C., it has often been argued that the best way to give a definition is to state the *essence* of the thing being defined. Thus, the classic example defines *man* as "a rational animal." (Today, to avoid sexist implications, instead of *man* we would say *human being* or *person*.) That is, the property of *rational animality* is taken to be the essence of every human creature, and so it must be mentioned in the definition of *man*. This statement guarantees that the definition is neither too broad nor too narrow. But philosophers have long criticized this alleged ideal type of definition, on several grounds, one of which is that no one can propose such definitions without assuming that the thing being defined has an essence in the first place—an assumption that is not necessary. Thus, we may want to define *causality,* or *explanation,* or even *definition* itself, but it is doubtful whether it is sound to assume that any of these things has an essence.

A much better way to provide a definition is to offer a set of **sufficient and necessary conditions.** Suppose we want to define the word *circle* and are conscious of the need to keep circles distinct from other geometrical figures such as rectangles and spheres. We might express our definition by citing sufficient and necessary conditions as follows: "Anything is a circle *if and only if* it is a closed plane figure and all points on the circumference are equidistant from the center." Using the connective "if and only if" (called the *biconditional*) between the definition and what is being defined helps to force into our consciousness the need to make the definition neither too exclusive (too narrow) nor too inclusive (too broad). Of course, for most ordinary purposes we don't require such a formally precise and explicit definition. Nevertheless, perhaps the best criterion to keep in mind when assessing a proposed definition is whether it can be stated in the "if and only if " form, and whether, if it is so stated, it is true; that is, if it truly specifies *all and only* the things covered by the word being defined.

Thus, to summarize, definitions can be given by

- Synonym,
- Example,
- Stipulation,
- Mention of the essence, and
- Statement of necessary and sufficient conditions.

Assumptions

We have already said that in the form of discourse known as argument certain statements are offered as reasons for other statements. But even the longest and most complex chain of reasoning or proof is fastened to **assumptions**—one or more *unexamined beliefs.* (Even if such a belief is shared by writer and reader, it is no less an assumption.) Benjamin Franklin argued against paying salaries to the holders of executive offices in the federal government on the grounds that men are moved by ambition (love of power) and by avarice (love of money) and that powerful positions conferring wealth incite men to do their worst. These assumptions he stated, though he felt no need to argue them at length because he assumed that his readers shared them.

An assumption may be unstated. A writer, painstakingly arguing specific points, may choose to keep one or more of the argument's assumptions tacit. Or the writer may be as unaware of some underlying assumption as of the surrounding air. For example, Franklin didn't even bother to state another assumption. He must have assumed that persons of wealth who accept an unpaying job (after all, only persons of wealth could afford to hold unpaid government jobs) will have at heart the interests of all classes of people, not only the interests of their own class. Probably Franklin did not state this assumption because he thought it was perfectly obvious, but if you think critically about the assumption, you may find reasons to doubt it. Surely one reason we pay our legislators is to make certain that the legislature does not consist only of people whose incomes may give them an inadequate view of the needs of others.

An Example: Assumptions in the Argument Permitting Abortion

1. Ours is a pluralistic society, in which we believe that the religious beliefs of one group should not be imposed on others.
2. Personal privacy is a right, and a woman's body is hers, not to be violated by laws that tell her she may not do certain things to her body.

But these (and other) arguments *assume* that a fetus is not—or not yet—a person and therefore is not entitled to the same protection against assaults that we are. Virtually all of us assume that it is usually wrong to kill a human being. Granted, we may find instances in which we believe it is acceptable to take a human life, such as self-defense against a would-be murderer. But even here we find a shared assumption that persons are ordinarily entitled not to be killed.

The argument about abortion, then, usually depends on opposed assumptions: For one group, the fetus is a human being and a potential person—and this potentiality is decisive. But for the other group it is not. Persons arguing one side or the other of the abortion issue ought to be aware that opponents may not share their assumptions.

Premises and Syllogisms

Premises are stated assumptions used as reasons in an argument. (The word comes from a Latin word meaning "to send before" or "to set in front.") A premise thus is a statement set down—assumed—before the argument is begun. The joining of two premises—two statements taken to be true—to produce a conclusion, a third statement, is called a **syllogism** (Greek for "a reckoning together"). The classic example is this:

Major premise:	All human beings are mortal.
Minor premise:	Socrates is a human being.
Conclusion:	Socrates is mortal.

Deduction

The mental process of moving from one statement ("All human beings are mortal") through another ("Socrates is a human being") to yet a further statement ("Socrates is mortal") is called **deduction,** from Latin for "lead down from." In this sense, deductive reasoning does not give us any new knowledge, although it is easy to construct examples that have so many premises, or premises that are so complex, that the conclusion really does come as news to most who examine the argument. Thus, the great detective Sherlock Holmes was credited by his admiring colleague, Dr. Watson, with unusual powers of deduction. Watson meant in part that Holmes could see the logical consequences of apparently disconnected reasons, the number and complexity of which left others at a loss. What is common in all cases of deduction is that the reasons or premises offered are supposed to contain within themselves, so to speak, the conclusion extracted from them.

Often a syllogism is abbreviated. Martin Luther King Jr., defending a protest march, wrote in "Letter from Birmingham Jail":

You assert that our actions, even though peaceful, must be condemned because they precipitate violence.

Fully expressed, the argument that King attributes to his critics would be stated thus:

Society must condemn actions (even if peaceful) that precipitate violence.

This action (though peaceful) will precipitate violence.

Therefore, society must condemn this action.

An incomplete or abbreviated syllogism in which one of the premises is
left unstated, of the sort found in King's original quotation, is called an
enthymeme (Greek for "in the mind").

Here is another, more whimsical example of an enthymeme, in
which both a premise and the conclusion are left implicit. Henry David
Thoreau remarked that "Circumstantial evidence can be very strong, as
when you find a trout in the milk." The joke, perhaps intelligible only to
people born before 1930 or so, depends on the fact that milk used to be
sold "in bulk"—that is, ladled out of a big can directly to the customer
by the farmer or grocer. This practice was finally prohibited in the 1930s
because for centuries the sellers, in order to increase their profit, were
diluting the milk with water. Thoreau's enthymeme can be fully expressed thus:

Trout live only in water.

This milk has a trout in it.

Therefore, this milk has water in it.

These enthymemes have three important properties: Their premises are
true, the form of their argument is *valid*, and they leave *implicit* either
the conclusion or one of the premises.

SOUND ARGUMENTS

The purpose of a syllogism is to present reasons that establish its conclusion. This is done by making sure that the argument satisfies both of two independent criteria:

- First, all of the premises must be *true.*
- Second, the syllogism must be *valid.*

Once these criteria are satisfied, the conclusion of the syllogism is guaranteed. Any such argument is said to establish or to prove its conclusion, or to use another term, it is said to be **sound.** Here's an example of a sound argument, a syllogism that proves its conclusion:

Extracting oil from the Arctic Wildlife Refuge would adversely affect the local ecology.

Adversely affecting the local ecology is undesirable, unless there is no better alternative fuel source.

Therefore, extracting oil from the Arctic Wildlife Refuge is undesirable, unless there is no better alternative fuel source.

Each premise is **true,** and the syllogism is **valid,** so it establishes its conclusion.

But how do we tell in any given case that an argument is sound? We perform two different tests, one for the truth of each of the premises and another for the validity of the argument.

The basic test for the **truth** of a premise is to determine whether what it asserts corresponds with reality; if it does, then it is true, and if it doesn't, then it is false. Everything depends on the content of the premise—what it asserts—and the evidence for it. (In the preceding syllogism, the truth of the premises can be tested by checking the views of experts and interested parties, such as policy makers, environmental groups, and experts on energy.)

The test for **validity** is quite different. We define a valid argument as one in which the conclusion follows from the premises, so that if all the premises are true then the conclusion *must* be true, too. The general test for validity, then, is this: If one grants the premises, one must also grant the conclusion. Or to put it another way, if one grants the premises but denies the conclusion, is one caught in a self-contradiction? If so, the argument is valid; if not, the argument is invalid.

The preceding syllogism passes this test. If you grant the information given in the premises but deny the conclusion, you have contradicted yourself. Even if the information were in error, the conclusion in this syllogism would still follow from the premises—the hallmark of a valid argument! The conclusion follows because the validity of an argument is a purely formal matter concerning the *relation* between premises and conclusion based on what they mean.

This relationship can be seen more clearly by examining an argument that is valid but that, because one or both of the premises are false, does *not* establish its conclusion. Here is an example of such a syllogism:

> The whale is a large fish.
>
> All large fish have scales.
>
> Therefore, whales have scales.

We know that the premises and the conclusion are false: Whales are mammals, not fish, and not all large fish have scales (sharks have no scales, for instance). But when the validity of the argument is being determined, the truth of the premises and the conclusion is beside the point. Just a little reflection assures us that *if* both of these premises were true, then the conclusion would have to be true as well. That is, anyone who grants the premises of this syllogism and yet denies the conclusion has contradicted herself. So the validity of an argument does not in any way depend on the truth of the premises or the conclusion.

A sound argument, as we said, is an argument that passes both the test of true premises and the test of valid inference. To put it another way, a sound argument passes the test of *content* (the premises are true, as a matter of fact) and the test of *form* (its premises and conclusion, by virtue of their very meanings, are so related that it is impossible for the premises to be true and the conclusion false).

Accordingly, an unsound argument, an argument that fails to prove its conclusion, suffers from one or both of two defects. First, not all of the premises are true. Second, the argument is invalid. Usually, we have in mind one or both of these defects when we object to someone's argument as "illogical." In evaluating someone's deductive argument, therefore, you must always ask: Is it vulnerable to criticism on the ground that one (or more) of its premises is false? Or is the inference itself vulnerable because even if all the premises are all true, the conclusion still wouldn't follow?

A deductive argument *proves* its conclusion if and only if *two conditions* are satisfied: (1) All the premises are *true*, and (2) it would be *inconsistent to assert the premises and deny the conclusions.*

A Word about False Premises   Suppose that one or more of the premises of a syllogism is false but the syllogism itself is valid. What does that tell us about the truth of the conclusion? Consider this example:

All Americans prefer vanilla ice cream to other flavors.

Tiger Woods is an American.

Therefore, Tiger Woods prefers vanilla ice cream to other flavors.

The first (or major) premise in this syllogism is false. Yet the argument passes our formal test for validity; it is clear that if one grants both premises, then one must accept the conclusion. So we can say that the conclusion *follows from* its premises, even though the premises *do not prove* the conclusion. This is not as paradoxical as it may sound. For all we know, the conclusion of this argument may in fact be true; Tiger Woods may indeed prefer vanilla ice cream, and the odds are that he does because consumption statistics show that a majority of Americans prefer vanilla. Nevertheless, if the conclusion in this syllogism is true, it is not because this argument proved it.

A Word about Invalid Syllogisms   Usually, one can detect a false premise in an argument, especially when the suspect premise appears in someone else's argument. A trickier business is the invalid syllogism. Consider this argument:

All terrorists seek publicity for their violent acts.

John Doe seeks publicity for his violent acts.

Therefore, John Doe is a terrorist.

In the preceding syllogism, let us grant that the first (major) premise is true. Let us also grant that the conclusion may well be true. Finally, the person mentioned in the second (minor) premise could indeed be a terrorist. But it is also possible that the conclusion is false; terrorists are not the only ones who seek publicity for their violent acts; think, for example, of the violence committed against doctors, clinic workers, and patients at clinics where abortions are performed. In short, the truth of the two premises is no guarantee that the conclusion is also true. It is possible to assert both premises and deny the conclusion without self-contradiction.

How do we tell, in general and in particular cases, whether a syllogism is valid? As you know, chemists use litmus paper to enable them to tell instantly whether the liquid in a test tube is an acid or a base. Unfortunately, logic has no litmus test to tell us instantly whether an argument is valid or invalid. Logicians beginning with Aristotle have developed techniques that enable them to test any given argument, no matter how complex or subtle, to determine its validity. But the results of their labors cannot be expressed in a paragraph or even a few pages; not for nothing are semester-long courses devoted to teaching formal deductive logic. Apart from advising you to consult Chapter 9, A Logician's View: Deduction, Induction, Fallacies, all we can do here is repeat two basic points.

First, validity of deductive arguments is a matter of their *form* or *structure*. Even syllogisms like the one on the Arctic Wildlife Refuge on page 53 come in a large variety of forms (256 different ones, to be precise), and only some of these forms are valid. Second, all valid deductive arguments (and only such arguments) pass this test: If one accepts all the premises, then one must accept the conclusion as well. Hence, if it is possible to accept the premises but reject the conclusion (without self-contradiction, of course), then the argument is invalid.

Let us exit from further discussion of this important but difficult subject on a lighter note. Many illogical arguments masquerade as logical. Consider this example: If it takes a horse and carriage four hours to go from Pinsk to Chelm, does it follow that a carriage with two horses will get there in two hours? Starting on page 230, we discuss at some length other kinds of deductive arguments, as well as **fallacies,** which are kinds of invalid reasoning.

Induction

Whereas deduction takes our beliefs and assumptions and extracts their hidden consequences, **induction** uses information about observed cases to reach a conclusion about unobserved cases. (The word comes from the Latin *in ducere,* "to lead into" or "to lead up to.") If we observe that the bite of a certain snake is poisonous, we may conclude on this evidence that another snake of the same general type is also poisonous. Our inference might be even broader. If we observe that snake after snake of a certain type has a poisonous bite and that these snakes are all rattlesnakes, we are tempted to **generalize** that all rattlesnakes are poisonous. By far the most common way to test the adequacy of a generalization is to confront it with one or more **counterexamples.** If the counterexamples are genuine and reliable, then the generalization must be false.

Unlike deduction, induction gives us conclusions that go beyond the information contained in the premises used in their support. Not surprisingly, the conclusions of inductive reasoning are not always true, even when all the premises are true. On page 44, we gave as an example our observation that on previous days a subway has run at 6:00 A.M. and that therefore we believe that it runs at 6:00 A.M. every day. Suppose, following this reasoning, we arrive at the subway platform just before 6:00 A.M. on a given day and wait an hour without a train. What inference should we draw to explain this? Possibly today is Sunday, and the subway doesn't run before 7:00 A.M. Or possibly there was a breakdown earlier this morning. Whatever the explanation, we relied on a sample that was not large enough (a larger sample might have included some early morning breakdowns) or not representative enough (a more representative sample would have included the later starts on holidays).

A Word about Samples   When we reason inductively, much depends on the size and the quality of the sample. We may interview five members of Alpha Tau Omega and find that all five are Republicans, yet we cannot legitimately conclude that all members of ATO are Republicans. The problem is not always one of failing to interview large numbers. A poll of ten thousand college students tells us very little about "college students" if all ten thousand are white males at the University of Texas. Such a sample, because it leaves out women and minority males, obviously is not sufficiently *representative* of "college students" as a group. Further, though not all of the students at the University of Texas are from Texas or even from the Southwest, it is quite likely that the student body is not fully representative (for instance, in race and in income) of American college students. If this conjecture is correct, even a truly representative sample of University of Texas students would not allow one to draw firm conclusions about American college students.

In short: An argument that uses samples ought to tell the reader how the samples were chosen. If it does not provide this information, the argument may rightly be treated with suspicion.

Evidence

Experimentation   Induction is obviously useful in arguing. If, for example, one is arguing that handguns should be controlled, one will point to specific cases in which handguns caused accidents or were used to commit crimes. If one is arguing that abortion has a traumatic effect on women, one will point to women who testify to that effect. Each instance constitutes **evidence** for the relevant generalization.

In a courtroom, evidence bearing on the guilt of the accused is introduced by the prosecution, and evidence to the contrary is introduced by the defense. Not all evidence is admissible (hearsay, for example, is not, even if it is true), and the law of evidence is a highly developed subject in jurisprudence. In the forum of daily life, the sources of evidence are less disciplined. Daily experience, a particularly memorable observation, an unusual event we witnessed—any or all of these may be used as evidence for (or against) some belief, theory, hypothesis, or explanation. The systematic study of what experience can yield is what science does, and one of the most distinctive features of the evidence that scientists can marshal on behalf of their claims is that it is the result of **experimentation.** Experiments are deliberately contrived situations that are often complex in their technology and designed to yield particular observations. What the ordinary person does with unaided eye and ear, the scientist does, much more carefully and thoroughly, with the help of laboratory instruments.

The variety, extent, and reliability of the evidence obtained in daily life and in the laboratory are quite different. It is hardly a surprise that in our civilization much more weight is attached to the "findings" of scientists than to the corroborative (much less the contrary) experiences of the ordinary person. No one today would seriously argue that the sun really does go around the earth just because it looks that way; nor would we argue that because viruses are invisible to the naked eye they cannot cause symptoms such as swellings and fevers, which are quite plainly visible.

Examples   One form of evidence is the **example.** Suppose that we argue that a candidate is untrustworthy and should not be elected to public office. We point to episodes in his career—his misuse of funds in 1998 and the false charges he made against an opponent in 2002—as examples of his untrustworthiness. Or if we are arguing that President Truman ordered the atom bomb dropped to save American (and, for that matter, Japanese) lives that otherwise would have been lost in a hard-fought invasion of Japan, we point to the stubbornness of the Japanese defenders in battles on the islands of Saipan, Iwo Jima, and Okinawa, where Japanese soldiers fought to the death rather than surrender.

These examples, we say, show us that the Japanese defenders of the main islands would have fought to their deaths without surrendering, even though they knew they would be defeated. Or if we argue that the war was nearly won when Truman dropped the bomb, we can cite secret peace feelers as examples of the Japanese willingness to end the war.

An example is a sample; these two words come from the same Old French word, *essample,* from the Latin *exemplum,* which means "something taken out"—that is, a selection from the group. A Yiddish proverb shrewdly says that " 'For example' is no proof," but the evidence of well-chosen examples can go a long way toward helping a writer to convince an audience.

In arguments, three sorts of examples are especially common:

- Real events,
- Invented instances (artificial or hypothetical cases), and
- Analogies.

We will treat each of these briefly.

REAL EVENTS   In referring to Truman's decision to drop the atom bomb, we have already touched on examples drawn from real events—the battles at Saipan and elsewhere. And we have also seen Ben Franklin pointing to an allegedly real happening, a fish that had consumed a smaller fish. The advantage of an example drawn from real life, whether a great historical event or a local incident, is that its reality gives it weight. It can't simply be brushed off.

On the other hand, an example drawn from reality may not provide as clear-cut an instance as could be wished for. Suppose, for instance, that someone cites the Japanese army's behavior on Saipan and on Iwo Jima as evidence that the Japanese later would have fought to the death in an American invasion of Japan and would therefore have inflicted terrible losses on themselves and on the Americans. This example is open to the response that in June and July 1945, Japanese diplomats sent out secret peace feelers, so that in August 1945, when Truman authorized dropping the bomb, the situation was very different.

Similarly, in support of the argument that nations will no longer resort to atomic weapons, some people have offered as evidence the fact that since World War I the great powers have not used poison gas. But the argument needs more support than this fact provides. Poison gas was not decisive or even highly effective in World War I. Moreover, the invention of gas masks made it obsolete.

In short, any *real* event is so entangled in its historical circumstances that it might not be adequate or even relevant evidence in the case being argued. In using a real event as an example (and real events certainly can be used), the writer ordinarily must demonstrate that the event can be taken out of its historical context and be used in the new context of argument. Thus, in an argument against using atomic weapons in warfare, the many deaths and horrible injuries inflicted on the Japanese at Hiroshima and Nagasaki can be cited as effects of nuclear weapons that would invariably occur and did not depend on any special circumstances of their use in Japan in 1945.

INVENTED INSTANCES   **Artificial** or **hypothetical cases—invented instances**—have the great advantage of being protected from objections of the sort just given. Recall Thoreau's trout in the milk; that was a colorful hypothetical case that nicely illustrated his point. An invented instance ("Let's assume that a burglar promises not to shoot a householder if the householder swears not to identify him. Is the householder bound by the oath?") is something like a drawing of a flower in a botany textbook or a diagram of the folds of a mountain in a geology textbook. It is admittedly false, but by virtue of its simplifications it sets forth the relevant details very clearly. Thus, in a discussion of rights, the philosopher Charles Frankel says,

> Strictly speaking, when we assert a right for X, we assert that Y has a duty. Strictly speaking, that Y has such a duty presupposes that Y has the capacity to perform this duty. It would be nonsense to say, for example, that a nonswimmer has a moral duty to swim to the help of a drowning man.

This invented example is admirably clear, and it is immune to charges that might muddy the issue if Frankel, instead of referring to a wholly abstract person, Y, talked about some real person, Jones, who did not rescue a drowning man. For then he would get bogged down over arguing about whether Jones *really* couldn't swim well enough to help, and so on.

Yet invented cases have their drawbacks. First and foremost, they cannot be used as evidence. A purely hypothetical example can illustrate a point or provoke reconsideration of a generalization, but it cannot substitute for actual events as evidence supporting an inductive inference. Sometimes such examples are so fanciful, so remote from life that they fail to carry conviction with the reader. Thus the philosopher Judith Jarvis Thomson, in the course of her argument entitled "A Defense of Abortion," asks you to imagine that you wake up one day and find that against your will a celebrated violinist whose body is not adequately functioning has been hooked up into your body, for life-support. Do you have the right to unplug the violinist? Readers of the essays in this book will have to decide for themselves whether the invented cases proposed by various authors are helpful or whether they are so remote that they hinder thought. Readers will have to decide, too, about when they can use invented cases to advance their own arguments.

But we add one point: Even a highly fanciful invented case can have the valuable effect of forcing us to see where we stand. We may say that we are, in all circumstances, against vivisection. But what would we say if we thought that an experiment on one mouse would save the life of someone we love? Or conversely, if one approves of vivisection, would one also approve of sacrificing the last giant panda to save the life of a senile stranger, a person who in any case probably would not live longer than another year? Artificial cases of this sort can help us to see that, well, no, we didn't really mean to say such-and-such when we said so-and-so.

ANALOGIES   The third sort of example, **analogy,** is a kind of comparison. Strictly, an analogy is an extended comparison in which different things are shown to be similar in several ways. Thus, if one wants to argue that a head of state should have extraordinary power during wartime, one can argue that the state at such a time is like a ship in a storm: The crew is needed to lend its help, but the decisions are best left to the captain. (Notice that an analogy compares things that are relatively *un*like. Comparing the plight of one ship to another or of one government to another is not an analogy; it is an inductive inference from one case of the same sort to another such case.) Or take another analogy: We have already glanced at Judith Thomson's hypothetical case in which the reader wakes up to find himself or herself hooked up to a violinist. Thomson uses this situation as an analogy in an argument about abortion. The reader stands for the mother, the violinist for the unwanted fetus. Whether this analogy is close enough to pregnancy to help illuminate our thinking about abortion is something that you may want to think about.

The problem with argument by analogy is this: Two admittedly different things are agreed to be similar in several ways, and the arguer goes on to assert or imply that they are also similar in another way—the point that is being argued. (That is why Thomson argues that if something is true of the reader-hooked-up-to-a-violinist, it is also true of the pregnant mother-hooked-up-to-a-fetus.) But the two things that are said to be analogous and that are indeed similar in characteristics *A*, *B*, and *C* are also different—let's say in characteristics *D* and *E*. As Bishop Butler is said to have remarked in the early eighteenth century, "Everything is what it is, and not another thing."

Analogies can be convincing, especially because they can make complex issues simple. "Don't change horses in midstream," of course, is not a statement about riding horses across a river but about choosing leaders in critical times. Still, in the end, analogies do not necessarily prove anything. What may be true about riding horses across a stream may not be true about choosing leaders in troubled times or about deciding on a given change of leadership. Riding horses across a stream and choosing leaders are, at bottom, different things, and however much these activities may be said to resemble one another, they remain different, and what is true for one need not be true for the other.

Analogies can be helpful in developing our thoughts. It is sometimes argued, for instance—on the analogy of the doctor-patient or the lawyer-client, or the priest-penitent relationship—that newspaper and television reporters should not be required to reveal their confidential sources. That is worth thinking about: Do the similarities run deep enough, or are there fundamental differences? Or take another example: Some writers who support abortion argue that the fetus is not a person any more than the acorn is an oak. That is also worth thinking about.

But one should also think about this response: A fetus is not a person, just as an acorn is not an oak, but an acorn is a potential oak, and a fetus is a potential person, a potential adult human being. Children, even new-born infants, have rights, and one way to explain this claim is to call attention to their potentiality to become mature adults. And so some people argue that the fetus, by analogy, has the rights of an infant, for the fetus, like the infant, is a potential adult.

While we're on this subject, let's consider a brief comparison made by Jill Knight, a member of the British Parliament, speaking about abortion:

> Babies are not like bad teeth, to be jerked out because they cause suffering.

Her point is effectively put; it remains for the reader to decide whether or not fetuses are *babies* and if a fetus is not a baby, *why* it can or can't be treated like a bad tooth. And yet a further bit of analogical reasoning, again about abortion: Thomas Sowell, an economist at the Hoover Institute, grants that women have a legal right to abortion, but he objects to a requirement that the government pay for abortions:

> Because the courts have ruled that women have a legal right to an abortion, some people have jumped to the conclusion that the government has to pay for it. You have a constitutional right to privacy, but the government has no obligation to pay for your window shades. (*Pink and Brown People*, p. 57)

We leave it to the reader to decide whether the analogy is compelling — that is, if the points of resemblance are sufficiently significant to allow one to conclude that what is true of people wanting window shades should be true of people wanting abortions.

Authoritative Testimony   Another form of evidence is **testimony,** the citation or quotation of authorities. In daily life we rely heavily on authorities of all sorts: We get a doctor's opinion about our health, we read a book because an intelligent friend recommends it, we see a movie because a critic gave it a good review, and we pay at least a little attention to the weather forecaster.

In setting forth an argument, one often tries to show that one's view is supported by notable figures, perhaps Jefferson, Lincoln, Martin Luther King Jr., or scientists who won the Nobel Prize. You may recall that in the second chapter, in talking about definitions of pornography, we referred to Kenneth Clark. To make certain that you were impressed by his testimony even if you had never heard of him, we described him as "probably the most influential English-speaking art critic of our time." But heed some words of caution:

- Be sure that the authority, however notable, is an authority on the topic in question (a well-known biologist might be an authority on vitamins but not on the justice of a war).
- Be sure that the authority is not biased. A chemist employed by the tobacco industry isn't likely to admit that smoking may be harmful, and a "director of publications" (that means a press agent) for a hockey team isn't likely to admit that watching or even playing ice hockey stimulates violence.
- Beware of nameless authorities: "a thousand doctors," "leading educators," "researchers at a major medical school."
- Be careful when using authorities who indeed were great authorities in their day but who now may be out of date (Adam Smith on economics, Julius Caesar on the art of war, Louis Pasteur on medicine).
- Cite authorities whose opinions your readers will value. William F. Buckley Jr.'s conservative/libertarian opinions mean a good deal to readers of the magazine that he founded, the *National Review*, but probably not to most liberal thinkers. Gloria Steinem's liberal/feminist opinions carry weight with the readers of the magazines that she cofounded, *New York* and *Ms.* magazine, but probably not much with persons who do not support the full social, economic, and political equality of men and women. If you are writing for the general reader, your usual audience, cite authorities who are likely to be accepted by the general reader.

One other point: *You* may be an authority. You probably aren't nationally known, but on some topics you perhaps can speak with the authority of personal experience. You may have been injured on a motorcycle while riding without wearing a helmet, or you may have escaped injury because you wore a helmet; you may have dropped out of school and then returned; you may have tutored a student whose native language is not English, or you may be such a student and you may have received tutoring. You may have attended a school with a bilingual education program. Your personal testimony on topics relating to these issues may be invaluable, and a reader will probably consider it seriously.

Statistics   The last sort of evidence we discuss here is quantitative or statistical. The maxim "More is better" captures a basic idea of quantitative evidence. Because we know that 90 percent is greater than 75 percent, we are usually ready to grant that any claim supported by experience in 90 percent of the cases is more likely to be true than an alternative claim supported by experience only 75 percent of the time. The greater the difference, the greater our confidence. Consider an example. Honors at graduation from college are often computed on a student's cumulative grade-point average (GPA). The undisputed assumption is that the nearer a student's GPA is to a perfect record (4.0), the better scholar he or she is and therefore the more deserving of highest honors. Consequently, a student with a GPA of 3.9 at the end of her senior year is a stronger candidate for graduating summa cum laude than another student with a GPA of 3.6. When faculty members on the honors committee argue over the relative academic merits of graduating seniors, we know that these quantitative, statistical differences in student GPAs will be the basic (even if not the only) kind of evidence under discussion.

GRAPHS, TABLES, NUMBERS   Statistical information can be marshaled and presented in many forms, but it tends to fall into two main types: the graphic and the numerical. Graphs, tables, and pie charts are familiar ways of presenting quantitative data in an eye-catching manner. (See pages 93–96.) To prepare the graphics, however, one first has to get the numbers themselves under control, and for some purposes it may be acceptable simply to stick with the numbers themselves.

But should the numbers be presented in percentages or in fractions? Should one report, say, that the federal budget underwent a twofold increase over the decade, that it increased by 100 percent, that it doubled, or that the budget at the beginning of the decade was one-half what it was at the end? Taken strictly, these are equivalent ways of saying the same thing. Choice among them, therefore, in an example like this perhaps will rest on whether one's aim is to dramatize the increase (a 100 percent increase looks larger than a doubling) or to play down the size of the increase.

THINKING ABOUT STATISTICAL EVIDENCE   Statistics often get a bad name because it is so easy to misuse them, unintentionally or not, and so difficult to be sure that they have been correctly gathered in the first place. (We remind you of the old saw "There are lies, damned lies, and statistics.") Every branch of social science and natural science needs statistical information, and countless decisions in public and private life are based on quantitative data in statistical form. It is important, therefore, to be sensitive to the sources and reliability of the statistics and to develop a healthy skepticism when confronted with statistics whose parentage is not fully explained.

Consider, for instance, statistics that kept popping up during the baseball strike of 1994. The owners of the clubs said that the average salary of a major-league player was $1.2 million. (The **average** in this case—technically the **mean**—is the result of dividing the total number of salary dollars by the number of players.) The players' union, however, did not talk about the average; rather, the union talked about the **median,** which was less than half of the average, a mere $500,000. (The *median* is the middle value in a distribution. Thus, of the 746 players, 363 earned less than $500,000, 361 earned more, and 22 earned exactly $500,000.) The union said, correctly, that *most* players earned a good deal less than the $1.2 million figure that the owners kept citing; but the $1.2 million average sounded more impressive to the general public, and that is the figure that the guy in the street mentioned when asked for an opinion about the strike.

One other example may help to indicate the difficulties of interpreting statistics. According to the San Francisco police department, in 1990 the city received 1,074 citizen complaints against the police. Los Angeles received only half as many complaints in the same period, and Los Angeles has five times the population of San Francisco. Does this mean that the police of San Francisco are much rougher than the police of Los Angeles? Possibly. But some specialists who have studied the statistics not only for these two cities but also for many other cities have concluded that a department with proportionately more complaints against it is not necessarily more abusive than a department with fewer complaints. According to these experts, the more confidence that the citizens have in their police force, the more the citizens will complain about police misconduct. The relatively small number of complaints against the Los Angeles police department thus may indicate that the citizens of Los Angeles are so intimidated and have so little confidence in the system that they do not bother to complain.

If it is sometimes difficult to interpret statistics, it is often at least equally difficult to establish accurate statistics. Consider this example:

> Advertisements are the most prevalent and toxic of the mental pollutants. From the moment your radio alarm sounds in the morning to the wee hours of late-night TV, microjolts of commercial pollution flood into your brain at the rate of about three thousand marketing messages per day. (Kalle Lasn, *Culture Jam,* 18–19)

Lasn's book includes endnotes as documentation, so, curious about the statistics, we turn to the appropriate page and we find this information concerning the source of his data:

> "three thousand marketing messages per day." Mark Landler, Walecia Konrad, Zachary Schiller, and Lois Therrien, "What Happened to Advertising?" *BusinessWeek*, September 23, 1991, page 66. Leslie Savan in *The Sponsored Life* (Temple University Press, 1994), page 1, estimated that "16,000 ads flicker across an individual's consciousness daily." I did an informal survey in March 1995 and found the number to be closer to 1,500 (this included all marketing messages, corporate images, logos, ads, brand names, on TV, radio, billboards, buildings, signs, clothing, appliances, in cyberspace, etc., over a typical twenty-four hour period in my life). (219)

Well, this endnote is odd. In the earlier passage, you will recall, the author asserted that "about three thousand marketing messages per day" flood into a person's brain. Now, in the documentation, he helpfully cites a source for that statistic, from *BusinessWeek*—though we have not the faintest idea of how the authors of the article in *BusinessWeek* came up with that figure. Oddly, he goes on to offer a very different figure (16,000 ads), and then, to our utter confusion, he offers yet a third figure, 1,500, based on his own "informal survey." Probably the one thing we can safely say about all three figures is that none of them means very much. Even if the compilers of the statistics told us exactly how they counted—let's say that among countless other criteria they assumed that the average person reads one magazine per day and that the average magazine contains 124 advertisements—it would be hard to take them seriously. After all, in leafing through a magazine, some people may read many ads, some may read none. Some people may read some ads carefully—but perhaps to enjoy their absurdity. Our point: Although the author in his text said, without implying any uncertainty, that "about three thousand marketing messages per day" reach an individual, it is evident (if one checks the endnote) that even he is confused about the figure he gives.

We are not suggesting, of course, that everyone who uses statistics is trying to deceive or even that many who use statistics are unconsciously deceived by them. We mean only to suggest that statistics are open to widely different interpretations and that often those columns of numbers, so precise with their decimal points, are in fact imprecise and possibly even worthless because they may be based on insufficient or biased samples.

A CHECKLIST FOR EVALUATING STATISTICAL EVIDENCE

Regard statistical evidence (like all other evidence) cautiously, and don't accept it until you have thought about these questions:

☐ Was it compiled by a disinterested source? Of course, the name of the source does not always reveal its particular angle (for example, People for the American Way), but sometimes the name lets you know what to expect (National Rifle Association, American Civil Liberties Union).

☐ Is it based on an adequate sample? (A study pointed out that criminals have an average IQ of 91 to 93, whereas the general population has an IQ of 100. The conclusion drawn was that criminals have a lower IQ than the general population. This reading may be accurate, but some doubts have been expressed. For instance, because the entire sample of criminals consisted only of *convicted* criminals, this sample may be biased; possibly the criminals with higher IQs have enough intelligence not to get caught. Or if they are caught, perhaps they are smart enough to hire better lawyers.)

☐ Is the statistical evidence recent enough to be relevant?

☐ How many of the factors likely to be relevant were identified and measured?

☐ Are the figures open to a different and equally plausible interpretation?

☐ If a percent is cited, is it the *average* (or *mean*), or is it the *median*?

Quiz

What is wrong with the following statistical proof that children do not have time for school?

> One-third of the time they are sleeping (about 122 days);
> One-eighth of the time they are eating (three hours a day, totaling 45 days);
> One-fourth of the time is taken up by summer and other vacations (91 days);
> Two-sevenths of the year is weekends (104 days).
> Total: 362 days — so how can a kid have time for school?

NONRATIONAL APPEALS

Satire, Irony, Sarcasm, Humor

In talking about definition, deduction, and evidence, we have been talking about means of rational persuasion. But as mentioned earlier, there are also other means of persuasion. Take force, for example. If X kicks Y, threatens to destroy Y's means of livelihood, or threatens Y's life, X may persuade Y to cooperate. One form of irrational but sometimes highly effective persuasion is **satire**—that is, witty ridicule. A cartoonist may persuade viewers that a politician's views are unsound by caricaturing (and thus ridiculing) the politician's appearance or by presenting a grotesquely distorted (funny, but unfair) picture of the issue.

Satiric artists often use caricature; satiric writers, also seeking to persuade by means of ridicule, often use **verbal irony.** Irony of this sort contrasts what is said and what is meant. For instance, words of praise may be meant to imply blame (when Shakespeare's Cassius says, "Brutus is an honorable man," he means his hearers to think that Brutus is dishonorable), and words of modesty may be meant to imply superiority ("Of course, I'm too dumb to understand this problem"). Such language, when heavy-handed, is called **sarcasm** ("You're a great guy," said to someone who will not lend the speaker ten dollars). If it is witty—if the jeering is in some degree clever—it is called irony rather than sarcasm.

Although ridicule is not a form of argument (because it is not a form of reasoning), passages of ridicule, especially verbal irony, sometimes appear in essays that are arguments. These passages, like reasons, or for that matter like appeals to the emotions, are efforts to persuade the hearer to accept the speaker's point of view. For example, in Judy Brady's famous essay "I Want a Wife," the writer, a woman, does not really mean that she wants a wife. The pretense that she wants a wife gives the essay a playful, joking quality; her words must mean something other than what they seem to mean. But that she is not merely joking (satire has been defined as "joking in earnest") is evident; she is seeking to persuade. She has a point, and she could argue it straight, but that would produce a very different sort of essay.

We have said that Brady's essay has a playful quality—which is not to say that it merely clowns around. She clearly is serious, but she is also entertaining. The great trick in using humor in an argument is, on the one hand, to avoid mere wisecracking, which makes the writer seem like a smart aleck, and, on the other hand, to avoid mere clownishness, which makes the writer seem like a fool. Later in this chapter (p. 74), we print an essay by George F. Will, that is (or seeks to be?) humorous in places. You be the judge.

Emotional Appeals

It is sometimes said that good argumentative writing appeals only to reason, never to emotion, and that any sort of emotional appeal is illegitimate, irrelevant. Logic textbooks may even stigmatize with Latin labels the various sorts of emotional appeal—for instance, *argumentum ad populam* (appeal to the prejudices of the mob, as in "Come on, we all know that schools don't teach anything anymore") and *argumentum ad misericordiam* (appeal to pity, as in "No one ought to blame this poor kid for stabbing a classmate because his mother was often institutionalized for alcoholism and his father beat him").

True, appeals to emotion may get in the way of the facts of the case; they may blind the audience by, in effect, throwing dust in its eyes or by stimulating tears. A classic example is found in Shakespeare's *Julius Caesar,* when Marc Antony addresses the Roman populace after Brutus, Cassius, and others have assassinated Caesar. The real issue is whether Caesar was becoming tyrannical (as the assassins claim) and would therefore curtail the freedom of the people. Antony turns from the evidence and stirs the mob against the assassins by appealing to its emotions. In the ancient Roman biographical writing that Shakespeare drew on, Sir Thomas North's translation of Plutarch's *Lives of the Noble Grecians and Romans,* Plutarch says that Antony,

> perceiving that his words moved the common people to compassion, . . .
> framed his eloquence to make their hearts yearn [that is, grieve] the
> more, and, taking Caesar's gown all bloody in his hand, he laid it open
> to the sight of them all, showing what a number of cuts and holes it
> had upon it. Therewithal the people fell presently into such a rage and
> mutiny that there was no more order kept.

Here are a few extracts from Antony's speeches in Shakespeare's play. Antony begins by asserting that he will speak only briefly:

> Friends, Romans, countrymen, lend me your ears;
> I come to bury Caesar, not to praise him.

After briefly offering some rather insubstantial evidence that Caesar gave no signs of behaving tyrannically (for example, "When that the poor have cried, Caesar hath wept"), Antony begins to play directly on the emotions of his hearers. Descending from the platform so that he may be in closer contact with his audience (like a modern politician, he wants to work the crowd), he calls attention to Caesar's bloody toga:

If you have tears, prepare to shed them now.
You all do know this mantle; I remember
The first time ever Caesar put it on:
'Twas on a summer's evening, in his tent,
That day he overcame the Nervii.
Look, in this place ran Cassius' dagger through;
See what a rent the envious Casca made;
Through this, the well-belovèd Brutus stabbed. . . .

In these few lines Antony first prepares the audience by suggesting to them how they should respond ("If you have tears, prepare to shed them now"), then flatters them by implying that they, like Antony, were intimates of Caesar (he credits them with being familiar with Caesar's garment), then evokes a personal memory of a specific time ("a summer's evening")—not just any old specific time but a very important one, the day that Caesar won a battle against the Nervii (a particularly fierce tribe in what is now France). In fact, Antony was *not* at the battle, and he did not join Caesar until three years later.

Antony does not mind being free with the facts; his point here is not to set the record straight but to stir the mob against the assassins. He goes on, daringly but successfully, to identify one particular slit in the garment with Cassius's dagger, another with Casca's, and a third with Brutus's. Antony cannot know which slit was made by which dagger, but his rhetorical trick works.

Notice, too, that Antony arranges the three assassins in climactic order, since Brutus (Antony claims) was especially beloved by Caesar:

Judge, O you gods, how dearly Caesar loved him!
This was the most unkindest cut of all;
For when the noble Caesar saw him stab,
Ingratitude, more strong than traitor's arms,
Quite vanquished him. Then burst his mighty heart. . . . (3.2.75–188)

Nice. According to Antony, the noble-minded Caesar—Antony's words have erased all thought of the tyrannical Caesar—died not from the wounds inflicted by daggers but from the heartbreaking perception of Brutus's ingratitude. Doubtless there was not a dry eye in the house. We can all hope that if we are ever put on trial, we have a lawyer as skilled in evoking sympathy as Antony.

The oration is obviously successful in the play and apparently was successful in real life, but it is the sort of speech that prompts logicians to write disapprovingly of attempts to stir feeling in an audience. (As mentioned earlier in this chapter, the evocation of emotion in an audience is called **pathos,** from the Greek word for "emotion" or "suffering.") There is nothing inherently wrong in stimulating our audience's emotions, but when an emotional appeal confuses the issue that is being argued about or shifts the attention away from the facts of the issue, we can reasonably speak of the fallacy of emotional appeal.

No fallacy is involved, however, when an emotional appeal heightens the facts, bringing them home to the audience rather than masking them. If we are talking about legislation that would govern police actions, it is legitimate to show a photograph of the battered, bloodied face of an alleged victim of police brutality. True, such a photograph cannot tell the whole truth; it cannot tell us if the subject threatened the officer with a gun or repeatedly resisted an order to surrender. But it can tell us that the victim was severely beaten and (like a comparable description in

A CHECKLIST FOR ANALYZING AN ARGUMENT

- ☐ What is the writer's claim or thesis? Ask yourself:
  - ☐ What claim is being asserted?
  - ☐ What assumptions are being made—and are they acceptable?
  - ☐ Are important terms satisfactorily defined?
- ☐ What support (evidence) is offered on behalf of the claim? Ask yourself:
  - ☐ Are the examples relevant, and are they convincing?
  - ☐ Are the statistics (if any) relevant, accurate, and complete? Do they allow only the interpretation that is offered in the argument?
  - ☐ If authorities are cited, are they indeed authorities on this topic, and can they be regarded as impartial?
  - ☐ Is the logic—deductive and inductive—valid?
  - ☐ If there is an appeal to emotion—for instance, if satire is used to ridicule the opposing view—is this appeal acceptable?
- ☐ Does the writer seem to you to be fair? Ask yourself:
  - ☐ Are counterarguments adequately considered?
  - ☐ Is there any evidence of dishonesty or of a discreditable attempt to manipulate the reader?
  - ☐ How does the writer establish the image of himself or herself that we sense in the essay?

words) evoke in us emotions that may properly enter into our decision about the permissible use of police evidence. Similarly, an animal rights activist who is arguing that calves are cruelly confined might reasonably tell us about the size of the pen in which the beast—unable to turn around or even to lie down—is kept. Others may argue that calves don't much care about turning around or have no right to turn around, but the verbal description, which unquestionably makes an emotional appeal, can hardly be called fallacious or irrelevant.

In appealing to emotions then, the important things are

- Not to falsify (especially by oversimplifying) the issue and
- Not to distract attention from the facts of the case.

Focus on the facts and concentrate on offering reasons (essentially, statements linked with "because"), but you may also legitimately bring the facts home to your readers by seeking to induce in them the appropriate emotions. Your words will be fallacious only if you stimulate emotions that are not rightly connected with the facts of the case.

DOES ALL WRITING CONTAIN ARGUMENTS?

Our answer to the question we have just posed is no—but probably *most* writing *does* contain an argument of sorts. Or put it this way: The writer wants to persuade the reader to see things the way the writer sees them—at least until the end of the essay. After all, even a recipe for a cherry pie in a food magazine—a piece of writing that is primarily expository (how to do it) rather than argumentative (how a reasonable person ought to think about this topic)—probably includes, near the beginning, a sentence with a hint of an argument in it, such as "*Because* [a sign that a *reason* will be offered] this pie can be made quickly and with ingredients (canned cherries) that are always available, give it a try, and it will surely become one of your favorites." Clearly, such a statement cannot stand as a formal argument—a discussion that takes account of possible counterarguments, that relies chiefly on logic and little if at all on emotional appeal, and that draws a conclusion that seems irrefutable. Still, the statement is something of an argument on behalf of making a pie with canned cherries. In this case, a claim is made (the pie will become a favorite), and two *reasons* are offered in support of this claim:

- It can be made quickly, and
- The chief ingredient—because it is canned—can always be at hand.

The underlying *assumptions* are

- You don't have a great deal of time to waste in the kitchen, and
- Canned cherries are just as tasty as fresh cherries—and even if they aren't, well, you wouldn't know the difference.

When we read a lead-in to a recipe, then, we won't find a formal argument, but we probably will get a few words that seek to persuade us to keep reading. And most writing does contain such material—sentences that give us a reason to keep reading, that engage our interests, and that make us want to stay with the writer for at least a little longer. If the recipe happens to be difficult and time-consuming, the lead-in may say, "Although this recipe for a cherry pie, using fresh cherries that you will have to pit, is a bit more time-consuming than the usual recipe that calls for canned cherries, once you have tasted it you will never go back to canned cherries." Again, although the logic is scarcely compelling, the persuasive element is evident. The assumption here is that you have a discriminating palate; once you have tasted a pie made with fresh cherries, you will never again enjoy the canned stuff. The writer is not giving us a formal argument, with abundant evidence and with a detailed refutation of counterarguments, but we do know where the writer stands and how the writer wishes us to respond.

AN EXAMPLE: AN ARGUMENT AND A LOOK AT THE WRITER'S STRATEGIES

This essay concerns President George W. Bush's proposal that drilling be allowed in part of the Arctic National Wildlife Refuge (ANWR, pronounced "An-war"). The section of the ANWR that is proposed for drilling is called the "1002 area," as defined by Section 1002 of the Alaska National Interest Lands Conservation Act of 1980. In March 2003, the Senate rejected the Bush proposal, but the issue remains alive.

We follow George F. Will's essay with some comments about the ways in which he constructs his argument.

GEORGE F. WILL

George F. Will, a syndicated columnist whose writing appears in 460 newspapers, was born in Champaign, Illinois, in 1941, and educated at Trinity College (Hartford), Oxford University, and Princeton University. Will has served as the Washington, D.C., editor of the National Review *and now writes a regular column for* Newsweek. *His essays have been collected in several books.*

Being Green at Ben and Jerry's

Some Environmental Policies Are Feel-Good Indulgences for an Era of Energy Abundance

If you have an average-size dinner table, four feet by six feet, put a dime on the edge of it. Think of the surface of the table as the Arctic National Wildlife Refuge in Alaska. The dime is larger than the piece of the coastal plain that would have been opened to drilling for oil and natural gas. The House of Representatives voted for drilling, but the Senate voted against access to what Sen. John Kerry, Massachusetts Democrat and presidential aspirant, calls "a few drops of oil." ANWR could produce, for 25 years, at least as much oil as America currently imports from Saudi Arabia.

Six weeks of desultory Senate debate about the energy bill reached an almost comic culmination in . . . yet another agriculture subsidy. The subsidy is a requirement that will triple the amount of ethanol, which is made from corn, that must be put in gasoline, ostensibly to clean America's air, actually to buy farmers' votes.

Over the last three decades, energy use has risen about 30 percent. But so has population, which means per capita energy use is unchanged. And per capita GDP has risen substantially, so we are using 40 percent less energy per dollar output. Which is one reason there is no energy crisis, at least none as most Americans understand such things—a shortage of, and therefore high prices of, gasoline for cars, heating oil for furnaces and electricity for air conditioners.

In the absence of a crisis to concentrate the attention of the inattentive American majority, an intense faction—full-time environmentalists—goes to work. Spencer Abraham, the secretary of Energy, says "the previous administration . . . simply drew up a list of fuels it *didn't* like—nuclear energy, coal, hydropower, and oil—which together account for 73 percent of America's energy supply." Well, there are always windmills.

Sometimes lofty environmentalism is a cover for crude politics. The 5
United States has the world's largest proven reserves of coal. But Mike
Oliver, a retired physicist and engineer, and John Hospers, professor
emeritus of philosophy at USC, note that in 1996 President Clinton put
68 billion tons of America's cleanest-burning coal, located in Utah, off-
limits for mining, ostensibly for environmental reasons. If every existing
U.S. electric power plant burned coal, the 68 billion tons could fuel them
for 45 years at the current rate of consumption. Now power companies
must import clean-burning coal, some from mines owned by Indonesia's
Lippo Group, the heavy contributor to Clinton, whose decision about
Utah's coal vastly increased the value of Lippo's coal.

The United States has just 2.14 percent of the world's proven reserves of oil, so some people say it is pointless to drill in places like
ANWR because "energy independence" is a chimera. Indeed it is. But domestic supplies can provide important insurance against uncertain foreign supplies. And domestic supplies can mean exporting hundreds of
billions of dollars less to oil-producing nations, such as Iraq.

Besides, when considering proven reserves, note the adjective. In
1930 the United States had proven reserves of 13 billion barrels. We then
fought the Second World War and fueled the most fabulous economic
expansion in human history, including the electricity-driven "New
Economy." (Manufacturing and running computers consume 15 percent
of U.S. electricity. Internet use alone accounts for half of the growth in
demand for electricity.) So by 1990 proven reserves were . . . 17 billion
barrels, not counting any in Alaska or Hawaii.

In 1975 proven reserves in the Persian Gulf were 74 billion barrels.
In 1993 they were 663 billion, a ninefold increase. At the current rate of
consumption, today's proven reserves would last 150 years. New discov-
eries will be made, some by vastly improved techniques of deep-water
drilling. But environmental policies will define opportunities. The government estimates that beneath the U.S. outer continental shelf, which
the government owns, there are at least 46 billion barrels of oil. But only
2 percent of the shelf has been leased for energy development.

Opponents of increased energy production usually argue for decreased consumption. But they flinch from conservation measures. A
new $1 gasoline tax would dampen demand for gasoline, but it would
stimulate demands for the heads of the tax increasers. After all,
Americans get irritable when impersonal market forces add 25 cents to
the cost of a gallon. Tougher fuel-efficiency requirements for vehicles
would save a lot of energy. But who would save the legislators who
passed those requirements? Beware the wrath of Americans who like to
drive, and autoworkers who like to make cars that are large, heavy and
safer than the gasoline-sippers that environmentalists prefer.

Some environmentalism is a feel-good indulgence for an era of en-   10
ergy abundance, which means an era of avoided choices. Or ignored
choices—ignored because if acknowledged, they would not make the
choosers feel good. Karl Zinsmeister, editor in chief of *The American
Enterprise* magazine, imagines an oh-so-green environmentalist enjoy-
ing the most politically correct product on the planet—Ben & Jerry's ice
cream. Made in a factory that depends on electricity-guzzling refrigeration, a gallon of ice cream requires four gallons of milk. While making
that much milk, a cow produces eight gallons of manure, and flatulence
with another eight gallons of methane, a potent "greenhouse" gas. And
the cow consumes lots of water plus three pounds of grain and hay,
which is produced with tractor fuel, chemical fertilizers, herbicides and
insecticides, and is transported with truck or train fuel:

"So every time he digs into his Cherry Garcia, the conscientious environmentalist should visualize (in addition to world peace) a pile of
grain, water, farm chemicals, and energy inputs much bigger than his
ice cream bowl on one side of the table, and, on the other side of the
table, a mound of manure eight times the size of his bowl, plus a balloon
of methane that would barely fit under the dining room table."

Cherry Garcia. It's a choice. *Bon appétit.*

Now let's look at Will's essay, to see some of the techniques that he
uses, techniques that enable him to engage a reader's interest and perhaps enable him to convince the reader, or at least make the reader
think, that Will probably is on to something.

The title, "Being Green at Ben and Jerry's," does not at all prepare
the reader for an argument about drilling in the National Arctic Wildlife
Refuge, but if you have read any of Will's other columns in *Newsweek*,
you probably know that he is conservative and that he will be poking
some fun at the green folk—the environmentalists. Will can get away
with using a title that is not focused because he has a body of loyal readers—people who will read him because they want to read him, whatever
the topic is—but the rest of us writers have to give our readers some
idea of what we will be talking about. In short, let your readers know
early, perhaps in the title, where you will be taking them.

The subtitle, "Some Environmental Policies Are Feel-Good In-
dulgences for an Era of Energy Abundance" perhaps added by an editor
of the magazine, does suggest that the piece will concern energy, and the
words "feel-good indulgence" pretty clearly tell readers that Will believes
the environmentalists are indulging themselves.

Paragraph 1 offers a striking comparison. Will wants us to believe
that the area proposed for drilling is tiny, so he says that if we imagine

the entire Arctic National Wildlife Refuge as a dinner table, the area proposed for drilling is the size of a dime. We think you will agree that this opening seizes a reader's attention. Assuming the truth of the figure—but there seems to be some dispute, since opponents have said that the area would be more like the size of a dinner plate—the image is highly effective. A dime is so small! And is worth so little! Still, one might ask—but probably one doesn't, because Will's figure is so striking—if the tininess of the area really is decisive. One might easily, and apparently with reason, dismiss as absurd the idea that a minuscule tsetse fly could kill a human being, or that the plague is spread by fleas that have bitten rats, because these proposals sound ridiculous—but they are true. One other point about the first paragraph: Will's voice sounds like a voice you might hear in your living room: "If you have an average-size dinner table," "the dime is larger," "at least as much oil." Don't think that in your own essays you need to adopt a highly formal style. Your reader should think of you as serious but not solemn.

Will goes on to say that Senator John Kerry, an opponent of drilling and therefore on the side that Will opposes, dismisses the oil in the refuge as "a few drops." Will replies that it "could produce, for 25 years, at least as much oil as America currently imports from Saudi Arabia." Kerry's "a few drops" is, of course, not to be taken literally; he means, in effect, that the oil is a drop in the bucket. But when one looks into the issue, one finds that estimates by responsible sources vary considerably, from 3.2 billion barrels to 11.5 billion barrels.

Paragraph 2 dismisses the Senate's debate ("almost comic," "actually to buy farmers' votes").

Paragraph 3 offers statistics to make the point that "there is no energy crisis." Here, as in the first paragraph, where he showed his awareness of Kerry's view, Will indicates that he is familiar with views other than his own. In arguing a case, it is important for the writer to let readers know that indeed there are other views—which the writer then goes on to show are less substantial than the writer's. Will is correct in saying that "per capita energy use is unchanged," but those on the other side might say, "Yes, per capita consumption has not increased, but given the population increase, the annual amount has vastly increased, which means that resources are being depleted and that pollution is increasing."

Paragraph 4 asserts again that there is no energy crisis, pokes at "full-time environmentalists" (perhaps there is a suggestion that such people really ought to get a respectable job), and ends with a bit of whimsy: These folks probably think we should go back to using windmills.

Paragraph 5, in support of the assertion that "Sometimes lofty environmentalism is a cover for crude politics," cites an authority (often an effective technique), and, since readers are not likely to recognize the name, it also identifies him ("professor emeritus of philosophy at USC"), and it then offers further statistics (again effective). The paragraph begins by talking about "crude politics" and ends with the assertion that "Now power companies must import clean-burning coal, some from mines owned by Indonesia's Lippo Group, the heavy contributor to Clinton." In short, Will does what he can to suggest that the views of at least some environmentalists are rooted in money and politics.

Paragraph 6 offers another statistic ("The United States has just 2.14 percent of the world's proven reserves of oil"), and he turns it *against* those who argue that therefore it is pointless for us to drill in Alaska. In effect, he is replying to people like Senator Kerry who say that the Arctic refuge provides only "a few drops of oil." The point, Will suggests, is not that we can't achieve independence; the point is that "domestic supplies can provide important insurance against uncertain foreign supplies."

Paragraph 7 begins nicely with a transition, "Besides," and then offers additional statistics concerning the large amount of oil that we have. It was, for instance, enough to fuel "the most fabulous economic expansion in human history."

Paragraph 8 offers additional statistics, first about "proven reserves" in the Persian Gulf and then about an estimate—but it is only an estimate—of oil "beneath the U.S. outer continental shelf." We are not certain of Will's point, but in any case the statistics suggest to a reader that the author has done his homework.

Paragraph 9 summarizes the chief position (as Will sees it) of those on the other side: They usually argue for decreased consumption, but they are afraid to argue for the sort of tax on gasoline that might indeed decrease consumption because they know that many Americans want to drive large, heavy cars. Further, the larger, heavier cars that the environmentalists object to are in fact "safer than the gasoline-sippers that environmentalists prefer."

Paragraph 10 uses the term "feel-good indulgence," which is also found in the subtitle of the essay, and now, in the third sentence of the paragraph, we hear again of Ben and Jerry, who have not been in our minds since the title of the essay, "Being Green at Ben and Jerry's." Perhaps we have been wondering all this while why Ben and Jerry are in the title. Almost surely the reader knows that Ben and Jerry are associated with ice cream and therefore with cows and meadows, and probably many readers know, at least vaguely, that Ben and Jerry are somehow associated with environmentalism and with other causes often thought to be on the left. Will (drawing on an article by Karl Zinsmeister, editor of *The American Enterprise*), writes what we consider an extremely amusing paragraph in which he points out that the process of making ice cream "depends on electricity-guzzling refrigeration" and that the cows are, so to speak, supported by fuel that transports fertilizers, herbicides, and insecticides. Further, in the course of producing the four gallons of milk that are required for one gallon of ice cream, the cows themselves—those darlings of environmentalists—contribute "eight gallons of manure, and flatulence with another eight gallons of methane, a potent 'greenhouse' gas." As we see when we read Will's next paragraph, the present paragraph is in large measure a lead-in for the following quotation. Will knows it is is *not* enough to give a quotation; a writer has to *make use* of the quotation—has to lead into it or, after quoting, has to comment on it, or do both.

Paragraph 11 is entirely devoted to quoting Zinsmeister, who imagines an environmentalist digging into a dish of one of Ben and Jerry's most popular flavors, Cherry Garcia. We are invited to see the bowl of ice cream on one side of the table—here Will effectively evokes the table of his first paragraph—and a pile of manure on the other side, "plus a balloon of methane that would barely fit under the dining room table." Vulgar, no doubt, but funny too. George Will knows that humor as well as logic (and statistics and other kinds of evidence) can be among the tools a writer uses in getting an audience to accept or at least to consider an argument.

Paragraph 12 consists of three short sentences, adding up to less than a single line of type: "Cherry Garcia. It's a choice. *Bon appétit.*" None of the sentences mentions oil or the Arctic Refuge or statistics, and therefore this ending might seem utterly irrelevant to the topic, but we think Will is very effectively saying, "Sure, you have a choice about drilling in the Arctic Refuge; any sensible person will choose the ice cream (drilling) rather than the manure and the gas (not drilling).

Topics for Critical Thinking and Writing

1. What, if anything, makes Will's essay interesting? What, if anything, makes it highly persuasive? How might it be made more persuasive?

2. In paragraph 10, Will clowns a bit about the gas that cows emit, but apparently this gas, which contributes to global warming, is no laughing matter. The government of New Zealand, in an effort to reduce livestock emissions of methane and nitrous oxide, proposed a tax that would subsidize future research on the emissions. The tax would cost the average farmer $300 a year. Imagine that you are a New Zealand farmer. Write a letter to your representative, arguing for or against the tax.

3. Senator Barbara Boxer, campaigning against the proposal to drill in ANWR, spoke of the refuge as "God's gift to us" (*New York Times*, March

20, 2002). How strong an argument is she offering? Some opponents of drilling have said that drilling in ANWR is as unthinkable as drilling in Yosemite or the Grand Canyon. Again, how strong is this argument? Can you imagine circumstances in which you would support drilling in these places? Do we have a moral duty to preserve certain unspoiled areas?

4. The Inupiat (Eskimo) who live in and near ANWR by a large majority favor drilling, seeing it as a source of jobs and a source of funding for schools, hospitals, and police. But the Ketchikan Indians, who speak of themselves as the "Caribou People," see drilling as a threat to the herds that they depend on for food and hides. How does one balance the conflicting needs of these two groups?

5. Opponents of drilling in ANWR argue that over its lifetime of fifty years, the area would produce less than 1 percent of the fuel we need during the period and that therefore we should not risk disturbing the area. Further, they argue that drilling in ANWR is an attempt at a quick fix to U.S. energy needs, whereas what is needed are sustainable solutions, such as the development of renewable energy sources (e.g., wind and sun) and fuel-efficient automobiles. How convincing do you find these arguments?

6. Proponents of drilling include a large majority — something like 75 percent of the people of Alaska, including its governor and its two senators. How much attention should be paid to their voices?

4

Visual Rhetoric:
Images as Arguments

SOME USES OF IMAGES

Most visual materials that accompany written arguments serve one of two functions—they appeal to the emotions (a photograph of a calf in a pen so narrow that the calf cannot turn, in an essay on animal liberation) or they clarify numerical data (a graph showing five decades of male and female law school enrollments). There are of course additional uses for pictures, for example cartoons may add a welcome touch of humor or satire, but in this chapter we concentrate on appeals to emotion and briefly on graphs and related images.

APPEALS TO THE EYE

We began the preceding chapter by distinguishing between *argument,* which we said relies on reason (*logos*), and *persuasion,* which we said is a broad term that can include appeal to the emotions (*pathos*)—for example, an appeal to pity. Threats, too, can be persuasive. As Al Capone famously said, "You can get a lot more done with a kind word and a gun than with a kind word alone." Indeed, most of the remarks that we can think of link persuasion not with the power of reason but with the power of emotional appeals, of flattery, of threats, and of appeals to self-interest. We have in mind passages spoken not only by the likes of the racketeer Al Capone, but by more significant figures. Consider these two remarks, which both use the word *interest* in the sense of "self-interest":

> Would you persuade, speak of Interest, not Reason
> — Ben Franklin

> There are two levers for moving men—interest and fear.
> —Napoleon Bonaparte

An appeal to self-interest is obviously at the heart of most advertisements: "Buy *X* automobile, and members of the opposite sex will find you irresistible," "Use *Y* instant soup, and your family will love you more," "Try *Z* cereal and enjoy regularity." We will look at advertisements later in this chapter, but first let's talk a bit more about the use and abuse of visual material in persuasion.

When we discussed the appeal to emotion (p. 69), we quoted from Mark Antony's speech to the Roman populace in Shakespeare's *Julius Caesar*, you will recall, Antony stirred the mob by displaying Caesar's blood-stained mantle, that is, by supplementing his words with visual material:

> Look, in this place ran Cassius' dagger through;
> See what a rent the envious Casca made;
> Through this, the well-belovèd Brutus stabbed. . . .

In courtrooms today, trial lawyers and prosecutors still do this sort of thing when they exhibit photos of a bloody corpse, or when they introduce as witnesses small children who sob as they describe the murder of their parents. The appeal clearly is not to reason but to the jurors' emotions—and yet, can we confidently say that this sort of visual evidence—this attempt to stir anger at the alleged perpetrator of the crime and pity for the victims — is irrelevant? Why shouldn't jurors vicariously experience the assault?

When we think about it—and it takes only a moment of thinking— the appeal in the courtroom to the eye and then to the heart or mind is evident even in smaller things, such as the clothing that the lawyers wear and the clothing that they advise their clients to wear. To take the most obvious, classic example: The mugger who normally wears jeans, a T-shirt, and a leather jacket appears in court in a three-piece suit, dress shirt, and necktie. Lawyers know that in arguing a case, visuals make statements—perhaps not logical arguments but nevertheless meaningful statements that will attract or repel jurors.

Another sort of visual appeal connected with some arguments should be mentioned briefly—the visual appeal of the specific setting in which the argument occurs. Martin Luther King Jr.'s great speech of August 28, 1963, "I Have a Dream," still reads very well on the page, but

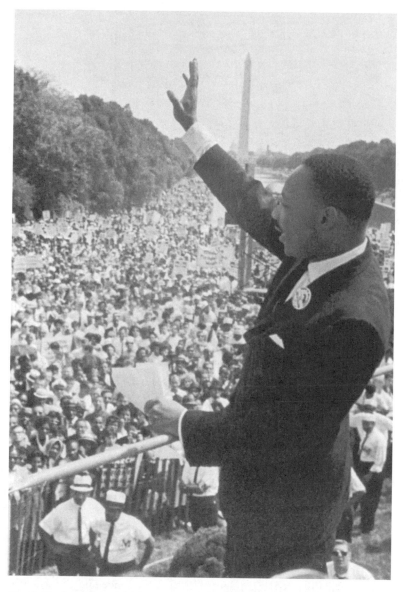

Martin Luther King Jr. delivering his "I Have a Dream" speech on August 28, 1963, from the steps of the Lincoln Memorial. The visual aspects — the setting (the Lincoln Memorial with the Washington Monument and the Capitol in the distance) and King's gestures — are part of the persuasive rhetoric of the speech.

(© ARS, NY. Lithograph printed in black; Matthew T. Mellon Fund, The Museum of Modern Art, NYC; Licensed by SCALA/Art Resource.)

part of its immense appeal when it was first given was due to its setting: King spoke to some 200,000 people in Washington, D.C., as he stood on the steps of the Lincoln Memorial. That setting was part of King's argument.

Pictures—and here we get to our chief subject—are also sometimes used as parts of arguments because pictures make statements. Some pictures, like Edvard Munch's *The Scream* (this page), make obvious statements: The swiftly receding diagonal lines of the fence and the walkway, the wavy sky, and the vibrating vertical lines to the right of the figure all convey the great agitation experienced by the figure in the woodcut. Some pictures, like the photographs shown to members of Congress during the debate over whether permission should be given to drill in the

Arctic National Wildlife Refuge are a bit less obvious: Opponents of drilling showed beautiful pictures of polar bears frolicking, wildflowers in bloom, and caribou on the move; proponents of drilling showed bleak pictures of what they called "barren land" and "a frozen wasteland." Both sides knew very well that images are powerful persuaders, and they did not hesitate to use images as supplements to words.

We again invite you to think about the appropriateness of using images in arguments. Should argument be entirely a matter of reason, of logic, without appeals to the emotions? Or can images of the sort that we have already mentioned provide visual (and emotional) support for reasons that are offered? The statement that "The Arctic National Wildlife Refuge is a home for abundant wildlife, notably polar bears, caribou, and wildflowers" may not mean much until it is reinforced with breathtaking images. (And, similarly, the statement that "Most of the ANWR land is barren" may not mean much until it is corroborated by images of the vast bleakness.)

> *A Rule for Writers:* If you think that pictures will help you to make the point you are arguing, include them with captions explaining sources and relevance.

ARE SOME IMAGES NOT FIT TO BE SHOWN?

Images of suffering—human or, as animal rights activists have made us see, animal—can be immensely persuasive. In the nineteenth century, for instance, the antislavery movement made extremely effective use of images in its campaign. We reproduce two antislavery images on page 86, as well as a counterimage that sought to assure viewers that slavery is a beneficent system. But are there some images not fit to print?

Until recently, many newspapers did not print pictures of lynched African Americans, hanged and burned and maimed. The reasons for not printing such images probably differed in the South and North: Southern papers may have considered the images to be discreditable to whites, while Northern papers may have deemed the images too revolting. Even today, when it is commonplace to see in newspapers and on television screens pictures of dead victims of war, or famine, or traffic accidents, one rarely sees bodies that are horribly maimed. (For traffic accidents, the body is usually covered, and we see only the smashed car.) The United States government has refused to release photographs showing the bodies of American soldiers killed in the war in Iraq, and it has

DESCRIPTION OF A SLAVE SHIP.

Images played an important role in the activities of the antislavery movement in the nineteenth century. On the top left is a diagram that shows how human cargo was packed into a slave ship; it was distributed with Thomas Clarkson's Essay on the Slavery and Commerce of the Human Species *(1804). On the top right is Frederick W. Mercer's photograph (April 2, 1863) of Gordon, a "badly lacerated" runaway slave. Images such as the slave ship and Gordon were used against the claims of slaveowners that slavery was a humane institution—claims that also were supported by illustrations, such as the woodcut at the bottom from Josiah Priest's* In Defense of Slavery.

been most reluctant to show pictures of dead Iraqi soldiers and civilians. Only after many Iraqis refused to believe that Saddam Hussein's two sons had been killed did the United States government reluctantly release pictures showing the blood-spattered faces of the two men — and some American newspapers and television programs refused to use the images.

There have been notable exceptions to this practice, such as Huynh Cong (Nick) Ut's 1972 photograph of children fleeing a napalm attack in Vietnam (below), which was widely reproduced in the United States and won the photographer a Pulitzer Prize in 1973. The influence of this particular photograph cannot be measured, but it is widely felt to have played a substantial role in increasing public pressure to end the Vietnam War. Another widely reproduced picture of horrifying violence is Eddie Adams's picture (1968) of a South Vietnamese chief of police firing a pistol into the head of a Viet Cong prisoner.

The issue remains: Are some images unacceptable? For instance, although capital punishment is legal in parts of the United States — by methods including lethal injection, hanging, shooting, and electrocution — every state in the Union prohibits the publication of pictures showing a criminal being executed. (On this topic, see Wendy Lesser, *Pictures at an Execution* [1993].) The most famous recent example of an image widely thought to be unprintable concerns the murder of Daniel Pearl, a Jewish reporter for the *Wall Street Journal.* Pearl was captured and murdered in June 2002 by Islamic terrorists in Pakistan. His killers videotaped Pearl reading a statement denouncing American policy, and being decapitated. The video also shows a man's arm holding Pearl's head. The video ends with the killers making several demands (such as the release of the Muslim prisoners being held by the United States in Guantánamo Bay, Cuba) and asserting that "If our demands are not met, this scene will be repeated again and again."

The chief arguments against reproducing in newspapers material from this video were that

- The video and even still images from it are unbearably gruesome;
- Showing the video would traumatize the Pearl family; and
- The video is propaganda by an enemy.

Those who favored broadcasting the video on television and printing still images from it in newspapers tended to argue that

- The photo will show the world what sort of enemy that the United States is fighting;
- Newspapers have published pictures of other terrifying sights (notably, people leaping out of windows of New York's twin towers and endless pictures of the space shuttle *Challenger* exploding); and
- No one was worried about protecting the families of these other victims from seeing painful images.

But ask yourself if the comparison of the Daniel Pearl video to the photos of the twin towers and of the *Challenger* is valid. You may respond that the individuals in the twin towers pictures are not specifically identifiable and that the images of the *Challenger*, though horrifying, are not as visually revolting as the picture of a severed head held up for view.

The *Boston Phoenix*, a weekly newspaper, published some images from the Daniel Pearl video and also put a link to the video (with a warning that the footage is "extremely graphic") on its Web site. The editor of the *Phoenix* justified publication on the three grounds we list. Pearl's wife, Mariane Pearl, was quoted in various newspapers as condemning the "heartless decision to air this despicable video," and a spokeswoman for the Pearl family, when asked for comment, referred reporters to a statement issued earlier, which said that broadcasters who show the video

> fall without shame into the terrorists' plan. . . . Danny believed that journalism was a tool to report the truth and foster understanding — not perpetuate propaganda and sensationalize tragedy. We had hoped that no part of this tape would ever see the light of day. . . . We urge all networks and news outlets to exercise responsibility and not aid the terrorists in spreading their message of hate and murder.[1]

Although some journalists expressed regret that Pearl's family was distressed, they insisted that journalists have a right to reproduce such material and that the images can serve the valuable purpose of shocking viewers into awareness.

---

[1]Quoted in the *Hartford Courant*, June 5, 2002, and reproduced on the Internet by the Freedom of Information Center, under the heading "Boston Paper Creates Controversy."

Topic for Critical Thinking and Writing

Marvin Kalb, a distinguished journalist, was quoted as saying that the public has a right to see the tape of Daniel Pearl's murder but that "common sense, decency, [and] humanity would encourage editors . . . to say 'no, it is not necessary to put this out.' There is no urgent demand on the part of the American people to see Daniel Pearl's death." Your view?

READING ADVERTISEMENTS

Advertising is one of the most common forms of visual persuasion we encounter in everyday life. None of us is so unsophisticated these days as to believe everything we see in an ad, yet the influence of advertising in our culture is pervasive and subtle. Consider, for example, a much-reproduced poster sponsored by Gatorade and featuring Michael Jordan. Such an image costs an enormous amount to produce and disseminate, and nothing in it is left to chance. The photograph of Jordan is typical, his attitude simultaneously strained and graceful, his face exultant, as he performs the feat for which he is so well known and about which most of us could only dream. We are aware of a crowd watching him, but the people in this crowd appear tiny, blurred, and indistinct compared to the huge image in the foreground; the photograph, like the crowd, focuses solely on Jordan. He is a legend, an icon of American culture. He is dressed not in his Chicago Bulls uniform but in a USA jersey, connecting his act of gravity-defying athleticism with the entire nation and with our sense of patriotism. The red, white, and blue of the uniform strengthens this impression in the original color photograph of the advertisement.

What do we make of the verbal message boldly written along the left-hand margin of the poster, "Be like Mike"? We are certainly not foolish enough to believe that drinking Gatorade will enable us to perform like Michael Jordan on the basketball court. But who among us wouldn't like to "Be like Mike" in some small way, to enjoy even a glancing association with his athletic grace and power—to say nothing of his fame, wealth, and sex appeal? Though the makers of Gatorade surely know we will not all rush out to buy their drink to improve our game, they are banking on the expectation that the association of their name with Jordan, and our memory of their logo in association with Jordan's picture, will create a positive impression of their product. If Mike drinks Gatorade—well, why shouldn't I give it a try? The good feelings and impressions created by the ad will, the advertisers hope, travel with us the next time we consider buying a sports drink.

As we discuss the power of advertising, it is appropriate to say a few words about the corporate logos that appear everywhere these days — on billboards, in newspapers and magazines, on television, and on T-shirts. It is useful to think of a logo as a sort of advertisement in shorthand. It is a single, usually simple, image that carries with it a world of associations and impressions. (The makers of Gatorade would certainly hope that we will be reminded of Michael Jordan and his slam dunk when we see their product name superimposed over the orange lightning bolt.)

Let's look at an advertisement that combines pictures with verbal text. The ad has two head shots, pictures of the sort that show "Ten Most Wanted Men." Both faces are widely known — Martin Luther King Jr. and Charles Manson — and viewers may initially wonder why they are juxtaposed. Then the large type above the pictures captures our attention with its size and a bold statement of fact:

> The man on the left is 75 times more likely to be stopped by the police while driving than the man on the right.

We presume that the statement is true — that is, that dark-skinned people are stopped by police officers seventy-five times more often than whites — and we probably know why. Almost surely we do *not* conclude that dark people are far more likely than white to speed, go through red lights, or cross lanes. We have heard about racial profiling and racial prejudice, and we may also have heard about the wry offense of which all African Americans are guilty, "driving while black." The small print on this ad goes on to tell us that, every day, "Police stop drivers based on their skin color rather than for the way they are driving," and it supports this assertion with a fact: "For example, in Florida 80% of those stopped and searched were black and Hispanic, while they constituted only 5% of all drivers." We assume that these statistics are true and that most readers find the statement alarming. The poster might have had these very words without the two pictures, but would we then have read the small print?

Incidentally, the American Civil Liberties Union did not print this poster for any reason related to Martin Luther King Jr. or Charles Manson. The poster's purpose appears in very small letters at the end of the caption:

> Support the ACLU.

We think that this ad is highly effective, and we invite you to perform a thought experiment. Suppose that the two pictures were omitted and that the text of the large type at the top of the ad was different, something like this:

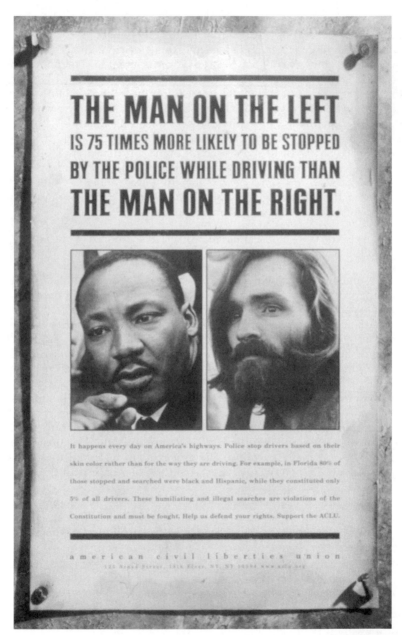

(Courtesy DeVito/Verdi, New York.)

> Persons of color, notably African Americans and non-white Hispanics, are 75 times more likely than white people to be stopped by the police when driving.

And then suppose the rest of the text consisted of the words in the present ad. Do you think this alternate version would make nearly the impact that the ACLU ad makes? The text is essentially the same, the statistics are still shocking, but the impact is gone. When we see the ACLU ad, we are for only a tiny fraction of a second, puzzled: What can the two faces—a civil rights leader and a serial killer—have in common? The large print almost immediately lets us know why these faces are paired, and we are probably hooked by (a) the shocking juxtaposition of faces and (b) the astounding fact that is asserted. So we probably go on to read the small print, though ordinarily we would not bother to read such tiny writing.

Incidentally, the writing beneath the picture could have been as large, or almost as large, as the print above the picture, merely by reducing the blank space at the top and bottom of the page. Why do you suppose the writing beneath the pictures is small? Do you think the ad would have been as compelling if the type above and below were of approximately equal size? Why or why not?

One other point: The pictures of King and Manson catch the interest of a wide audience, an audience much wider than the group that would normally be targeted as persons who might contribute money or energy to an association chiefly concerned with civil liberties. That is, this ad speaks to almost anyone who may be concerned with fairness or decency.

VISUALS AS AIDS TO CLARITY: MAPS, GRAPHS, TABLES, AND PIE CHARTS

Maps were obviously part of the argument in the debate over drilling in the Arctic National Wildlife Refuge. Advocates of drilling argued that drilling would take place only in such a *tiny* area. Their map showed Alaska, with an indication (in gray) of the much smaller part of Alaska that was the Refuge, and a further indication (cross-hatched) of what these advocates of drilling emphasized was a minuscule part of the Refuge. Opponents, however, showed maps indicating the path of migrating caribou, and the roads that would have to be constructed across the refuge to get *to* the area where the drilling would take place.

Graphs, tables, and pie charts usually present quantitative data in visual form, helping writers clarify mind-numbing statistical assertions.

A CHECKLIST FOR ANALYZING IMAGES (ESPECIALLY ADVERTISEMENTS)

☐ What is the overall effect of the design? Colorful and busy (suggesting activity)? Quiet and understated (for instance, chiefly white and grays, with lots of empty space)? Old fashioned or cutting edge?

☐ What about the image immediately gets your attention? Size? Position on the page? Beauty of the image? Grotesqueness of the image? Humor?

☐ What is the audience for the image? Affluent young men? Housewives? Retired persons?

☐ Does the text make a logical appeal ("Tests at a leading university prove that . . . ," "If you believe X, you should vote 'No' on this referendum")?

☐ Does the image appeal to the emotions? Examples: Images of starving children or maltreated animals appeal to our sense of pity; images of military valor may appeal to our patriotism; images of luxury may appeal to our envy; images of sexually attractive people may appeal to our desire to be like them; images of violence or of extraordinary ugliness (as, for instance, in some ads showing a human fetus being destroyed) may seek to shock us.

☐ Does the image make an ethical appeal—that is, does it appeal to our character as a good human being? Ads by charitable organizations often appeal to our sense of decency, fairness, and pity, but ads that appeal to our sense of prudence (ads for insurance companies or for investment houses) also essentially are making an ethical appeal.

☐ What is the relation of print to image? Does the image do most of the work, or does it serve to attract us and to lead us on to read the text?

For instance, a line graph may tell us how many immigrants came to the United States in each decade of the last century.

A bar graph (the bars can run either horizontally or vertically) offers similar information; we can see at a glance that, say, the second bar is almost double the length of the first, indicating that the number is almost double.

A pie chart is a circle divided into wedges so that we can see—literally see—how a whole is divided into its parts. We can see, for instance,

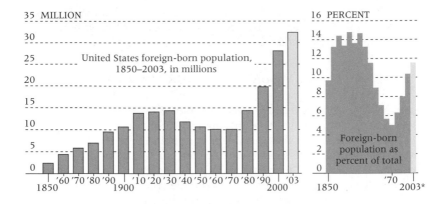

COMING TO AMERICA . . .
Both the percentage and number of foreign-born people in the United States dropped during much of the 20th century, but after 1970, the tide was turning again.

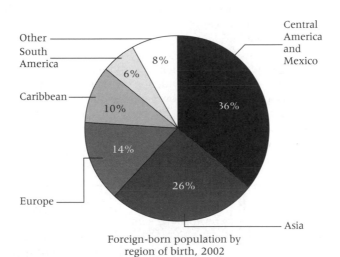

Foreign-born population by
region of birth, 2002

*Most recent estimate
Source: United States Census Bureau

. . . FROM NEAR AND FAR
Central America, Mexico, and Asia contribute most to the foreign-born population.

that of the entire pie—which may represent registered voters in a certain state—one fourth are registered Democrats, one fifth are registered Republicans, and the remainder do not give a party affiliation.

A NOTE ON USING VISUALS IN YOUR OWN PAPER

Every paper uses some degree of visual persuasion, merely in its appearance: perhaps a title page, certainly margins (ample—but not so wide that they tell the reader that the writer is unable to write a paper of the assigned length), double-spacing for the convenience of the reader, paragraphing (again for the convenience of the reader), and so on. But you may also want to use images—for example, pictures, graphs, or pie charts. Keep a few guidelines in mind as you begin to work with images, "writing" visuals into your own argument with at least as much care as you would read them in others':

- Consider the needs and attitudes of your audience, and select the type of visuals—graphs, drawings, photographs—likely to be most persuasive to that audience.
- Consider the effect of color, composition, and placement within your document. Because images are most effective when they appear near the text that supplements them, do not group all of your images at the end of the paper.

Remember especially that images are almost never self-supporting or self-explanatory. They may be evidence for your argument (Ut's photograph of napalm victims is *very* compelling evidence of suffering), but they are not arguments themselves. Be sure to explain each image that you use, integrating it into the verbal text that provides the logic and principal support of our thesis.

(DILBERT © Scott Adams. Reprinted by permission of United Features Syndicate, Inc.)

5

Writing an Analysis of an Argument

ANALYZING AN ARGUMENT

Examining the Author's Thesis

Most of your writing in other courses will require you to write an analysis of someone else's writing. In a course in political science you may have to analyze, say, an essay first published in *Foreign Affairs*, perhaps reprinted in your textbook, that argues against raising tariff barriers to foreign trade. Or a course in sociology may require you to analyze a report on the correlation between fatal accidents and drunk drivers under the age of twenty-one. Much of your writing, in short, will set forth reasoned responses to your reading as preparation for making an argument of your own.

Obviously you must understand an essay before you can analyze it thoughtfully. You must read it several times—not just skim it—and (the hard part) you must think about it. Again, you'll find that your thinking is stimulated if you take notes and if you ask yourself questions about the material. Notes will help you to keep track of the writer's thoughts and also of your own responses to the writer's thesis. The writer probably *does* have a thesis, a claim, a point, and if so, you must try to locate it. Perhaps the thesis is explicitly stated in the title or in a sentence or two near the beginning of the essay or in a concluding paragraph, but perhaps you will have to infer it from the essay as a whole.

Notice that we said the writer *probably* has a thesis. Much of what you read will indeed be primarily an argument; the writer explicitly or implicitly is trying to support some thesis and to convince you to agree with it. But some of what you read will be relatively neutral, with the argument just faintly discernible—or even with no argument at all. A work may, for instance, chiefly be a report: Here are the data, or here is what X, Y, and Z said; make of it what you will. A report might simply state how various ethnic groups voted in an election. In a report of this sort, of course, the writer hopes to persuade readers that the facts are correct, but no thesis is advanced, at least not explicitly or perhaps even consciously; the writer is not evidently arguing a point and trying to change our minds. Such a document differs greatly from an essay by a political analyst who presents similar findings to persuade a candidate to sacrifice the votes of this ethnic bloc and thereby get more votes from other blocs.

Examining the Author's Purpose

While reading an argument, try to form a clear idea of the author's **purpose.** Judging from the essay or the book, was the purpose to persuade, or was it to report? An analysis of a pure report (a work apparently without a thesis or argumentative angle) on ethnic voting will deal chiefly with the accuracy of the report. It will, for example, consider whether the sample poll was representative.

Much material that poses as a report really has a thesis built into it, consciously or unconsciously. The best evidence that the prose you are reading is argumentative is the presence of two kinds of key terms:

- **Transitions that imply the drawing of a conclusion:** *therefore, because, for the reason that, consequently;*
- **Verbs that imply proof:** *confirms, verifies, accounts for, implies, proves, disproves, is (in)consistent with, refutes, it follows that.*

Keep your eye out for such terms, and scrutinize their precise role whenever, or wherever they appear. If the essay does not advance a thesis, think of a thesis (a hypothesis) that it might support or some conventional belief that it might undermine.

Examining the Author's Methods

If the essay advances a thesis, you will want to analyze the strategies or methods of argument that allegedly support the thesis.

- Does the writer quote authorities? Are these authorities really competent in this field? Are equally competent authorities who take a different view ignored?

- Does the writer use statistics? If so, are they appropriate to the point being argued? Can they be interpreted differently?
- Does the writer build the argument by using examples or analogies? Are they satisfactory?
- Are the writer's assumptions acceptable?
- Does the writer consider all relevant factors? Has he or she omitted some points that you think should be discussed? For instance, should the author recognize certain opposing positions and perhaps concede something to them?
- Does the writer seek to persuade by means of ridicule? If so, is the ridicule fair: Is it supported also by rational argument?

In writing your analysis, you will want to tell your reader something about the author's purpose and something about the author's **methods.** It is usually a good idea at the start of your analysis—if not in the first paragraph then in the second or third—to let the reader know the purpose (and thesis, if there is one) of the work you are analyzing and then to summarize the work briefly.

Next you will probably find it useful (your reader will certainly find it helpful) to write out *your* thesis (your evaluation or judgment). You might say, for instance, that the essay is impressive but not conclusive, or is undermined by convincing contrary evidence, or relies too much on unsupported generalizations, or is wholly admirable, or whatever. Remember, because your paper is itself an argument, it needs its own thesis.

And then, of course, comes the job of setting forth your analysis and the support for your thesis. There is no one way of going about this work. If, say, your author gives four arguments (for example, an appeal to common sense, the testimony of authorities, the evidence of comparisons, and an appeal to self-interest), you might want to do one of the following:

- Take up these four arguments in sequence.
- Discuss the simplest of the four and then go on to the more difficult ones.
- Discuss the author's two arguments that you think are sound and then turn to the two that you think are not sound (or perhaps the reverse).
- Take one of these approaches and then clinch your case by constructing a fifth argument that is absent from the work under scrutiny but in your view highly important.

In short, the organization of your analysis may or may not follow the organization of the work you are analyzing.

Examining the Author's Persona

You will probably also want to analyze something a bit more elusive than the author's explicit arguments: the author's self-presentation. Does the author seek to persuade readers partly by presenting himself or herself as conscientious, friendly, self-effacing, authoritative, tentative, or in some other light? Most writers do two things:

- They present evidence, and
- They present themselves (or, more precisely, they present the image of themselves that they wish us to behold).

In some persuasive writing this **persona** or **voice** or presentation of the self may be no less important than the presentation of evidence.

In establishing a persona, writers adopt various rhetorical strategies, ranging from the use of characteristic words to the use of a particular form of organization. For instance, the writer who speaks of an opponent's "gimmicks" instead of "strategy" is trying to downgrade the opponent and also to convey the self-image of a streetwise person. On a larger scale, consider the way in which evidence is presented and the kind of evidence offered. One writer may first bombard the reader with facts and then spend relatively little time drawing conclusions. Another may rely chiefly on generalizations, waiting until the end of the essay to bring the thesis home with a few details. Another may begin with a few facts and spend most of the space reflecting on these. One writer may seem professorial or pedantic, offering examples of an academic sort; another, whose examples are drawn from ordinary life, may seem like a regular guy. All such devices deserve comment in your analysis.

The writer's persona, then, may color the thesis and help it develop in a distinctive way. If we accept the thesis, it is partly because the writer has won our goodwill by persuading us of his good character (*ethos*, in Aristotle's terms). Later we talk more about the appeal to the character of the speaker—the so-called *ethical appeal.*

The author of an essay may, for example, seem fair minded and open minded, treating the opposition with great courtesy and expressing interest in hearing other views. Such a tactic is itself a persuasive device. Or take an author who appears to rely on hard evidence such as statistics. This reliance on seemingly objective truths is itself a way of seeking to persuade—a rational way, to be sure, but a mode of persuasion nonetheless.

Especially in analyzing a work in which the author's persona and ideas are blended, you will want to spend some time commenting on the persona. Whether you discuss it near the beginning of your analysis or near the end will depend on your own sense of how you want to construct your essay, and this decision will partly depend on the work you are analyzing. For example, if the author's persona is kept in the background and is thus relatively invisible, you may want to make that point fairly early to get it out of the way and then concentrate on more interesting matters. If, however, the persona is interesting—and perhaps seductive, whether because it seems so scrupulously objective or so engagingly subjective—you may want to hint at this quality early in your essay and then develop the point while you consider the arguments.

Summary

In the last few pages we have tried to persuade you that, in writing an analysis of your reading, you must do the following:

- Read and reread thoughtfully. Writing notes will help you to think about what you are reading.
- Be aware of the purpose of the material to which you are responding.

We have also tried to point out these facts:

- Most of the nonliterary material that you will read is designed to argue, to report, or to do both.
- Most of this material also presents the writer's personality, or voice, and this voice usually merits attention in an analysis. An essay on, say, nuclear war, in a journal devoted to political science, may include a voice that moves from an objective tone to a mildly ironic tone to a hortatory tone, and this voice is worth commenting on.

Possibly all this explanation is obvious. There is yet another point, though, equally obvious but often neglected by students who begin by writing an analysis and end up by writing only a summary, a shortened version of the work they have read:

- Although your essay is an analysis of someone else's writing, and you may have to include a summary of the work you are writing about, your essay is *your* essay. The thesis, the organization, and the tone are yours. Your thesis, for example, may be that although the author is convinced she has presented a strong case, her case is far from proved. The organization of your paper may be deeply indebted to the work you are analyzing, but it need not be. The author may have begun with specific examples and then gone on to make generalizations and to draw conclusions, but you may begin with the conclusions. Similarly, your tone may resemble your subject's (let's say the voice is courteous academic), but it will nevertheless have its own ring, its own tone of (say) urgency, caution, or coolness.

AN ARGUMENT, ITS ELEMENTS, AND A STUDENT'S ANALYSIS OF THE ARGUMENT

LISA SCHIFFREN

Lisa Schiffren was a speechwriter for former Vice President Dan Quayle. We reprint an essay that originally was published in the New York Times *on March 23, 1996. When Schiffren's essay was published, it seemed likely that Hawaii would legalize gay marriages. In fact, Hawaii did not do so, but some years later, in November 2003, the Massachusetts Supreme Judicial Court (the highest court in the state) ruled that the state constitution gives gay couples the right to marry. There is now much talk about the possibility of amending the federal constitution to prohibit such marriages.*

Gay Marriage, an Oxymoron

As study after study and victim after victim testify to the social devastation of the sexual revolution, easy divorce, and out-of-wedlock motherhood, marriage is fashionable again. And parenthood has transformed many baby boomers into advocates of bourgeois norms.

Indeed, we have come so far that the surprise issue of the political season is whether homosexual "marriage" should be legalized. The Hawaii courts will likely rule that gay marriage is legal, and other states will be required to accept those marriages as valid.

Considering what a momentous change this would be—a radical redefinition of society's most fundamental institution—there has been almost no real debate. This is because the premise is unimaginable to many, and the forces of political correctness have descended on the discussion, raising the cost of opposition. But one may feel the same affection for one's homosexual friends and relatives as for any other and be genuinely pleased for the happiness they derive from relationships while opposing gay marriage for principled reasons.

"Same-sex marriage" is inherently incompatible with our culture's understanding of the institution. Marriage is essentially a lifelong compact between a man and woman committed to sexual exclusivity and the creation and nurture of offspring. For most Americans, the marital union—as distinguished from other sexual relationships and legal and economic partnerships—is imbued with an aspect of holiness. Though many of us are uncomfortable using religious language to discuss social and political issues, Judeo-Christian morality informs our view of family life.

Though it is not polite to mention it, what the Judeo-Christian tra- 5 dition has to say about homosexual unions could not be clearer. In a diverse, open society such as ours, tolerance of homosexuality is a necessity. But for many, its practice depends on a trick of cognitive dissonance that allows people to believe in the Judeo-Christian moral order while accepting, often with genuine regard, the different lives of homosexual acquaintances. That is why, though homosexuals may believe that they are merely seeking a small expansion of the definition of marriage, the majority of Americans perceive this change as a radical deconstruction of the institution.

Some make the conservative argument that making marriage a civil right will bring stability, an end to promiscuity, and a sense of fairness to gay men and women. But they miss the point. Society cares about stability in heterosexual unions because it is critical for raising healthy children and transmitting the values that are the basis of our culture.

Whether homosexual relationships endure is of little concern to society. That is also true of most childless marriages, harsh as it is to say. Society has wisely chosen not to differentiate between marriages, because it would require meddling into the motives and desires of everyone who applies for a license.

In traditional marriage, the tie that really binds for life is shared responsibility for the children. (A small fraction of gay couples may choose to raise children together, but such children are offspring of one partner and an outside contributor.) What will keep gay marriages together when individuals tire of each other?

Similarly, the argument that legal marriage will check promiscuity by gay males raises the question of how a "piece of paper" will do what the threat of AIDS has not. Lesbians seem to have little problem with monogamy or the rest of what constitutes "domestication," despite the absence of official status.

Finally, there is the so-called fairness argument. The government gives   10
tax benefits, inheritance rights, and employee benefits only to the married. Again, these financial benefits exist to help couples raise children. Tax reform is an effective way to remove distinctions among earners.

If the American people are interested in a radical experiment with same-sex marriages, then subjecting it to the political process is the right route. For a court in Hawaii to assume that it has the power to radically redefine marriage is a stunning abuse of power. To present homosexual marriage as a fait accompli, without national debate, is a serious political error. A society struggling to recover from thirty years of weakened norms and broken families is not likely to respond gently to having an institution central to most people's lives altered.

Let's examine Schiffren's essay with an eye to identifying those elements we mentioned earlier in this chapter (pp. 97–101) that deserve notice when examining *any* argument: The author's *thesis, purpose, methods,* and *persona*. And while we're at it, let's also notice some other features of Schiffren's essay that will help us appreciate its effect and evaluate its strength's and weaknesses. All this will put us in a better position to write an evaluation or to write an argument of our own confirming, extending, or rebutting Schiffren's argument.

Title   Schiffren's title—"Gay Marriage, An Oxymoron"—is a bit risky, since it includes a fairly unusual word, but because she was publishing in the *New York Times* she must have felt (probably correctly) that most of her readers would be familiar with the word. (*The Times* is known to have a highly educated readership.) An *oxymoron* (from Greek words for "pointedly foolish") uses contradictory terms, such as "deafening silence," "hateful love," "bittersweet," "wise fool." Readers familiar with the word would probably (if they oppose gay marriage) might silently say, "Yes, well said, right on" or (if they favor gay marriage) might silently say, "Oh come on, let's not be so dismissive." In either case they would probably go on to read the essay. But what of readers who are unfamiliar with the word? Perhaps they too are hooked: "What in the world is an oxymoron?" and presumably they might read the essay in order to learn.

In any case, Schiffren in her title indicates her *topic* (gay marriage) and her *thesis* or point (gay marriage is an absurdity), and she also indicates something of her *persona:* She is (a) highly educated (*oxymoron* is the evidence) and (b) she is hard-hitting, not afraid to call a spade a spade.

Thesis   What is the basic thesis that Schiffren is arguing? The title gave us a good idea, but the first paragraph seems to backtrack a bit, or, more precisely, it approaches the topic indirectly. In the opening paragraph Schiffren indicates clearly that she is unhappy with "the sexual revolution," a movement that has produced "victim after victim," a movement that she says is characterized by "easy divorce, and out-of-wedlock motherhood." Given her title, we realize that she will see gay marriage as yet another assault on marriage. The second paragraph, in harmony with the first, asserts that gay marriage would be "a momentous change" in our society, and in the first sentence of the third paragraph she explicitly states her thesis: "'Same-sex marriage' is inherently incompatible with our culture's understanding of the institution." Schiffren's title more or less stated her thesis, but with a somewhat unusual word; here, in the beginning of the third paragraph, she states it with the utmost clarity. Writers need not announce their thesis in so many words, but they do need to have a thesis, a point they want to make, and they ought to make their point evident fairly soon—as Schiffren does.

Purpose   There's no doubt that Schiffren's *purpose* in this essay is to *persuade* the reader to adopt her view that gay marriage is a threat to our society. This amounts to trying to persuade us that her thesis (stated above) is *true.* Schiffren does not, however, show that her essay is argumentative or persuasive by using the key terms that normally mark argumentative prose. She doesn't speak of her "reasons," she doesn't say things like "thus it follows," and she doesn't connect clauses or sentences with "therefore" or "because."

But this doesn't matter. The argumentative nature of her essay is revealed by the *judgment* she states in her title (gay marriage is nonsense) and by the clear implications in the first three paragraphs that gay marriage is a serious threat to our society. Any author who has a thesis as obvious as Schiffren's is likely to want to persuade her readers to agree with it. To persuade them, she needs to try to *support* it; accordingly, the bulk of the essay constitutes just such support.

Method   Although Schiffren introduces the Judeo-Christian objection to homosexuality early in her argument—that is, she appeals to authority, and to tradition—for the most part her method is to state the arguments on behalf of gay marriage and then to rebut them. Thus, her sixth paragraph introduces the opponent's claim that gay marriage "brings stability" to homosexual unions, but she goes on to say, in effect, that society doesn't much care whether homosexual unions are stable or not because the two people involved are not bringing up children. Next she summarizes the pro-gay marriage argument that marriage will "check promiscuity," an argument she responds to—which is *not* to say that she conclusively refutes it—by saying that if AIDS hasn't checked promiscuity, a peice of paper won't. Finally, she turns to the fairness argument, an argument concerning such things as tax benefits. She counters this argument by saying, again, that financial benefits exist in order to help parents bring up children, for the good of society.

Persona   Schiffren presents herself as a no-nonsense defender of traditional marriage. Her forthrightness may add little or nothing to the soundness of her arguments, but it surely adds to the persuasive effect. By presenting herself as she does—plain-speaking and righteously indignant—she effectively jars the reader's complacency (surely, all sensible folks must *oppose* gay marriage!), and she wins at least the reader's grudging respect (she says what she thinks, and we admire people who speak their mind). Further, even readers who disagree with Schiffren will have to admit that she at least is familiar with some of the opposing arguments and that she offers responses that deserve thought.

The chief danger, we think, is that her frankness verges on abrasiveness; readers may feel that she is, well, not someone they would like to spend much time with. She herself recognizes that she may sometimes tread on toes when, at the start of her fifth paragraph, she writes, *"Though it is not polite to mention it* [our italics], what the Judeo-Christian tradition has to say about homosexual unions could not be clearer." Similarly, in her seventh paragraph we also see that Schiffren is aware that her tone is sharp: "Whether homosexual relationships endure is of little concern to society. That is also true of most childless marriages, harsh as it is to say."

We call attention to these moments when the persona in this essay is a bit prickly, but we think that Schiffren on the whole manages to maintain the reader's sense that she is a decent person who is seriously concerned about an important issue.

Closing Paragraph   Schiffren ends with a suggestion that seems to be open-minded but that in effect hammers her argument home: "If the American people are interested in a radical experiment with same-sex marriages, then subjecting it to the political process is the right route."

But of course she assumes that the American people are *not* interested in a "radical experiment," and the rest of the paragraph makes clear her objections to such an experiment:

> A society struggling to recover from thirty years of weakened norms and broken families is not likely to respond gently to having an institution central to most people's lives altered.

Let's turn now to a student's analysis of Schiffren's essay—and then to our analysis of the student's analysis.

Jacob Cohen

English 2B

Professor Lee

March 23 2004

Is the Idea of Gay Marriage Really a Self-Contradiction?

Lisa Schiffren's "Gay Marriage, an Oxymoron" is an engaging piece of writing, but it is an unconvincing argument.
Schiffren writes forcefully — her title gets our attention, partly
because the word "oxymoron" is unusual and partly because if
one does know the meaning of this word the title is hard-
hitting — and the rest of her essay indicates that she is aware
of opposing views. That is, in reading her essay, a reader can't
say simply, "She doesn't know what she is talking about." She
does know a good deal about the pros and cons of her topic,
so a reader has to take seriously her view that gay marriage
just doesn't make any sense. In all probability, readers who
oppose gay marriage will feel that she makes a convincing
case. Still — and not surprisingly, because her essay is short
and the issue is complicated — her essay is not totally convincing, and indeed I think some points can be refuted.

Her first argument — the first place where she begins
to give reasons — is in her fourth paragraph, where she says
that same-sex marriage "is inherently incompatible with our
culture's understanding of the institution . . . [because] marriage is essentially a lifelong compact between a man and a
woman committed to sexual exclusivity and the creation and
nurture of offspring (p. 103). As my brackets around "because"
indicate, Schiffren does not use the word because but the construction of her sentences certainly indicates that she is giving
a reason, she is arguing a case. What are we to make of her

view that "marriage is essentially a lifelong compact . . . committed to sexual exclusivity and the creation and nurture of offspring." First, let's think about "a lifelong compact." We live in an age of prenuptial agreements and, more important, in a world where something like fifty percent of the marriages of ten years ago have ended in divorce. Many people participate in marriages where they swear to remain married "until death do us part," but almost no one seems to remember such a vow when he or she seeks a divorce. Second, in an age where many women now hold jobs outside of the house, the "creation and nurture of offspring" is often put on hold, sometimes indefinitely. Later (in her seventh paragraph) Schiffren indicates that she is not much concerned with childless marriages, but lots of other people are — the people who for one reason or another do not wish to have children and the people who for one reason or another cannot have children but who wish to get married and who <u>do</u> get married.

    Schiffren's next argument, in her fifth paragraph, is that "the Judeo-Christian tradition" opposes gay marriage. She is right, to a degree. Certainly the Hebrew Bible opposes it. Leviticus 20.13 says, "If a man also lie with mankind, as he lieth with a woman, both of them have committed an abomination: they shall surely be put to death," and I have been told that St. Paul somewhere in the New Testament seems to oppose homosexuality, but I have also been told that Jesus nowhere mentions it. Still, I grant that the Judeo-Christian <u>tradition</u> (though not the explicit teaching of Jesus) opposes homosexuality. For me, however, this is not a compelling argument: Although the Pledge of Allegiance includes the words "one nation under God," and some of our coins bear the motto "In God we trust," our nation is not a theocracy governed by either Jewish or Christian law. True, some of our laws correspond to the Ten Commandments — "Thou shalt not kill," for instance — but, on the other hand, we do <u>not</u> have a law that says we must honor our father and our mother, and we do <u>not</u> have a law that forbids the making of "graven images." In fact, many of our churches themselves contain images. Further, in all probability most people — even those who point to Leviticus 20, condemning homosexuality — would not approve of a law that executed all homosexuals. If there are people who approve of executing homosexuals in accordance with Leviticus 20.13, I wonder if they also approve of another passage in the Hebrew Bible, Deuteronomy 22.15–24, which says that persons guilty of engaging in premarital sex or adultery shall be stoned to death. And how many Americans today believe we follow Genesis 29.15–30, which recognizes the practice of polygamy? (When Utah was admitted to the Union, it was only after its residents agreed to outlaw polygamy). In short, although I myself am a churchgoer and am not gay, I cannot accept as an argument against legalizing gay marriage Schiffren's assertion — even though it is true — that the Judeo-Christian tradition has not supported homosexual relationships.

Schiiffren's next argument (paragraph 6) is a reply to the argument that legalizing gay marriage "will bring stability, an end to promiscuity" among gay people. Her answer, given in this paragraph and the next three, is that no one much cares whether or not these childless marriages are stable, and that if AIDS hasn't reduced promiscuity, a marriage license (a "piece of paper") won't reduce it either. Schiffren grants that "a small fraction of gay couples may choose to raise children together," but she dismisses this group by saying that "such children are offspring of one partner and an outside contributor (paragraph 8). What has that got to do with the issue of legalizing marriage? Further, this "small fraction" probably would be much larger if gay marriage were legalized, and if adoption agencies were not prejudiced against gay couples. Schiffren might (although she doesn't raise the issue at all) say that such families, lacking either a mother or a father, are not as stable and nourishing as straight couples, but there seems to be no evidence to support such a view. In any case, I think she fails to face the argument that gay couples might indeed contribute to society by raising children.

Her final arguments concerns "the so-called fairness argument" (paragraph 10), and here she returns to her earlier point that the laws that favor straight marriage do so in order to encourage the creation of families. She is probably right, but the fact remains that many heterosexual couples do not have children, and it is evident that some heterosexual couples — let's say a man and woman who marry in their sixties — cannot have children. In my view, the argument that society favors straight marriage because such marriage leads to the production of children and the care of these children in a stable relationship is, even if true, not a compelling reason to deny homosexual men and lesbian women the opportunity to marry and to thereby gain all of the benefits — psychological and financial — of marriage.

Schiffren several times supports her position by arguing that "most Americans" and "a majority of Americans" believe such-and-such. But the Declaration of Independence — a very

American document, a document that is cherished by "most Americans" and by "a majority of Americans" — says that we are all entitled to "the pursuit of happiness." Despite the high divorce rate in America today, countless happily married people would agree that much of their happiness depends on the fact that they are <u>married</u>. Why should homosexual people be denied this particular kind of happiness?

AN ANALYSIS OF THE STUDENT'S ANALYSIS

Jacob Cohen's essay seems to us to be excellent, doubtless the product of a good deal of thoughtful revision. He does not cover every possible aspect of Schiffren's essay—he concentrates on Schiffren's reasoning and says nothing about her style, her tone, her persona—but we think that, given the limits of 500–750 words, he does a good job. What makes his essay effective? We can list the chief reasons:

- The essay has a title that is of at least a little interest—it is more interesting than "An Analysis of an Essay" or "On Lisa Schiffren's Essay"—and it gives a hint of what is to follow. How does it give a hint? The word "Really" and the question mark hint that Cohen is going to say, in effect, "*No*, gay-marriage is not inherently self-contradictory."
- The author identifies his subject (he names the writer and the title of the essay he is writing about) early.
- He reveals his thesis early. His topic is Schiffren's essay; his thesis or point is that the essay is intelligent but unpersuasive.
- He takes up all of Schiffren's main points.
- He uses a few brief quotations to let us hear Schiffren's voice and to assure us that he is staying close to her text, but he does not pad his essay with long quotations.

- The essay has a reasonable organization. Cohen begins with the beginning of Schiffren's essay and then he takes up each of her arguments, in order.
- He concludes (without the stiffness of saying "in conclusion") by introducing a point that more or less turns the tables on Schiffren. In her essay she several times alludes to cherished American traditions, so Cohen introduces the phrase "the pursuit of happiness," a phrase that appears in the Declaration of Independence, a document that surely Schiffren values highly. Further, he says (and surely Schiffren would agree) that a good marriage yields a particular happiness that cannot be found elsewhere. Why, then, he asks, should gays not be allowed to pursue the happiness that marriage offers?
- Notice, finally, that he sticks closely to Schiffren's essay. He does not go off on a tangent and argue that the ancient Greeks practiced homosexuality, or that Schiffren's case might have been stronger if she had pointed out that once gay marriage is legalized, the next step might be the legalization of polygamy or bestiality.

Query: Good though this essay is, would it be better if Jacob Cohen, in his first paragraph, had briefly summarized Schiffren's essay?

Topic for Critical Thinking and Writing

1. It is sometimes said that gay marriage "devalues" marriage. Putting aside your personal feelings about the issue, write the best paragraph you can, refuting this view. Next, write the best paragraph you can in support of the view that gay marriage devalues marriage.
2. In the United States several states have laws prohibiting interracial marriages. These laws were struck down in 1967 when the U.S. Supreme Court, in *Loving v. Virginia,* ruled that "the freedom to marry has long been recognized as one of the vital personal rights essential to the orderly pursuit of happiness by free men." ("Loving" was the last name of an interracial couple, and Virginia is the state, not a woman). Do you think that this 1967 ruling, invalidating state laws prohibiting interracial marriage, is relevant to laws concerning gay marriage?

A CHECKLIST FOR WRITING AN ANALYSIS OF AN ARGUMENT

☐ Early in your essay have you fairly stated the writer's thesis (claim) and summarized his or her supporting reasons? And have you explained to your reader any disagreement about definitions of important terms?

☐ Have you, again fairly early in your essay, indicated where you will be taking your reader, i.e., have you indicated your general response to the essay you are analyzing?

☐ Have you called attention to the strengths, if any, and the weaknesses, if any, of the essay?

☐ Have you commented not only on the *logos* (logic, reasoning) but also on the *ethos* (character of the writer, as presented in the essay)? For instance, has the author convinced you that he or she is well-informed and is a person of goodwill? Or, on the other hand, does the writer seem to be chiefly concerned with ridiculing those who hold a different view?

☐ If there is an appeal to *pathos* (emotion, originally meaning "pity for suffering," but now interpreted more broadly to include appeals to patriotism, humor, or loyalty to family, for example), is it acceptable? If not, why not?

☐ Have you used occasional brief quotations to let your reader hear the author's tone and to ensure fairness and accuracy?

☐ Is your analysis effectively organized?

☐ Does your essay, perhaps in the concluding paragraphs, indicate your agreement or disagreement with the writer and but also your view of the essay as a piece of argumentative writing?

☐ Is your tone appropriate?

Exercise

Take one of the essays not yet discussed in class or an essay assigned now by your instructor, and in an essay of 500 words analyze and evaluate it.

6

Developing an Argument of Your Own

PLANNING, DRAFTING, AND REVISING AN ARGUMENT

First, hear the wisdom of Mark Twain: "When the Lord finished the world, He pronounced it good. That is what I said about my first work, too. But Time, I tell you, Time takes the confidence out of these incautious early opinions."

All of us, teachers and students, have our moments of confidence, but for the most part we know that it takes considerable effort to write clear, thoughtful, seemingly effortless prose. In a conversation we can cover ourselves with such expressions as "Well, I don't know, but I sort of think . . . ," and we can always revise our position ("Oh, well, I didn't mean it that way"), but once we have handed in the final version of our writing, we are helpless. We are (putting it strongly) naked to our enemies.

Getting Ideas

In Chapter 1 we quoted Robert Frost, "To learn to write is to learn to have ideas," and we offered suggestions about getting ideas, a process traditionally called **invention.** A moment ago we said that we often improve our ideas when we try to explain them to someone else. Partly, of course, we are responding to questions or objections raised by our companion in the conversation. But partly we are responding to ourselves: Almost as soon as we hear what we have to say, we may find that it won't do, and, if we are lucky, we may find a better idea surfacing. One of the best ways of getting ideas is to talk things over.

The process of talking things over usually begins with the text that you are reading: Your marginal notes, your summary, and your queries parenthetically incorporated within your summary are a kind of dialogue between you and the author you are reading. More obviously, when you talk with friends about your topic, you are trying out and developing ideas. Finally, after reading, taking notes, and talking, you may feel that you now have clear ideas and need only put them into writing. And so you take a sheet of blank paper, and perhaps a paralyzing thought suddenly strikes: "I have ideas but just can't put them into words."

Despite what many people believe,

- Writing is not only a matter of putting one's ideas into words.
- Just as talking with others is a way of getting ideas, *writing is a way of getting and developing ideas.*

Writing, in short, can be an important part of critical thinking. One big reason we have trouble writing is our fear of putting ourselves on record, but another big reason is our fear that we have no ideas worth putting down. But by jotting down notes—or even free associations—and by writing a draft, however weak, we can help ourselves to think our way toward good ideas.

Freewriting   Writing for five or six minutes, nonstop, without censoring what you produce is one way of getting words down on paper that will help to lead to improved thoughts. Some people who write on a computer find it useful to dim the screen so they won't be tempted to look up and fiddle too soon with what they have just written. Later they illuminate the screen, scroll back, and notice some keywords or passages that can be used later in drafting a paper.

Listing   Jotting down items, just as you do when you make a shopping list, is another way of getting ideas. When you make a shopping list, you write *ketchup,* and the act of writing it reminds you that you also need hamburger rolls—and *that* in turn reminds you (who knows how or why?) that you also need a can of tuna fish. Similarly, when you prepare a list of ideas for a paper, jotting down one item will generate another. Of course, when you look over the list, you will probably drop some of these ideas—the dinner menu will change—but you are making progress.

Diagramming   Sketching some sort of visual representation of an essay is a kind of listing. Three methods of diagramming are especially common:

- **Clustering**   Write, in the middle of a sheet of paper, a word or phrase summarizing your topic (for instance, *health care;* see diagram), circle it, and then write down and circle a related word (for example, *gov't-provided*). Perhaps this leads you to write *higher taxes,* and you then circle this phrase and connect it to *gov't-provided*. The next thing that occurs to you is *employer-provided*— and so you write this down and circle it. You will not connect this to *higher taxes,* but you will connect it to *health care* because it is a sort of parallel to *gov't-provided*. The next thing that occurs to you is *unemployed people*. This category does not connect easily with *employer-provided,* so you won't connect these two terms with a line, but you probably will connect *unemployed people* with *health care* and maybe also with *gov't-provided*. Keep going, jotting down ideas, and making connections where possible, indicating relationships.
- **Branching**   Some writers find it useful to build a tree, moving from the central topic to the main branches (chief ideas) and then to the twigs (aspects of the chief ideas).
- **Comparing in columns**   Draw a line down the middle of the page, and then set up two columns showing oppositions. For instance, if you are concerned with health care, you might head one column *gov't-provided* and the other *employer-provided*. Under the first column, you might write *covers unemployed,* and under the second column, you might write *omits unemployed*. You might

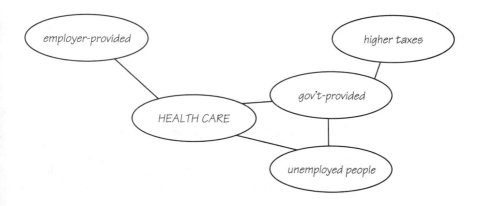

go on to write, under the first column, *higher taxes,* and under the second, *higher prices*—or whatever else relevant comes to mind.

All of these methods can, of course, be executed with pen and paper, but you may also be able to use them on your computer depending on the capabilities of your software.

Whether you are using a computer or a pen, you put down some words and almost immediately see that they need improvement, not simply a little polishing but a substantial overhaul. You write, "Race should be counted in college admissions for two reasons," and as soon as you write these words, a third reason comes to mind. Or perhaps one of those "two reasons" no longer seems very good. As E. M. Forster said, "How can I know what I think till I see what I say?" We have to see what we say, we have to get something down on paper, before we realize that we need to make it better.

Writing, then, is really **rewriting**—that is, **revising**—and a revision is a *re-vision,* a second look. The paper that you hand in should be clear and may even seem effortless to the reader, but in all likelihood the clarity and apparent ease are the result of a struggle with yourself, a struggle during which you greatly improved your first thoughts. You begin by putting down your ideas, such as they are, perhaps even in the random order in which they occurred, but sooner or later comes the job of looking at them critically, developing what is useful in them and chucking out what is not. If you follow this procedure you will be in the company of Picasso, who said that he "advanced by means of destruction."

Whether you advance bit by bit (writing a sentence, revising it, writing the next, and so on) or whether you write an entire first draft and then revise it and revise it again and again is chiefly a matter of temperament. Probably most people combine both approaches, backing up occasionally but trying to get to the end fairly soon so that they can see rather quickly what they know, or think they know, and can then start the real work of thinking, of converting their initial ideas into something substantial.

Asking Questions   Getting ideas, we said when we talked about **topics** and **invention** strategies in Chapter 1 (p. 11) is mostly a matter of asking (and then thinking about) questions. We append questions to the end of each argumentative essay in this book, not to torment you but to help you to think about the arguments—for instance, to turn your attention to especially important matters. If your instructor asks you to write an answer to one of these questions, you are lucky: Examining the question will stimulate your mind to work in a definite direction.

If a topic is not assigned, and you are asked to write an argument, you will find that some ideas (possibly poor ones, at this stage, but that doesn't matter because you will soon revise) will come to mind if you ask yourself questions. You can begin finding where you stand on an issue (**stasis**) by asking the following five basic questions:

1. What is *X*?
2. What is the value of *X*?
3. What are the causes (or the consequences) of *X*?
4. What should (or ought or must) we do about *X*?
5. What is the evidence for my claims about *X*?

Let's spend a moment looking at each of these questions.

1. **What is *X*?** We can hardly argue about the number of people sentenced to death in the United States in 2000—a glance at the appropriate government report will give the answer—but we can argue about whether or not capital punishment as administered in the United States is discriminatory. Does the evidence, we can ask, support the view that in the United States the death penalty is unfair? Similarly, we can ask whether a human fetus is a human being (in saying what something is, must we take account of its potentiality?), and, even if we agree that a fetus is a human being, we can further ask about whether it is a *person*. In *Roe v. Wade* the U.S. Supreme Court ruled that even the "viable" unborn human fetus is not a "person" as that term is used in the Fifth and Fourteenth Amendments. Here the question is this: Is the essential fact about the fetus that it is a person?

An argument of this sort makes a claim—that is, it takes a stand—but notice that it does not also have to argue for an action. Thus, it may argue that the death penalty is administered unfairly—that's a big enough issue—but it need not therefore go on to argue that the death penalty should be abolished. After all, another possibility is that the death penalty should be administered fairly. The writer of the essay may be doing enough if he or she establishes the truth of the claim and leaves to others the possible courses of action.

2. **What is the value of *X*?** No one can argue with you if you say you *prefer* the plays of Tennessee Williams to those of Arthur Miller. But as soon as you say that Williams is a *better* playwright than Miller, you have based your preference on implicit standards, and it is incumbent on you to support your preference by giving evidence about the relative skill, insight, and accomplishments of Williams and of Miller. Your

argument is an evaluation. The question now at issue is the merits of the two authors and the standards appropriate for such an appraisal.

In short, an essay offering an evaluation normally has two purposes: (1) to set forth an assessment and (2) to convince the reader that the assessment is reasonable. In writing an evaluation you will have to establish criteria, and these will vary depending on your topic. For instance, if you are comparing the artistic merit of the plays by Williams and by Miller, you may want to talk about the quality of the characterization, the significance of the theme, and so on. But if the topic is "Which playwright is more suitable to be taught in high school?," other criteria may be appropriate, such as the difficulty of the language, the sexual content of the scenes, and so on.

3. **What are the causes (or the consequences) of X?** Why did the rate of auto theft increase during a specific period? If we abolish the death penalty, will that cause the rate of murder to increase? Notice, by the way, that such problems may be complex. The phenomena that people usually argue about—say, such things as inflation, war, suicide, crime—have many causes, and it is therefore often a mistake to speak of *the* cause of *X*. A writer in *Time* mentioned that the life expectancy of an average American male is about sixty-seven years, a figure that compares unfavorably with the life expectancy of males in Japan and Israel. The *Time* writer suggested that an important cause of the relatively short life span is "the pressure to perform well in business." Perhaps. But the life expectancy of plumbers is no greater than that of managers and executives. Nutrition authority Jean Mayer, in an article in *Life*, attributed the relatively poor longevity of American males to a diet that is "rich in fat and poor in nutrients." Doubtless other authorities propose other causes, and in all likelihood no one cause accounts for the phenomenon.

4. **What should (or ought or must) we do about X?** Must we always obey the law? Should the law allow eighteen-year-olds to drink alcohol? Should eighteen-year-olds be drafted to do one year of social service? Should pornography be censored? Should steroid use by athletes be banned? Ought there to be Good Samaritan laws, making it a legal duty for a stranger to intervene to save a person from death or great bodily harm, when one might do so with little or no risk to oneself? These questions involve conduct and policy; how we answer them will reveal our values and principles.

An essay answering questions of this sort usually begins by explaining what the issue is, states why the reader should care about it, and then offers the proposal, paying attention to the counterarguments.

5. **What is the evidence for my claims about X?** Critical reading, writing, and thinking depend essentially on identifying and evaluating

the evidence for and against the claims one makes and encounters in the writings of others. It is not enough to have an *opinion* or belief one way or the other; you need to be able to support your opinions—the bare fact of your sincere belief in what you say or write is not itself any *evidence* that what you believe is true.

So what are good reasons for opinions, adequate evidence for one's beliefs? The answer, of course, depends on what kind of belief or opinion, assertion or hypothesis, claim or principle, you want to assert. For example, there is good evidence that President John F. Kennedy was assassinated on November 22, 1963, because this is the date for his death reported in standard almanacs. You could further substantiate the date by checking the back issues of the *New York Times*. But a different kind of evidence is needed to support the proposition that the chemical composition of water is H_2O. And you will need still other kinds of evidence to support your beliefs about the likelihood of rain tomorrow, the probability that the Red Sox will win the pennant this year, the twelfth digit in the decimal expansion of pi, the average cumulative grades of the graduating seniors over the past three years in your college, the relative merits of *Hamlet* and *Death of a Salesman,* and the moral dimensions of sexual harassment. None of these issues is merely a matter of opinion; yet on some of them, educated and informed people may disagree over the reasons and the evidence and what they show. Your job as a critical thinker is to be alert to the relevant reasons and evidence and to make the most of them as you present your views.

Again, an argument may take in two or more of these five issues. Someone who argues that pornography should (or should not) be censored will have to mark out the territory of the discussion by defining pornography (our first issue: What is *X*?). The argument probably will also need to examine the consequences of adopting the preferred policy (our third issue) and may even have to argue about its value (our second issue). Some people maintain that pornography produces crime, but others maintain that it provides a harmless outlet for impulses that otherwise might vent themselves in criminal behavior. Further, someone arguing about the wisdom of censoring pornography might have to face the objection that censorship, however desirable on account of some of its consequences, may be unconstitutional and that even if censorship were constitutional, it would (or might) have undesirable side effects, such as repressing freedom of political opinion. And one will always have to keep asking oneself the fifth question, What is the evidence for my claims?

Thinking about one or more of these questions may get you going. For instance, thinking about the first question, What is *X*?, will require you to produce a definition, and as you work at producing a satisfactory definition, you may find new ideas arising. If a question seems relevant, start writing, even if you write only a fragmentary sentence. You'll probably find that one word leads to another and that ideas begin to appear. Even if these ideas seem weak as you write them, don't be discouraged; you have put something on paper, and returning to these words, perhaps in five minutes or perhaps the next day, you will probably find that some are not at all bad and that others will stimulate you to better ones.

It may be useful to record your ideas in a special notebook reserved for the purpose. Such a **journal** can be a valuable resource when it comes time to write your paper. Many students find it easier to focus their thoughts on writing if during the period of gestation they have been jotting down relevant ideas on something more substantial than slips of paper or loose sheets. The very act of designating a notebook as your journal for a course can be the first step in focusing your attention on the eventual need to write a paper.

If what we have just said does not sound convincing, and you know from experience that you often have trouble getting started with your writing, don't despair; first aid is at hand in a sure-fire method that we will now explain.

The Thesis

Let's assume that you are writing an argumentative essay—perhaps an evaluation of an argument in this book—and you have what seems to be a pretty good draft or at least a bunch of notes that are the result of hard thinking. You really do have ideas now, and you want to present them effectively. How will you organize your essay? No one formula works best for every essayist and for every essay, but it is usually advisable to formulate a basic **thesis** (a claim, a central point, a chief position) and to state it early. Every essay that is any good, even a book-length one, has a thesis (a main point), which can be stated briefly. Remember Coolidge's remark on the preacher's sermon on sin: "He was against it." Don't confuse the **topic** (sin) with the thesis (sin is bad). The thesis is the argumentative theme, the author's primary claim or contention, the proposition that the rest of the essay will explain and defend. Of course, the thesis may sound commonplace, but the book or essay or sermon ought to develop it interestingly and convincingly.

Here are some sample theses:

- Smoking should be prohibited in all enclosed public places.
- Smoking should be limited to specific parts of enclosed public places and entirely prohibited in small spaces, such as elevators.

- Proprietors of public places such as restaurants and sports arenas should be free to determine whether they wish to prohibit, limit, or impose no limitations on smokers.

Imagining an Audience

Of course, the questions that you ask yourself to stimulate your thoughts will depend primarily on what you are writing about, but additional questions are always relevant:

- Who are my readers?
- What do they believe?
- What common ground do we share?
- What do I want my readers to believe?
- What do they need to know?
- Why should they care?

These questions require a little comment. The literal answer to the first probably is "my teacher," but (unless you are given instructions to the contrary) you should not write specifically for your teacher. Instead, you should write for an audience that is, generally speaking, like your classmates. In short, your imagined audience is literate, intelligent, and moderately well informed, but it does not know everything that you know, and it does not know your response to the problem that you are addressing.

The essays in this book are from many different sources, each with its own audience. An essay from the *New York Times* is addressed to the educated general reader; an essay from *Ms.* magazine is addressed to readers sympathetic to feminism. An essay from *Commonweal*, a Roman Catholic publication addressed to the nonspecialist, is likely to differ in point of view or tone from one in *Time*, even though both articles may advance approximately the same position. The writer of the article in *Commonweal* may, for example, effectively cite church fathers and distinguished Roman Catholic writers as authorities, whereas the writer of the *Time* article would probably cite few or even none of these figures because a non-Catholic audience might be unfamiliar with them or, even if familiar, might be unimpressed by their views.

The tone as well as the gist of the argument is in some degree shaped by the audience. For instance, popular journals, such as the *National Review* and *Ms.* magazine, are more likely to use ridicule than are journals chiefly addressed to, say, an academic audience.

The Audience as Collaborator

If you imagine an audience and keep asking yourself what this audience needs to be told and what it doesn't need to be told, you will find that material comes to mind, just as it comes to mind when a friend asks you what a film you saw was about, who was in it, and how you liked it.

Your readers do not have to be told that Thomas Jefferson was an American statesman in the early years of this country's history, but they do have to be told that Elizabeth Cady Stanton was a late-nineteenth-century American feminest. Why? You would need to identify Stanton because it's your hunch that your classmates never heard of her, or even if they may have heard the name, they can't quite identify it. But what if your class has been assigned an essay by Stanton? In that case your imagined reader knows Stanton's name and knows at least a little about her, so you don't have to identify Stanton as an American of the nineteenth century. But you do still have to remind your reader about relevant aspects of her essay, and you do have to tell your reader about your responses to them.

After all, even if the instructor has assigned an essay by Stanton, you cannot assume that your classmates know the essay inside out. Obviously, you can't say, "Stanton's third reason is also unconvincing," without reminding the reader, by means of a brief summary, of her third reason. Again,

- Think of your classmates—people like you—as your imagined readers; and
- Be sure that your essay does not make unreasonable demands.

If you ask yourself, "What do my readers need to know?" (and "What do I want them to believe?"), you will find some answers arising, and you will start writing.

We have said that you should imagine your audience as your classmates. But this is not the whole truth. In a sense, your argument is addressed not simply to your classmates but to the world interested in ideas. Even if you can reasonably assume that your classmates have read only one work by Stanton, you will not begin your essay by writing "Stanton's essay is deceptively easy." You will have to name the work; it is possible that a reader has read some other work by Stanton. And by precisely identifying your subject, you help to ease the reader into your essay.

Similarly, you won't begin by writing,

The majority opinion in <u>Walker v. City of Birmingham</u> was that . . .

Rather, you'll write something like this:

In <u>Walker v. City of Birmingham,</u> the U.S. Supreme Court ruled in 1966 that city authorities acted lawfully when they jailed Martin Luther King Jr. and other clergymen in 1963 for marching in Birmingham without a permit. Justice Potter Stewart delivered the majority opinion, which held that . . .

By the way, if you think you suffer from a writing block, the mere act of writing out such readily available facts will help you to get started. You will find that putting a few words down on paper, perhaps merely copying the essay's title or an interesting quotation from the essay, will stimulate you to jot down thoughts that you didn't know you had in you.

Here, again, are the questions about audience. If you write with a word processor, consider putting these questions into a file. For each assignment, copy (with the Copy command) the questions into the file you are currently working on, and then, as a way of generating ideas, *enter your responses, indented, under each question.*

- Who are my readers?
- What do they believe?
- What common ground do we share?
- What do I want my readers to believe?
- What do they need to know?
- Why should they care?

Thinking about your audience can help you to put some words on paper; even more important, it can help you to get ideas. Our second and third questions about the audience ("What do they believe?" and "How much common ground do we share?") will usually help you get ideas flowing. Presumably your imagined audience does not share your views, or at least does not fully share them. But why? How can these readers hold a position that to you seems unreasonable? If you try to put yourself into your readers' shoes, and if you think about what your audience knows or thinks it knows, you will find yourself getting ideas.

You do not believe (let's assume) that people should be allowed to smoke in enclosed public places, but you know that some people hold a different view. Why do they hold it? Try to state their view *in a way that would be satisfactory to them.* Having done so, you may come to perceive that your conclusions and theirs differ because they are based on different premises, perhaps different ideas about human rights. Examine the opposition's premises carefully, and explain, first to yourself and ultimately to your readers, why you find some premises unacceptable.

Possibly some facts are in dispute, such as whether nonsmokers may be harmed by exposure to tobacco. The thing to do, then, is to check the facts. If you find that harm to nonsmokers has not been proved, but you nevertheless believe that smoking should be prohibited in enclosed public places, of course you can't premise your argument on the wrongfulness of harming the innocent (in this case, the nonsmokers). You will have to develop arguments that take account of the facts, whatever they are.

Among the relevant facts there surely are some that your audience or your opponent will not dispute. The same is true of the values relevant to the discussion; the two of you are very likely to agree, if you stop to think about it, that you share belief in some of the same values (such as the principle mentioned above, that it is wrong to harm the innocent). These areas of shared agreement are crucial to effective persuasion in argument.

A Rule for Writers: If you wish to persuade, you'll have to begin by finding premises you can share with your audience.

There are two good reasons why you should identify and isolate the areas of agreement:

- There is no point in disputing facts or values on which you and your readers really agree.
- It usually helps to establish goodwill between you and your opponent when you can point to beliefs, assumptions, facts, and values that the two of you share.

In a few moments we will return to the need to share some of the opposition's ideas.

Recall that in writing college papers it is usually best to write for a general audience, an audience rather like your classmates but without the specific knowledge that they all share as students enrolled in one course. If the topic is smoking in public places, the audience presumably consists of smokers and nonsmokers. Thinking about our fifth question on page 123 — "What do readers need to know?" — may prompt you to give statistics about the harmful effects of smoking. Or if you are arguing on behalf of smokers, it may prompt you to cite studies claiming that no evidence conclusively demonstrates that cigarette smoking is harmful to nonsmokers. If indeed you are writing for a general audience and you are not advancing a highly unfamiliar view, our second question ("What does the audience believe?") is less important here, but if the audience is specialized, such as an antismoking group, a group of restaurant owners who fear that antismoking regulations will interfere with their business, or a group of civil libertarians, an effective essay will have to address their special beliefs.

In addressing their beliefs (let's assume that you do not share them or do not share them fully), you must try to establish some common ground. If you advocate requiring restaurants to provide nonsmoking areas, you should at least recognize the possibility that this arrangement will result in inconvenience for the proprietor. But perhaps (the good news) the restaurant will regain some lost customers or will attract some new customers. This thought should prompt you to think of kinds of evidence, perhaps testimony or statistics.

When you formulate a thesis and ask questions about it, such as who the readers are, what do they believe, what do they know, and what do they need to know, you begin to get ideas about how to organize the material or at least to see that some sort of organization will have to be worked out. The thesis may be clear and simple, but the reasons (the argument) may take many pages. The thesis is the point; the argument sets forth the evidence that is offered to support the thesis.

The Title

It's not a bad idea to announce your thesis in your **title.** If you scan the table of contents of this book, you will notice that a fair number of essayists use the title to let the readers know, at least in a very general way, what position will be advocated. Here are a few examples:

Gay Marriages: Make Them Legal

"Diversity" Is a Smoke Screen for Discrimination

Why Handguns Must Be Outlawed

True, these titles are not especially engaging, but the reader welcomes them because they give some information about the writer's thesis.

Some titles do not announce the thesis but they at least announce the topic:

Is All Discrimination Unfair?

On Racist Speech

Why Make Divorce Easy?

Although not clever or witty, these titles are informative.

Some titles seek to attract attention or to stimulate the imagination:

A First Amendment Junkie

A Crime of Compassion

Addicted to Health

All of these are effective, but a word of caution is appropriate here. In your effort to engage your reader's attention, be careful not to sound like a wise guy. You want to engage your readers, not turn them off.

Finally, be prepared to rethink your title *after* you have finished the last draft of your paper. A title somewhat different from your working title may be an improvement because the emphasis of your finished paper may have turned out to be rather different from what you expected when you first thought of a title.

The Opening Paragraphs

Opening paragraphs are difficult to write, so don't worry about writing an effective opening when you are drafting. Just get some words down on paper, and keep going. But when you revise your first draft—really a zero draft—you probably should begin to think seriously about the effect of your opening.

A good introduction arouses the reader's interest and helps prepare the reader for the rest of the paper. How? Opening paragraphs usually do at least one (and often all) of the following:

- Attract the reader's interest (often with a bold statement of the thesis or with an interesting statistic, quotation, or anecdote),
- Prepare the reader's mind by giving some idea of the topic and often of the thesis,
- Give the reader an idea of how the essay is organized, and
- Define a key term.

You may not wish to announce your thesis in your title, but if you don't announce it there, you should set it forth early in the argument, in your introductory paragraph or paragraphs. In her title "Human Rights and Foreign Policy," Jeanne J. Kirkpatrick merely announces her topic (subject) as opposed to her thesis (point), but she begins to hint at the thesis in her first paragraph, by deprecating President Jimmy Carter's policy:

> In this paper I deal with three broad subjects: first, the content and consequences of the Carter administration's human rights policy;

second, the prerequisites of a more adequate theory of human rights; and third, some characteristics of a more successful human rights policy.

Or consider this opening paragraph from Peter Singer's "Animal Liberation":

> We are familiar with Black Liberation, Gay Liberation, and a variety of other movements. With Women's Liberation some thought we had come to the end of the road. Discrimination on the basis of sex, it has been said, is the last form of discrimination that is universally accepted and practiced without pretense, even in those liberal circles which have long prided themselves on their freedom from racial discrimination. But one should always be wary of talking of "the last remaining form of discrimination." If we have learned anything from the liberation movements, we should have learned how difficult it is to be aware of the ways in which we discriminate until they are forcefully pointed out to us. A liberation movement demands an expansion of our moral horizons, so that practices that were previously regarded as natural and inevitable are now seen as intolerable.

Although Singer's introductory paragraph nowhere mentions animal liberation, in conjunction with its title it gives us a good idea of what Singer is up to and where he is going. Singer knows that his audience will be skeptical, so he reminds them that many of us in previous years were skeptical of reforms that we now take for granted. He adopts a strategy used fairly often by writers who advance unconventional theses: Rather than beginning with a bold announcement of a thesis that may turn off some of his readers because it sounds offensive or absurd, Singer warms up his audience, gaining their interest by cautioning them politely that although they may at first be skeptical of animal liberation, if they stay with his essay they may come to feel that they have expanded their horizons.

Notice, too, that Singer begins by establishing common ground with his readers; he assumes, probably correctly, that they share his view that other forms of discrimination (now seen to be unjust) were once widely practiced and were assumed to be acceptable and natural. In this paragraph, then, Singer is not only showing himself to be fair-minded but is also letting us know that he will advance a daring idea. His opening wins our attention and our goodwill. A writer can hardly hope to do more. (In a few pages we will talk a little more about winning the audience.)

In your introductory paragraphs,

- You may have to give some background information that your readers will need to keep in mind if they are to follow your essay.
- You may wish to define some terms that are unfamiliar or that you use in an unusual sense.

After announcing the topic, giving the necessary background, and stating your position (and perhaps the opposition's) in as engaging a manner as possible, it is usually a good idea to give the reader an idea of *how* you will proceed—that is, what the organization will be.

A Rule for Writers: In writing or at least in revising these paragraphs, keep in mind this question: What do my readers need to know? Remember, your aim throughout is to write *reader-friendly* prose, and keeping the needs and interests of your audience constantly in mind will help you achieve this goal.

Similarly, you may, for instance, want to announce fairly early that there are four common objections to your thesis and that you will take them up one by one, beginning with the weakest (or most widely held, or whatever) and moving to the strongest (or least familiar), after which you will advance your own view in greater detail. Not every argument begins with refuting the other side, though many arguments do. The point to remember is that you usually ought to tell your readers where you will be taking them and by what route.

Organizing and Revising the Body of the Essay

Most argumentative essays more or less follow this organization:

1. Statement of the problem
2. Statement of the structure of the essay
3. Statement of alternative solutions
4. Arguments in support of the proposed solution
5. Arguments answering possible objections
6. A summary, resolution, or conclusion

Let's look at each of these six steps:

1. **Statement of the problem**   Whether the problem is stated briefly or at length depends on the nature of the problem and the writer's audience. If you haven't already defined unfamiliar terms or terms you use in a special way, probably now is the time to do so. In any case, it is advisable here to state the problem objectively (thereby gaining the trust of the reader) and to indicate why the reader should care about the issue.

2. **Statement of the structure of the essay**   After stating the problem at the appropriate length, the writer often briefly indicates the structure of the rest of the essay. The commonest structure is suggested below, in points 3 and 4.

3. **Statement of alternative solutions**   In addition to stating the alternatives fairly, the writer probably conveys willingness to recognize not only the integrity of the proposers but also the (partial) merit of at least some of the alternative solutions.

The point made in the previous sentence is important and worth amplifying. Because it is important to convey your goodwill — your sense of fairness — to the reader, it is advisable to let your reader see that you are familiar with the opposition and that you recognize the integrity of those who hold that view. This you do by granting its merits as far as you can.

The next stage, which constitutes most of the body of the essay, usually is this:

4. **Arguments in support of the proposed solution**   The evidence offered will, of course, depend on the nature of the problem. Relevant statistics, authorities, examples, or analogies may come to mind or be available. This is usually the longest part of the essay.

5. **Arguments answering possible objections**   These arguments may suggest that

   a. The proposal won't work (perhaps it is alleged to be too expensive, to make unrealistic demands on human nature, or to fail to get to the heart of the problem);

   b. The proposed solution will create problems greater than the difficulty to be resolved. (A good example of a proposal that produced dreadful unexpected results is the law mandating a prison term for anyone over eighteen in possession of an illegal drug. Heroin dealers then began to use children as runners, and cocaine importers followed the practice.)

6. **A summary, resolution, or conclusion**   Here the writer may seek to accommodate the views of the opposition as far as

possible but clearly suggests that the writer's own position makes good sense. A conclusion—the word comes from the Latin *claudere*, "to shut"—ought to provide a sense of closure, but it can be much more than a restatement of the writer's thesis. It can, for instance, make a quiet emotional appeal by suggesting that the issue is important and that the ball is now in the reader's court.

Of course not every essay will follow this six-step pattern, but let's assume that in the introductory paragraphs you have sketched the topic (and have shown or nicely said, or implied, that the reader doubtless is interested in it) and have fairly and courteously set forth the opposition's view, recognizing its merits and indicating the degree to which you can share part of that view. You now want to set forth your arguments explaining why you differ on some essentials.

In setting forth your own position, you can begin either with your strongest reasons or your weakest. Each method of organization has advantages and disadvantages. If you begin with your strongest, the essay may seem to peter out; if you begin with the weakest, you build to a climax, but your readers may not still be with you because they may have felt at the start that the essay was frivolous. The solution to this last possibility is to make sure that even your weakest argument is an argument of some strength. You can, moreover, assure your readers that stronger points will soon be offered and you offer this point first only because you want to show that you are aware of it and that, slight though it is, it deserves some attention. The body of the essay, then, is devoted to arguing a position, which means offering not only supporting reasons but also refutations of possible objections to these reasons.

Doubtless you will sometimes be uncertain, as you draft your essay, whether to present a given point before or after another point. When you write, and certainly when you revise, try to put yourself into your reader's shoes: Which point do you think the reader needs to know first? Which point *leads to* which further point? Your argument should not be a mere list of points, of course; rather, it should clearly integrate one point with another in order to develop an idea. But in all likelihood you won't have a strong sense of the best organization until you have written a draft and have reread it.

---

*A **Rule** for Writers:* When you revise, make sure that your organization is clear to your readers.

Checking Paragraphs   When you revise your draft, watch out also for short paragraphs. Although a paragraph of only two or three sentences (like some in this chapter) may occasionally be helpful as a transition between complicated points, most short paragraphs are undeveloped paragraphs. (Newspaper editors favor very short paragraphs because they can be read rapidly when printed in the narrow columns typical of newspapers. Many of the essays reprinted in this book originally were published in newspapers, hence they consist of very short paragraphs. There is no reason for you to imitate this style in the argumentative essays you will be writing.)

In revising, when you find a paragraph of only a sentence or two or three, check first to see if it should be joined to the paragraph that precedes or follows. Second, if on rereading you are certain that a given paragraph should not be tied to what comes before or after, think about amplifying the paragraph with supporting detail (this is not the same as mere padding).

Checking Transitions   Make sure, too, in revising, that the reader can move easily from the beginning of a paragraph to the end and from one paragraph to the next. Transitions help the reader to perceive the connections between the units of the argument. For example ("For example" is a transition, of course, indicating that an illustration will follow), they may

- **Illustrate:** *for example, for instance, consider this case*;
- **Establish a sequence:** *a more important objection, a stronger example, the best reason*;
- **Connect logically:** *thus, as a result, therefore, so, it follows*;
- **Compare:** *similarly, in like manner, just as, analogously*;
- **Contrast:** *on the other hand, in contrast, however, but*;
- **Summarize:** *in short, briefly*.

Expressions such as these serve as guideposts that enable your reader to move easily through your essay.

When writers revise an early draft, they chiefly

- **Unify** the essay by eliminating irrelevancies;
- **Organize** the essay by keeping in mind an imagined audience;
- **Clarify** the essay by fleshing out thin paragraphs, by making certain that the transitions are adequate, and by making certain that generalizations are adequately supported by concrete details and examples.

We are not talking about polish or elegance; we are talking about fundamental matters. Be especially careful not to abuse the logical connectives (*thus*, *as a result*, and so on). If you write several sentences followed by *therefore* or a similar word or phrase, be sure that what you write after the *therefore* really *does follow* from what has gone before. Logical connectives are not mere transitional devices used to link disconnected bits of prose. They are supposed to mark a real movement of thought—the essence of an argument.

The Ending

What about concluding paragraphs, in which you try to summarize the main points and reaffirm your position? If you can look back over your essay and can add something that enriches it and at the same time wraps it up, fine, but don't feel compelled to say, "Thus, in conclusion, I have argued X, Y, and Z, and I have refuted Jones." After all, *conclusion* can have two meanings: (1) ending, or finish, as the ending of a joke or a novel, or (2) judgment or decision reached after deliberation. Your essay should finish effectively (the first sense), but it need not announce a judgment (the second).

If the essay is fairly short, so that a reader can more or less keep the whole thing in mind, you may not need to restate your view. Just make sure that you have covered the ground and that your last sentence is a good one. Notice that the student essay printed later in this chapter (p. 144) does not end with a formal conclusion, though it ends conclusively, with a note of finality.

By a note of finality we do *not* mean a triumphant crowing. It's usually far better to end with the suggestion that you hope you have by now indicated why those who hold a different view may want to modify it and accept yours.

If you study the essays in this book, or, for that matter, the editorials and op-ed pieces in a newspaper, you will notice that writers often provide a sense of closure by using one of the following devices:

- A return to something in the introduction,
- A glance at the wider implications of the issue (for example, if smoking is restricted, other liberties are threatened),
- An anecdote that engagingly illustrates the thesis, or
- A brief summary (but this sort of ending may seem unnecessary and even tedious, especially if the paper is short and if the summary merely repeats what has already been said).

Two Uses of an Outline

The Outline as a Preliminary Guide   Some writers find it useful to sketch an outline as soon as they think they know what they want to say, even before they write a first draft. This procedure can be helpful in planning a tentative organization, but remember that in revising a draft new ideas will arise, and the outline may have to be modified. A preliminary outline is chiefly useful as a means of getting going, not as a guide to the final essay.

The Outline as a Way of Checking a Draft   Whether or not you use a preliminary outline, we strongly suggest that after you have written what you hope is your last draft, you make an outline of it; there is no better way of finding out whether the essay is well organized.

Go through the draft and jot down the chief points in the order in which you make them. That is, prepare a table of contents—perhaps a phrase for each paragraph. Next, examine your jottings to see what kind of sequence they reveal in your paper:

1. Is the sequence reasonable? Can it be improved?
2. Are any passages irrelevant?
3. Does something important seem to be missing?

If no coherent structure or reasonable sequence clearly appears in the outline, then the full prose version of your argument probably doesn't have any either. Therefore, produce another draft, moving things around, adding or subtracting paragraphs—cutting and pasting into a new sequence, with transitions as needed—and then make another outline to see if the sequence now is satisfactory.

You are probably familiar with the structure known as a **formal outline.** Major points are indicated by I, II, III; points within major points are indicated by A, B, C; divisions within A, B, C are indicated by 1, 2, 3; and so on. Thus,

    I. Arguments for opening all Olympic sports to professionals
       A. Fairness
          1. Some Olympic sports are already open to professionals.
          2. Some athletes who really are not professionals are classified as professionals.
       B. Quality (achievements would be higher)

You may want to outline your draft according to this principle, or it may be enough if you simply jot down a phrase for each paragraph and indent the subdivisions. But keep these points in mind:

- It is not enough for the parts to be ordered reasonably;
- The order must be made clear to the reader, probably by means of transitions such as *for instance, on the other hand, we can now turn to an opposing view,* and so on.

Tone and the Writer's Persona

Although this book is chiefly about argument in the sense of rational discourse—the presentation of reasons in support of a thesis or conclusion—the appeal to reason is only one form of persuasion. Another form is the appeal to emotion—to pity, for example. Aristotle saw, in addition to the appeal to reason and the appeal to emotion, a third form of persuasion, the appeal to the character of the speaker. He called it the **ethical appeal** (the Greek word for this kind of appeal is **ethos,** "character"). The idea is that effective speakers convey the suggestion that they are

- Informed,
- Intelligent,
- Benevolent, and
- Honest.

Because they are perceived as trustworthy, their words inspire confidence in their listeners. It is, of course, a fact that when we read an argument we are often aware of the *person* or *voice* behind the words, and our assent to the argument depends partly on the extent to which we can share the speaker's assumptions, look at the matter from the speaker's point of view—in short, *identify* with this speaker.

How can a writer inspire the confidence that lets readers identify themselves with the writer? To begin with, the writer should possess the virtues Aristotle specified: intelligence or good sense, honesty, and benevolence or goodwill. As the Roman proverb puts it, "No one gives what he does not have." Still, possession of these qualities is not a guarantee that you will convey them in your writing. Like all other writers, you will have to revise your drafts so that these qualities become apparent, or, stated more moderately, you will have to revise so that nothing in the essay causes a reader to doubt your intelligence, honesty, and goodwill. A blunder in logic, a misleading quotation, a snide remark, even an error in spelling—all such slips can cause readers to withdraw their sympathy from the writer.

> *A Rule for Writers:* Present yourself so that your
> readers see you as knowledgeable, honest, open-
> minded, and interested in helping them to think
> about an issue of significance.

But of course all good argumentative essays do not sound exactly
alike; they do not all reveal the same speaker. Each writer develops his
or her own voice or (as literary critics and teachers call it) **persona.** In
fact, one writer will have several voices or personae, depending on the
topic and the audience. The president of the United States delivering an
address on the State of the Union has one persona; chatting with a
reporter at his summer home he has another. This change is not a matter of hypocrisy. Different circumstances call for different language. As
a French writer put it, there is a time to speak of "Paris" and a time to
speak of "the capital of the nation." When Lincoln spoke at Gettysburg,
he didn't say "Eighty-seven years ago," but "Four score and seven years
ago." We might say that just as some occasions required him to be the
folksy Honest Abe, the occasion of the dedication of hallowed ground
required him to be formal and solemn, and so the president of the
United States appropriately used biblical language. The election cam-
paigns called for one persona, and the dedication of a military cemetery
called for a different persona.

When we talk about a writer's persona, we mean the way in which
the writer presents his or her attitudes

- Toward *the self,*
- Toward *the audience*, and
- Toward *the subject.*

Thus, if a writer says,

> I have thought long and hard about this subject, and I can say with
> assurance that . . .

we may feel that we are listening to a self-satisfied ass who probably is
simply mouthing other people's opinions. Certainly he is mouthing
clichés: "long and hard," "say with assurance."

Let's look at a slightly subtler example of an utterance that reveals
an attitude. When we read that

> President Nixon was hounded out of office by journalists,

we hear a respectful attitude toward Nixon ("President Nixon") and a hostile attitude toward the press (they are beasts, curs who "hounded" our elected leader). If the writer's attitudes were reversed, she might have said something like this:

> The press turned the searchlight on Tricky Dick's criminal shenanigans.

"Tricky Dick" and "criminal" are obvious enough, but notice that "shenanigans" also implies the writer's contempt for Nixon, and of course, "turned the searchlight" suggests that the press is a source of illumination, a source of truth. The original version and the opposite version both say that the press was responsible for Nixon's resignation, but the original version ("President Nixon was hounded") conveys indignation toward journalists, whereas the revision conveys contempt for Nixon.

These two versions suggest two speakers who differ not only in their view of Nixon but also in their manner, including the seriousness with which they take themselves. Although the passage is very short, it seems to us that the first speaker conveys righteous indignation ("hounded"), whereas the second conveys amused contempt ("shenanigans"). To our ears the tone, as well as the point, differs in the two versions.

We are talking about **loaded words,** words that convey the writer's attitude and that by their connotations are meant to win the reader to the writer's side. Compare *freedom fighter* with *terrorist, pro-choice* with *pro-abortion,* or *pro-life* with *anti-choice. Freedom fighter, pro-choice,* and *pro-life* sound like good things; speakers who use these words are seeking to establish themselves as virtuous people who are supporting worthy causes. The **connotations** (associations, overtones) of these pairs of words differ, even though the **denotations** (explicit meanings, dictionary definitions) are the same, just as the connotations of *mother* and *female parent* differ, although the denotations are the same. Similarly, although Lincoln's "four score and seven" and "eighty-seven" both denote "thirteen less than one hundred," they differ in connotation.

Tone is not only a matter of connotations (*hounded out of office* versus, let's say, *compelled to resign,* or *pro-choice* versus *pro-abortion*); it is also a matter of such things as the selection and type of examples. A writer who offers many examples, especially ones drawn from ordinary life, conveys a persona different from that of a writer who offers no examples or only an occasional invented instance. The first of these probably is, one might say, friendlier, more down-to-earth.

Last Words on Tone   On the whole, when writing an argument, it is advisable to be courteous and respectful of your topic, of your audience, and of people who hold views you are arguing against. It is rarely good for one's own intellectual development to regard as villains or fools persons who hold views different from one's own, especially if some of them are in the audience. Keep in mind the story of the two strangers on a train who, striking up a conversation, found that both were clergymen, though of different faiths. Then one said to the other, "Well, why shouldn't we be friends? After all, we both serve God, you in your way and I in His."

Complacency is all right when telling a joke but not when offering an argument:

- Recognize opposing views,
- Assume they are held in good faith,
- State them fairly (if you don't, you do a disservice not only to the opposition but to your own position because the perceptive reader will not take you seriously), and
- Be temperate in arguing your own position: "If I understand their view correctly . . ."; "It seems reasonable to conclude that . . ."; "Perhaps, then, we can agree that. . . ."

We, One, or I?

The use of *we* in the last sentence brings us to another point: May the first-person pronouns *I* and *we* be used? In this book, because two of us are writing, we often use *we* to mean the two authors. And we sometimes use *we* to mean the authors and the readers, as in phrases like the one that ends the previous paragraph. This shifting use of one word can be troublesome, but we hope (clearly the *we* here refers only to the authors) that we have avoided any ambiguity. But can, or should, or must, an individual use *we* instead of *I*? The short answer is no.

If you are simply speaking for yourself, use *I*. Attempts to avoid the first person singular by saying things like "This writer thinks . . . ," and "It is thought that . . . ," and "One thinks that . . . ," are far more irritating (and wordy) than the use of *I*. The so-called editorial *we* is as odd sounding in a student's argument as is the royal *we*. Mark Twain said that the only ones who can appropriately say *we* are kings, editors, and people with a tapeworm. And because one *one* leads to another, making the sentence sound (James Thurber's words) "like a trombone solo," it's best to admit that you are the author, and to use *I*. But there is no need

---

A CHECKLIST FOR ATTENDING TO THE NEEDS OF THE AUDIENCE

☐ Do I have a sense of what the audience probably knows about the issue?

☐ Do I have a sense of what the audience probably thinks about the issue?

☐ How much common ground do we probably share?

☐ Have I, in the paper, tried to establish common ground and then moved on to advance my position?

☐ Have I supported my arguments with sufficient details?

☐ Have I used the appropriate language (for instance, defined terms that are likely to be unfamiliar)?

☐ Have I indicated *why* my readers should care about the issue and should accept or at least take seriously my views?

☐ Is the organization clear?

☐ Have I presented myself as a person who is (a) fair, (b) informed, and (c) worth listening to?

---

to preface every sentence with "I think." The reader knows that the essay is yours; just write it, using *I* when you must, but not needlessly.

Avoiding Sexist Language

Courtesy as well as common sense requires that you respect the feelings of your readers. Many people today find offensive the implicit sexism in the use of male pronouns to denote not only men but also women ("As the reader follows the argument, he will find . . ."). And sometimes the use of the male pronoun to denote all people is ridiculous: "An individual, no matter what his sex, . . ."

In most contexts there is no need to use gender-specific nouns or pronouns. One way to avoid using *he* when you mean any person is to use *he or she* (or *she or he*) instead of *he,* but the result is sometimes a bit cumbersome—although it is superior to the overly conspicuous *he/she* and to *s/he.*

Here are two simple ways to solve the problem:

- *Use the plural* ("As readers follow the argument, they will find . . ."), or

- *Recast the sentence* so that no pronoun is required ("Readers following the argument will find . . .").

Because *man* and *mankind* strike many readers as sexist when used in such expressions as "Man is a rational animal" and "Mankind has not yet solved this problem," consider using such words as *human being, person, people, humanity,* and *we.* (*Examples:* "Human beings are rational animals"; "We have not yet solved this problem.")

PEER REVIEW

Your instructor may suggest—or may even require—that you submit an early draft of your essay to a fellow student or small group of students for comment. Such a procedure benefits both author and readers: You get the responses of a reader and the student-reader gets experience in thinking about the problems of developing an argument, especially in thinking about such matters as the degree of detail that a writer needs to offer to a reader and the importance of keeping the organization evident to a reader.

A STUDENT'S ESSAY, FROM ROUGH NOTES TO FINAL VERSION

While we were revising this textbook, we asked the students in one of our classes to write a short essay (500-750 words) on some ethical problem that concerned them. Because this assignment was the first writing assignment in the course, we explained that a good way to get ideas is to ask oneself some questions, jot down responses, question those responses, and write freely for ten minutes or so, not worrying about contradictions. We invited our students to hand in their initial jottings along with the finished essay, so that we could get a sense of how they proceeded as writers. Not all of them chose to hand in their jottings, but we were greatly encouraged by those who did. What was encouraging was the confirmation of an old belief, the belief—we call it a fact—that students will hand in a thoughtful essay if before they prepare a final version they nag themselves, ask themselves *why* they think this or that, jot down their responses, and are not afraid to change their minds as they proceed.

A PEER REVIEW CHECKLIST FOR
A DRAFT OF AN ARGUMENT

Read the draft through, quickly. Then read it again, with the following questions in mind.

☐ Does the draft show promise of fulfilling the assignment?

☐ Looking at the essay as a whole, what thesis (main idea) is advanced?

☐ Are the needs of the audience kept in mind? For instance, do some words need to be defined? Is the evidence (for instance, the examples, and the testimony of authorities) clear and effective?

☐ Can you accept the assumptions? If not, why not?

☐ Is any obvious evidence (or counterevidence) overlooked?

☐ Is the writer proposing a solution? If so,

  ☐ Are other equally attractive solutions adequately examined?

  ☐ Has the writer overlooked some unattractive effects of the proposed solution?

☐ Looking at each paragraph separately,

  ☐ What is the basic point?

  ☐ How does each paragraph relate to the essay's main idea or to the previous paragraph?

  ☐ Should some paragraphs be deleted? Be divided into two or more paragraphs? Be combined? Be put elsewhere? (If you outline the essay by jotting down the gist of each paragraph, you will get help in answering these questions.)

  ☐ Is each sentence clearly related to the sentence that precedes and to the sentence that follows?

  ☐ Is each paragraph adequately developed? Are there sufficient details, perhaps brief supporting quotations from the text?

  ☐ Are the introductory and concluding paragraphs effective?

☐ What are the paper's chief strengths?

☐ Make at least two specific suggestions that you think will assist the author to improve the paper.

Here are the first jottings of a student, Emily Andrews, who elected to write about whether to give money to street beggars. She simply put down ideas, one after the other.

Help the poor? Why do I (sometimes) do it?

I feel guilty, and think I should help them: poor, cold, hungry (but also some of them are thirsty for liquor, and will spend the money on liquor, not on food).

I also feel annoyed by them — most of them:

Where does the expression "the deserving poor" come from?

And "poor but honest"? Actually, that sounds a bit odd. Wouldn't "rich but honest" make more sense?

Why don't they work? Fellow with red beard, always by bus stop in front of florist's shop, always wants a handout. He is a regular, there all day every day, so I guess he is in a way "reliable," so why doesn't he put the same time in on a job?

Or why don't they get help? Don't they know they need it? They <u>must</u> know they need it.

Maybe that guy with the beard is just a con artist. Maybe he makes more money by panhandling than he would by working, and it's a lot easier!

Kinds of poor — how to classify??
    drunks, druggies, etc.
    mentally ill (maybe drunks belong here too)
    decent people who have had terrible luck

Why private charity?

Doesn't it make sense to say we (fortunate individuals) should give something — an occasional handout — to people who have had terrible luck? (I suppose some people might say that there is no need for any of us to give anything — the government takes care of the truly needy — but I <u>do</u> believe in giving charity. A month ago a friend of the family passed away, and the woman's children suggested that people might want to make a donation in her name, to a shelter for battered women. I know my parents made a donation.)

BUT how can I tell who is who, which are which? Which of these people asking for "spare change" really need (deserve???) help, and which are phonies? Impossible to tell.

Possibilities:
> Give to no one
> Give to no one but make an annual donation, maybe to United Way
> Give a dollar to each person who asks. This would probably not cost me even a dollar a day
> Occasionally do without something — maybe a CD — or a meal in a restaurant — and give the money I save to people who seem worthy.

WORTHY? What am I saying? How can I, or anyone, tell? The neat-looking guy who says he just lost his job may be a phony, and the dirty bum — probably a drunk — may desperately need food. (OK, so what if he spends the money on liquor instead of food? At least he'll get a little pleasure in life. No! It's not all right if he spends it on drink.)

Other possibilities:
> Do some volunteer work?
> To tell the truth, I don't want to put in the time. I don't feel <u>that</u> guilty.

So what's the problem?

Is it, How I can help the very poor (handouts, or through an organization)? or

How I can feel less guilty about being lucky enough to be able to go to college, and to have a supportive family?

I can't quite bring myself to believe I should help every beggar who approaches, but I also can't bring myself to believe that I should do nothing, on the grounds that:
> a. it's probably their fault
> b. if they are deserving, they can get gov't help. No, I just can't believe that. Maybe some are too proud to look for government help, or don't know that they are entitled to it.

What to do?

On balance, it seems best to
> a. give to United Way
> b. maybe also give to an occasional individual, if I happen to be moved, without worrying about whether he or she is "deserving" (since it's probably impossible to know).

A day after making these notes Emily reviewed them, added a few points, and then made a very brief selection from them to serve as an outline for her first draft:

Opening para.: "poor but honest"? Deserve "spare change"?

Charity: private or through organizations?
     pros and cons
     guy at bus
     it wouldn't cost me much, but . . . better to
     give through organizations

Concluding para.: still feel guilty?
       maybe mention guy at bus again?

After writing and revising a draft, Emily Andrews submitted her essay to a fellow student for peer review. She then revised her work in light of the suggestions she received and in light of her own further thinking.

On the next page we give the final essay. If after reading the final version you reread the early jottings, you will notice that some of the jottings never made it into the final version. But without the jottings, the essay probably could not have been as interesting as it is. When the writer made the jottings, she was not so much putting down her ideas as *finding* ideas by the process of writing.

Emily Andrews

Professor Barnet

English 102

January 16, 2004

Why I Don't Spare "Spare Change"

"Poor but honest." "The deserving poor." I don't know the origin of these quotations, but they always come to mind when I think of "the poor." But I also think of people who, perhaps through alcohol or drugs, have ruined not only their own lives but also the lives of others in order to indulge in their own pleasure. Perhaps alcoholism and drug addiction really are "diseases," as many people say, but my own feeling — based, of course, not on any serious study — is that most alcoholics and drug addicts can be classified with the "undeserving poor." And that is largely why I don't distribute spare change to panhandlers.

But surely among the street people there are also some who can rightly be called "deserving." Deserving what? My spare change? Or simply the government's assistance? It happens that I have been brought up to believe that it is appropriate to make contributions to charity — let's say a shelter for battered women — but if I give some change to a panhandler, am I making a contribution to charity and thereby helping someone, or, on the contrary, am I perhaps simply encouraging someone not to get help? Or maybe even worse, am I supporting a con artist?

If one believes in the value of private charity, one can give either to needy individuals or to charitable organizations. In giving to a panhandler one may indeed be helping a person who badly needs help, but one cannot be certain that one is giving to a needy individual. In giving to an organization such as the United Way, on the other hand, one can feel that one's money is likely to be used wisely. True, confronted by a beggar one may feel that <u>this</u> particular unfortunate individual needs help at <u>this</u> moment — a cup of coffee or a sandwich — and the need will not be met unless I put my hand in my pocket right now. But I have come to think that the beggars whom I encounter can get along without my spare change, and indeed perhaps they are actually better off for not having money to buy liquor or drugs.

It happens that in my neighborhood I encounter few panhandlers. There is one fellow who is always by the bus stop where I catch the bus to the college, and I never give him anything precisely because he is always there. He is such a regular that, I think, he ought to be able to hold a regular job. Putting him aside, I probably don't encounter more than three or four beggars in a week. (I'm not counting street musicians. These people seem quite able to work for a living. If they see their "work" as playing or singing, let persons who enjoy their performances pay them. I do not consider myself among their audience.) The truth of the matter is that, since I meet so few beggars, I could give each one a dollar and hardly feel the loss. At most, I might go without seeing a movie some week. But I know nothing about these people, and it's my impression — admittedly based on almost no evidence — that they simply prefer begging to working. I am not

Andrews 3

generalizing about street people, and certainly I am not talking about street people in the big urban centers. I am talking
only about the people whom I actually encounter.

That's why I usually do not give "spare change," and I
don't think I will in the future. These people will get along
without me. Someone else will come up with money for their
coffee or their liquor, or, at worst, they will just have to do
without. I will continue to contribute occasionally to a
charitable organization, not simply (I hope) to salve my con-
science but because I believe that these organizations
actually do good work. But I will not attempt to be a
mini-charitable organization, distributing (probably to the
unworthy) spare change.

Finally, here are a few comments about the essay:

- *The title is informative,* alerting the reader to the topic and the
author's position. (By the way, the student told us that in her next-
to-last draft the title was "Is It Right to Spare 'Spare Change'?"
This title, like the revision, introduces the topic but not the
author's position. The revised version seems to us to be more
striking.)
- *The opening paragraph holds a reader's interest,* partly by alluding
to the familiar phrase "the deserving poor" and partly by introducing the *un*familiar phrase "the *un*deserving poor." Notice, too,
that this opening paragraph ends by clearly asserting the author's
thesis. Of course, writers need not always announce their thesis
early, but it is usually advisable to do so. Readers like to know
where they are going.

- *The second paragraph* begins by voicing what probably is the reader's somewhat uneasy—perhaps even negative—response to the first paragraph. That is, *the writer has a sense of her audience;* she knows how her reader feels, and she takes account of the feeling.

- *The third paragraph clearly sets forth the alternatives.* A reader may disagree with the writer's attitude, but the alternatives seem to be stated fairly.

- *The last two paragraphs are more personal* than the earlier paragraphs. The writer, more or less having stated what she takes to be the facts, now is entitled to offer a highly personal response to them.

- *The final paragraph nicely wraps things up* by means of the words "spare change," which go back to the title and to the end of the first paragraph. The reader thus experiences a sensation of completeness. The essayist, of course, has not solved the problem for all of us for all time, but she presents a thoughtful argument and ends the essay effectively.

Exercise

In an essay of 500 words, state a claim and support it with evidence. Choose an issue in which you are genuinely interested and about which you already know something. You may want to interview a few experts and do some reading, but don't try to write a highly researched paper. Sample topics:

1. Students in laboratory courses should not be required to participate in the dissection of animals.
2. Washington, D.C., should be granted statehood.
3. Puerto Rico should be granted statehood.
4. Women should, in wartime, be exempted from serving in combat.
5. The annual Miss America contest is an insult to women.
6. The government should not offer financial support to the arts.
7. The chief fault of the curriculum in high school was . . .
8. Grades should be abolished in college and university courses.
9. No specific courses should be required in colleges or universities.

7

Using Sources

WHY USE SOURCES?

We have pointed out that one gets ideas by writing. In the exercise of writing a draft, ideas begin to form, and these ideas stimulate further ideas, especially when one questions—when one *thinks* about—what one has written. But of course in writing about complex, serious questions, nobody is expected to invent all the answers. On the contrary, a writer is expected to be familiar with the chief answers already produced by others and to make use of them through selective incorporation and criticism. In short, writers are not expected to reinvent the wheel; rather, they are expected to make good use of it and perhaps round it off a bit or replace a defective spoke. In order to think out your own views in writing, you are expected to do some preliminary research into the views of others.

We use the word *research* broadly. It need not require taking copious notes on everything written on your topic; rather, it can involve no more than familiarizing yourself with at least some of the chief responses to your topic. In one way or another, almost everyone does some research. If we are going to buy a car, we may read an issue or two of a magazine or visit a Web site that rates cars, or we may talk to a few people who own models that we are thinking of buying, and then we visit a couple of dealers to find out who is offering the best price.

Research, in short, is not an activity conducted only by college professors or by students who visit the library in order to write research papers. It is an activity that all of us engage in to some degree. In writing a research paper, you will engage in it to a great degree. But doing research is not the whole of a research paper. The reader expects the writer to have *thought* about the research and to develop an argument based on the findings. Many businesses today devote an entire division to research and development. That's what is needed in writing, too. The reader wants not only a lot of facts but also a developed idea, a point to which the facts lead. Don't let your reader say of your paper what Gertrude Stein said of her hometown, Oakland, California: "When you get there, there isn't any *there* there."

Consider arguments about whether athletes should be permitted to take anabolic steroids, drugs that supposedly build up muscle, restore energy, and enhance aggressiveness. A thoughtful argument on this subject will have to take account of information that the writer can gather only by doing some research. Do steroids really have the effects commonly attributed to them? And are they dangerous? If they are dangerous, how dangerous are they? (After all, competitive sports are inherently dangerous, some of them highly so. Many boxers, jockeys, and football players have suffered severe injury, even death, from competing. Does anyone believe that anabolic steroids are more dangerous than the contests themselves?) Obviously, again, a respectable argument about steroids will have to show awareness of what is known about them.

Or take this question: Why did President Truman order that atomic bombs be dropped on Hiroshima and Nagasaki? The most obvious answer is to end the war, but some historians believe he had a very different purpose. In their view, Japan's defeat was ensured before the bombs were dropped, and the Japanese were ready to surrender; the bombs were dropped not to save American (or Japanese) lives but to show Russia that the United States would not be pushed around. Scholars who hold this view, such as Gar Alperovitz in *Atomic Diplomacy*, argue that Japanese civilians in Hiroshima and Nagasaki were incinerated not to save the lives of American soldiers who otherwise would have died in an invasion of Japan but to teach Stalin a lesson. Dropping the bombs, it is argued, marked not the end of the Pacific War but the beginning of the cold war.

One must ask: What evidence supports this argument or claim or thesis, which assumes that Truman could not have thought the bomb was needed to defeat the Japanese because the Japanese knew they were defeated and would soon surrender without a hard-fought defense that would cost hundreds of thousands of lives? What about the momentum that had built up to use the bomb? After all, years of effort and $2 billion had been expended to produce a weapon with the intention of using it to end the war against Germany. But Germany had been defeated without the use of the bomb. Meanwhile, the war in the Pacific continued unabated. If the argument we are considering is correct, all this background counted for little or nothing in Truman's decision, a decision purely diplomatic and coolly indifferent to human life. The task for the writer is to evaluate the evidence available and then to argue for or against the view that Truman's purpose in dropping the bomb was to impress the Soviet government.

A student writing on the topic will certainly want to read the chief books on the subject (Alperovitz's, cited above, Martin Sherwin's *A World Destroyed*, and John Toland's *The Rising Sun*) and perhaps reviews of them, especially the reviews in journals devoted to political science. (Reading a searching review of a serious scholarly book is a good way to identify quickly some of the book's main contributions and controversial claims.) Truman's letters and statements and books and articles about Truman are also clearly relevant, and doubtless important articles are to be found in recent issues of scholarly journals and electronic sources. In fact, even an essay on such a topic as whether Truman was morally justified in using the atomic bomb for *any* purpose will be a stronger essay if it is well informed about such matters as the estimated loss of life that an invasion would have cost, the international rules governing weapons, and Truman's own statements about the issue.

How does one go about finding the material needed to write a well-informed argument? We will provide help, but first we want to offer a few words about choosing a topic.

CHOOSING A TOPIC

We will be brief. If a topic is not assigned, choose one that

- Interests you and
- Can be researched with reasonable thoroughness in the allotted time.

Topics such as censorship, the environment, and sexual harassment obviously impinge on our lives, and it may well be that one such topic is of especial interest to you. But the scope of these topics makes researching them potentially overwhelming. Type the word *censorship* into an **Internet** search engine, and you will be referred to thousands of information sources.

This brings us to our second point—a manageable topic. Any of the topics above would need to be narrowed substantially before you could begin searching in earnest. Similarly, a topic such as the causes of World War II can hardly be mastered in a few weeks or argued in a ten-page paper. It is simply too big.

You can, however, write a solid paper analyzing, evaluating, and arguing for or against General Eisenhower's views on atomic warfare. What were they, and when did he hold them? (In his books of 1948 and 1963 Eisenhower says that he opposed the use of the bomb before Hiroshima and that he argued with Secretary of War Henry Stimson against dropping it, but what evidence supports these claims? Was Eisenhower attempting to rewrite history in his books?) Eisenhower's own writings and books and other information sources on Eisenhower will, of course, be the major sources for a paper on this topic, but you will also want to look at books and articles about Stimson and at publications that contain information about the views of other generals, so that, for instance, you can compare Eisenhower's view with Marshall's or MacArthur's.

Your instructor understands that you are not going to spend a year writing a 200-page book, but you should understand that you must do more than consult a single Web site on Eisenhower and the article on atomic energy in an encyclopedia.

FINDING MATERIAL

Your sources will, of course, depend on your topic. Some topics will require no more than a trip to the library or an afternoon spent at your personal computer, but others may require interviews. If you are writing about some aspect of AIDS, for instance, you probably will find it useful to consult your college or community health center.

For facts, you ought to try to consult experts—for instance, members of the faculty or other local authorities on art, business, law, and so forth; for opinions and attitudes, you will usually consult interested laypersons. Remember, however, that experts have their biases and that "ordinary" people may have knowledge that experts lack. When interviewing experts, keep in mind Picasso's comment: "You mustn't always believe what I say. Questions tempt you to tell lies, particularly when there is no answer."

INTERVIEWING PEERS
AND LOCAL AUTHORITIES

If you are interviewing your peers, you will probably want to make an effort to get a representative sample. Of course, even within a group not all members share a single view—many African Americans favor affirmative action but not all do, and many gays favor legalizing gay marriage but, again, some don't. Make an effort to talk to a range of people who might be expected to offer varied opinions. You may learn some unexpected things.

Here we will concentrate, however, on interviews with experts.

1. **Finding subjects for interviews**   If you are looking for expert opinions, you may want to start with a faculty member on your campus. You may already know the instructor, or you may have to scan the catalog to see who teaches courses relevant to your topic. Department secretaries and college Web sites are good sources of information about the special interests of the faculty and also about lecturers who will be visiting the campus.

2. **Doing preliminary homework**   (1) Know something about the person whom you will be interviewing. Biographical reference works such as *Who's Who in America, Who's Who among Black Americans, Who's Who of American Women,* and *Directory of American Scholars* may include your interviewee, or, again, a departmental secretary may be able to provide a vita for a faculty member. (2) In requesting the interview, make evident your interest in the topic and in the person. (If you know something about the person, you will be able to indicate why you are asking him or her.) (3) Request the interview, preferably in writing, a week in advance, and ask for ample time—probably half an hour to an hour. Indicate whether or not the material will be confidential, and (if you want to use a recorder) ask if you may record the interview. (4) If the person accepts the invitation, ask if he or she recommends any preliminary reading, and establish a time and a suitable place, preferably not the cafeteria during lunchtime.

3. **Preparing thoroughly**   (1) If your interviewee recommended any reading or has written on the topic, read the material. (2) Tentatively formulate some questions, keeping in mind that (unless you are simply gathering material for a survey of opinions) you want more than yes or no answers. Questions beginning with *Why* and *How* will usually require the interviewee to go beyond yes and no.

Even if your subject has consented to let you bring a recorder, be prepared to take notes on points that strike you as especially significant; without written notes, you will have nothing if the recorder has malfunctioned. Further, by taking occasional notes you will give the interviewee some time to think and perhaps to rephrase or to amplify a remark.

4. **Conducting the interview**   (1) Begin by engaging in brief conversation, without taking notes. If the interviewee has agreed to let you use a recorder, settle on the place where you will put it. (2) Come prepared with an opening question or two, but as the interview proceeds, don't hesitate to ask questions that you had not anticipated

asking. (3) Near the end (you and your subject have probably agreed on the length of the interview) ask the subject if he or she wishes to add anything, perhaps by way of clarifying some earlier comment. (4) Conclude by thanking the interviewee and by offering to provide a copy of the final version of your paper.

5. **Writing up the interview**   (1) As soon as possible—certainly within twenty-four hours after the interview—review your notes and clarify them. At this stage, you can still remember the meaning of your abbreviated notes and shorthand devices (maybe you have been using *n* to stand for *nurses* in clinics where abortions are performed), but if you wait even a whole day you may be puzzled by your own notes. If you have recorded the interview, you may want to transcribe all of it—the laboriousness of this task is one good reason why many interviewers do not use recorders—and you may then want to scan the whole and mark the parts that now strike you as especially significant. If you have taken notes by hand, type them up, along with your own observations, for example, "Jones was very tentative on this matter, but she said she was inclined to believe that. . . ." (2) Be especially careful to indicate which words are direct quotations. If in doubt, check with the interviewee.

USING THE LIBRARY

Most topics, as we have said, will require research in the library. Notice that we have spoken of a topic, not of a thesis or even of a *hypothesis* (tentative thesis). Advanced students, because they are familiar with the rudiments of a subject (say, the origins of the cold war) usually have not only a topic but also a hypothesis or even a thesis in mind. Less experienced students are not always in this happy position: Before they can offer a hypothesis, they have to find a problem. Some instructors assign topics; others rely on students to find their own topics, based on readings in the course or in other courses.

When you have a *topic* ("Eisenhower and the atomic bomb") and perhaps a *thesis* (an attitude toward the topic, a claim that you want to argue, such as "Eisenhower's disapproval of the bomb was the product of the gentleman-soldier code that he had learned at West Point"), it is often useful to scan a relevant book. You may already know of a relevant book, and it is likely in turn to cite others. If, however, you don't know of any book, you can find one by consulting the catalog in the library, which lists books not only by author and by title but also by subject. There are many computerized cataloguing systems; your librarian can teach you how to use the one in your college or university library.

If there are many books on the topic, how do you choose just one? Choose first a fairly thin one, of fairly recent date, published by a reputable publisher. You may even want to jot down two or three titles and then check reviews of these books before choosing one book to skim. Your college or university library may subscribe to *Books in Print with Reviews,* an electronic database that contains citations and the full text of book reviews from several reliable journals and magazines. Many other more specialized databases exist for scholarly book reviews, or you might find one of these print indexes helpful:

> *Book Review Digest* (1905–)
>
> *Book Review Index* (1965–)
>
> *Humanities Index* (1974–)
>
> *Index to Book Reviews in the Humanities* (1960–)
>
> *Social Sciences Index* (1974–)

Book Review Digest includes brief extracts from the reviews, and so look there first, but its coverage is not as broad as the other indexes.

Skimming a recent academic book is a good way to get an overview of a topic, and it may help you to form a tentative thesis and focus your research further. But because the publication process takes a year or more, even a book with a publication date of this year may have been written at least a year earlier (and on some issues—for instance, regulations concerning cloning or censorship of the Internet—some of the information in the source may be outdated). Articles in academic journals, too, usually are written many months before they are published, but magazines and newspapers or their electronic equivalents can provide you with up-to-date information. Articles, whether in academic journals or in current magazines, have the further advantage of being short, so they are likely to be more focused than a book; they therefore may speak more directly to your tentative thesis.

To find articles in periodicals, begin with the computerized search tools that now are available in most college and university libraries. Two of the most popular search tools are *InfoTrac* and the *Readers' Guide to Periodical Literature.* Your library probably has at least one of these CD-ROM systems, each of which indexes hundreds of popular and semi-popular magazines (like *Time* and *Scientific American*) and well-respected newspapers (like the *New York Times* and the *Washington Post*). If your topic is one in which there is wide public interest, these **databases** will point you toward many potential research sources. Using these systems is simply a matter of launching the appropriate software, typing in one or two keywords related to your topic, and perhaps narrowing the search with additional words if the database turns up more than a few references to the terms you enter.

Even better than *InfoTrac* and the *Readers' Guide*, however, are the many specialized academic indexes now available on CD-ROM. These indexes, which list scholarly books and articles in specialized academic journals, are up-to-date and therefore are among the most valued tools. To find articles in journals, consult the *Humanities Index* and the *MLA International Bibliography* for topics in the humanities; for topics in psychology and other social sciences, consult *PsycLit* and the *Social Science Index*. Your college librarian can guide you to indexes for engineering and hard sciences, business and industry, education, the arts, or whatever field you are working in. Some of these indexes (such as the popular education index *ERIC* and the *Newspaper Abstracts*) not only provide bibliographic information but also include abstracts, or short summaries, of the articles they index or even the full text of the printed article. Which search tools you use will depend both on your topic and on what is available in your library. All of the major systems are designed to be easy to use, but if you experience difficulty, don't hesitate to ask the librarian for advice about which system to use and how to use it.

Annual print versions of many of these bibliographies and indexes also exist. If you prefer to use a print document or if your library doesn't have the CD-ROM database you need, ask your librarian for advice about using a more traditional search method.

FINDING INFORMATION ONLINE

If you have an Internet connection, you don't have to go any further than your personal computer to access a wealth of information for your research paper. This information may come from a number of online sources, including text archives, listservs (e-mail discussion groups), and Usenet newsgroups. But unless you already know of a particular source for your paper, the best place to begin an Internet search is with the **World Wide Web.** In addition, a good Web site will often, along with providing information, point to other on- and offline sources of related interest.

Dozens of search engines are available to help you start your research, two of the most popular being Google and Yahoo! If you do not already have a favorite, ask teachers, a librarian, or friends about their preferences, and experiment with several of them to find one you like. Most search engines give you two options for how to find relevant documents and information. The first is a keyword search in which you type in a word or phrase and the engine scans the Net for documents containing that word or phrase. If your topic is highly focused and you have very specific search terms in mind, a keyword search may work well for you, but entering a broad topic like *affirmative action* or *euthanasia* will result in thousands of hits, many of them of little value to you. The other type of search is topic based. This allows you to select from a menu of broad topic areas, such as *government* or *entertainment*, and narrow the topic through a series of menus until you reach a more specific topic, like *divorce law* or *television violence.* Many search engines select the references that appear under their topic searches, filtering out those whose content is particularly suspect.

We have two words of caution if you plan to use the Internet for serious research. First, the early stages of your research may take longer than planned. The Net is huge, fast-changing, and chaotic, and navigating it is not easy. Computer systems crash, Web pages move or disappear altogether, and the discourse surrounding a controversial topic like censorship or abortion can change overnight. Second, remember that the Net is highly democratic; anyone who can get online can express an opinion. The advantage is that knowledgeable people can offer information quickly, but the disadvantage is that careless scholars, blowhards, and liars can shed misinformation. It is always important for researchers to evaluate their sources, but evaluation is especially important when the source is online.

EVALUATING SOURCES

Finding a source of information related to your topic is not sufficient; you must be sure that the source is both valid and appropriate for your purposes. A quick evaluation of your sources before you begin carefully reading and taking notes on them may save you an enormous amount of time and frustration. Skim each source quickly, and keep the following in mind as you skim.

A recent book or article is usually preferable to an older one. Not only should your information be as up-to-date as possible, but recent works often effectively summarize previous research. (An exception to the rule "newer is better" would be if you have chosen an older work for a specific purpose, such as to compare it to more recent work to demonstrate changing attitudes.) In the case of Internet sources, sites will often indicate when they were last updated; if the one you use doesn't, you have no way of knowing reliably how fresh the information is.

As far as possible, try to determine the credibility of the author. The author's credentials are often briefly described on the book jacket or at

A CHECKLIST FOR EVALUATING PRINT SOURCES

For Books:

☐ Is the book recent? If not, is the information you will be using from it likely or unlikely to change over time?

☐ How credible is the author?

☐ Is the book published by a respectable press?

☐ Is the book broad enough in its focus and written in a style you can understand?

☐ Does the book relate directly to your tentative thesis, or is it of only tangential interest?

☐ Do the arguments in the book seem sound, based on what you have learned about skillful critical reading and writing?

For Articles from Periodicals:

☐ Is the periodical recent?

☐ Is the author's name given? Does he or she seem a credible source?

☐ Is the periodical respectable and serious?

☐ How directly does the article speak to your topic and tentative thesis?

☐ If the article is from a scholarly journal, are you sure you understand it?

the back of the book; these may reveal if the author is indeed an expert in the field and even if he or she has possible biases about the topic. But what if the work is anonymous, as many newspaper articles and Internet sources are? Anonymous articles are not necessarily bad sources, but approach them with a bit of caution; why might an author not have put his or her name on a piece?

You will also want to determine the credibility of the publisher (especially in the case of anonymous works). Though publisher credibility may be difficult for you to judge, you can usually trust large, nationally recognized companies and presses associated with universities more than smaller, less well-known publishers. (If you have doubts, ask your instructor or librarian about a particular publisher.) Remember that academic journals tend to be more respectable than popular magazines

A CHECKLIST FOR EVALUATING ELECTRONIC SOURCES

An enormous amount of valuable material is available on the World Wide Web—but so is an enormous amount of junk. True, there is also plenty of junk in books and journals, but most printed material has been subjected to a review process: Book publishers and editors of journals send manuscripts to specialized readers who evaluate them and recommend whether the material should or should not be published. Publishing on the Web is quite different. Anyone can publish on the Web with no review process: All that is needed is the right software.

☐ What person or organization produced the site (a commercial entity, a non-profit entity, a student, an expert)? Check the electronic address in order to get a clue about the authorship. If there is a link to the author's homepage, check it out to learn about the author. Does the author have an affiliation with a respectable institution?

☐ What is the purpose of the site? Is the site in effect an infomercial, or is it an attempt to contribute to a thoughtful discussion?

☐ Are the sources of information indicated and verifiable? If possible, check the sources.

☐ Is the site authoritative enough to use? (If it seems to contain review materials or class handouts, you probably don't want to take it too seriously.)

☐ When was the page made available? Is it out of date?

and that among magazines a hierarchy exists; an article from *Newsweek* usually is more credible than one from *People*. A similar hierarchy exists for newspapers: the *Washington Post* is powerfully credible, while tabloids such as the *Midnight Globe* are not. With online sources you often can tell, either from the document itself or from a close look at the Internet address, if a Web site, archive, or other source is associated with a reliable institution, such as a university, library, or government agency. While this kind of association does not guarantee accuracy, it does help to establish the credibility of the information. A final word about Internet sources: Don't let a flashy, expensive-looking Web site distract you from thinking critically about the site's content. While graphics, fancy fonts, audio and video clips, and the like can enhance a good site, a reliable source must offer more than a good show.

If you were researching a paper on reform of divorce law, for instance, how would you evaluate the Web site shown below? Both the text and graphics for this Web site suggest immediately that it is not a scholarly source but the Internet equivalent of a popular magazine. The colors are bright, and there are ads for "relationship advice" and professional services. It is, in short, a commercial venture designed to provide people in the process of divorce with advice and support while, not incidentally, making some money for the advertisers and sponsors of the site.

Does this mean the site is unreliable and will be useless for your paper? Not necessarily. There may well be hidden nuggets here that could enrich your paper, perhaps recent statistics on numbers of divorces or a pertinent quotation from someone engaged in the process of divorce. It does, however, mean that you must exercise caution if you choose to cite this information. At the very least, your paper will need to acknowledge the nature of your information source, so that your readers will know up front the potential bias of the site. Certainly you would want the paper to include information from some more scholarly sources as well.

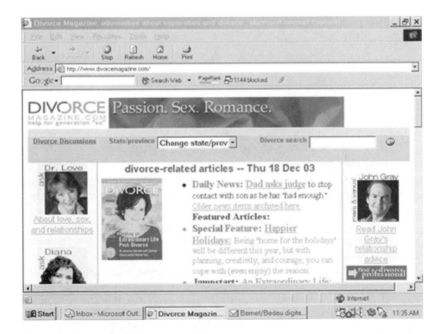

TAKING NOTES

When it comes to taking notes, all researchers have their own habits that they swear by, and they can't imagine any other way of working. We still prefer to take notes on four- by six-inch index cards, while others use a notebook or a computer for note-taking. Whatever method you use, the following techniques should help you maintain consistency and keep organized during the research process:

1. If you use a notebook or cards, write in ink (pencil gets smudgy), and write on only one side of the card or paper. (Notes on the backs of cards tend to get lost, and writing on the back of paper will prevent you from later cutting up and rearranging your notes.)

2. Put only one idea in each notebook or computer entry or on each card (though an idea may include several facts).

3. Put a brief heading on each entry or card, such as "Truman's last words on A-bomb."

4. Summarize, for the most part, rather than quote at length.

5. Quote only passages in which the writing is especially effective, or passages that are in some way crucial.

6. Make sure that all quotations are exact. Enclose quoted words within quotation marks, indicate omissions by ellipses (three spaced periods: . . .), and enclose within square brackets ([ ]) any insertions or other additions you make.

7. *Never* copy a passage, changing an occasional word. *Either* copy it word for word, with punctuation intact, and enclose it within quotation marks, *or* summarize it drastically. If you copy a passage but change a word here and there, you may later make the mistake of using your note verbatim in your essay, and you will be guilty of plagiarism.

8. Give the page number of your source, whether you summarize or quote. If a quotation you have copied runs in the original from the bottom of page 210 to the top of page 211, in your notes put a diagonal line (/) after the last word on page 210, so that later, if in your paper you quote only the material from page 210, you will know that you must cite 210 and not 210-11.

9. Indicate the source. The author's last name is enough if you have consulted only one work by the author; but if you consult more than one work by an author, you need further identification, such as the author's name and a short title.

10. Add your own comments about the substance of what you are recording. Such comments as "but contrast with Sherwin" or "seems illogical" or "evidence?" will ensure that you are thinking as well as writing and will be of value when you come to transform your notes into a draft. Be sure, however, to enclose such notes within double diagonals (//), or to mark them in some other way, so that later you will know they are yours and not your source's. If you use a computer for note taking, you may wish to write your comments in italics or in a different font.

11. In a separate computer file or notebook page or on separate index cards, write a bibliographic entry for each source. The information in each entry will vary, depending on whether the source is a book, a periodical, an electronic document, and so forth. The kind of information (for example, author and title) needed for each type of source can be found in the sections on MLA Format: The List of Works Cited (p. 177) or APA Format: The List of References (p. 189).

A WORD ABOUT PLAGIARISM

Plagiarism is the unacknowledged use of someone else's work. The word comes from a Latin word for "kidnapping," and plagiarism is indeed the stealing of something engendered by someone else. We won't deliver a sermon on the dishonesty (and folly) of plagiarism; we intend only to help you understand exactly what plagiarism is. The first thing to say is that plagiarism is not limited to the unacknowledged quotation of words.

A *paraphrase* is a sort of word-by-word or phrase-by-phrase translation of the author's language into your language. True, if you paraphrase you are using your own words, but you are also using someone else's ideas, and, equally important, you are using this other person's sequence of thoughts. Even if you change every third word in your source, and you give the author credit, you are plagiarizing. Here is an example of this sort of plagiarism, based on the previous sentence:

> Even if you alter every third or fourth word from your source, and you give credit to the author, you will be guilty of plagiarism.

Even if the writer of this paraphrase had cited a source after it, the writer would still be guilty of plagiarism because the passage borrows not only the idea but the shape of the presentation, the sentence structure. The writer of this passage hasn't really written anything; he or she has only adapted something. What the writer needs to do is to write something like this:

> Changing an occasional word does not free the writer from the obligation to cite a source.

And the source would still need to be cited, if the central idea were not a commonplace one.

You are plagiarizing if without giving credit you use someone else's ideas—even if you put these ideas entirely into your own words. When you use another's ideas, you must indicate your indebtedness by saying something like "Alperovitz points out that . . ." or "Secretary of War Stimson, as Martin Sherwin notes, never expressed himself on this point." Alperovitz and Sherwin pointed out something that you had not thought of, and so you must give them credit if you want to use their findings.

Again, even if after a paraphrase you cite your source, you are plagiarizing. How, you may wonder, can you be guilty of plagiarism if you cite a source? Easy. A reader assumes that the citation refers to information or an opinion, *not* to the presentation or development of the idea; and of course, in a paraphrase you are not presenting or developing the material in your own way.

Now consider this question: *Why* paraphrase? Often there is no good answer. Since a paraphrase is as long as the original, you may as well quote the original, if you think that a passage of that length is worth quoting. Probably it is *not* worth quoting in full; probably you should *not* paraphrase but rather should drastically *summarize* most of it, and perhaps quote a particularly effective phrase or two. As we explained on pages 28–31, the chief reason to paraphrase a passage is to clarify it— that is, to make certain that you and your readers understand a passage that—perhaps because it is badly written—is obscure.

Generally what you should do is to take the idea and put it entirely into your own words, perhaps reducing a paragraph of a hundred words to a sentence of ten words, but you must still give credit for the idea. If you believe that the original hundred words are so perfectly put that they cannot be transformed without great loss, you'll have to quote them and cite your source. But clearly there is no point in paraphrasing the author's hundred words into a hundred of your own. Either quote or summarize, but cite the source.

Keep in mind, too, that almost all generalizations about human nature, no matter how common and familiar (for instance, "males are innately more aggressive than females") are not indisputable facts; they are at best hypotheses on which people differ and therefore should either not be asserted at all or should be supported by some cited source

A CHECKLIST FOR AVOIDING PLAGIARISM

☐ In my notes did I *always* put quoted material within quotation marks?

☐ In my notes did I summarize *in my own words* and give credit to the source for the idea?

☐ In my notes did I *avoid paraphrasing*, i.e., did I avoid copying, keeping the structure of the source's sentences but using some of my own words? (Paraphrases of this sort, even with a footnote citing the source, are *not* acceptable, since the reader incorrectly assumes that the writing is essentially yours.)

☐ If in my paper I set forth a borrowed idea, do I give credit, even though the words and the shape of the sentences are entirely my own?

☐ If in my paper I quote directly, do I put the words within quotation marks and cite the source?

☐ Do I *not* cite material that can be considered common knowledge (material that can be found in numerous reference works, such as the date of a public figure's birth or the population of San Francisco or the fact that *Hamlet* is regarded as a great tragedy) without citing?

☐ If I have the slightest doubt about whether I should or should not cite a source, have I taken the safe course and cited the source?

or authority. Similarly, because nearly all statistics (whether on the intelligence of criminals or the accuracy of lie detectors) are the result of some particular research and may well have been superseded or challenged by other investigators, it is advisable to cite a source for any statistics you use unless you are convinced they are indisputable, such as the number of registered voters in Memphis in 1988.

On the other hand, there is something called **common knowledge,** and the sources for such information need not be cited. The term does not, however, mean exactly what it seems to. It is common knowledge, of course, that Ronald Reagan was an American president (so you don't cite a source when you make that statement), and under the conventional interpretation of this doctrine, it is also common knowledge that he was born in 1911. In fact, of course, few people other than Reagan's wife and children know this date. Still, information that can be found in many places and that is indisputable belongs to all of us; therefore, a writer need not cite her source when she says that Reagan was born in 1911. Probably she checked a dictionary or an encyclopedia for the date, but the source doesn't matter. Dozens of sources will give exactly the same information, and in fact, no reader wants to be bothered with a citation on such a point.

Some students have a little trouble developing a sense of what is and what is not common knowledge. Although, as we have just said, readers don't want to hear about the sources for information that is indisputable and can be documented in many places, if you are in doubt about whether to cite a source, cite it. Better risk boring the reader a bit than risk being accused of plagiarism.

COMPILING AN ANNOTATED BIBLIOGRAPHY

When several sources have been identified and gathered, many researchers prepare an annotated bibliography. This is a list providing all relevant bibliographic information (just as it will appear in your Works Cited list or References list) as well as a brief descriptive and evaluative summary of each source—perhaps one to three sentences. Your instructor may ask you to provide an annotated bibliography for your research project.

An annotated bibliography serves four main purposes.

- First, constructing such a document helps you to master the material contained in any given source. To find the heart of the argument presented in an article or book, phrase it briefly, and comment on it, you must understand it fully.

- Second, creating an annotated bibliography helps you to think about how each portion of your research fits into the whole of your project, how you will use it, and how it relates to your topic and thesis.

- Third, an annotated bibliography helps your readers: They can quickly see which items may be especially helpful in their own research.

- Fourth, in constructing an annotated bibliography at this early stage, you will get some hands-on practice at bibliographic format, thereby easing the job of creating your final bibliography (the Works Cited list or References list for your paper).

Below are two examples of entries for an annotated bibliography in MLA (Modern Language Association) format for a project on the effect of violence in the media. The first is for a book, the second for an article from a periodical. Notice that each

- Begins with a bibliographic entry—author (last name first), title, and so forth—and then
- Provides information about the content of the work under consideration, suggesting how each may be of use to the final research paper.

Clover, Carol J. Men, Women, and Chain Saws: Gender in the Modern Horror Film. Princeton: Princeton UP, 1992. The author focuses on Hollywood horror movies of the 1970s and 1980s. She studies representations of women and girls in these movies and the responses of male viewers to female characters, suggesting that this relationship is more complex and less exploitative than the common wisdom claims.

Winerip, Michael. "Looking for an Eleven O'Clock Fix." New York Times Magazine 11 Jan. 1998: 30–40. The article focuses on the rising levels of violence on local television news and highlights a station in Orlando, Florida, that tried to reduce its depictions of violence and lost viewers as a result. Winerip suggests that people only claim to be against media violence, while their actions prove otherwise.

WRITING THE PAPER

Organizing Your Notes

If you have read thoughtfully, taken careful (and, again, thoughtful) notes on your reading, and then (yet again) thought about these notes, you are well on the way to writing a good paper. You have, in fact, already written some of it, in your notes. By now you should clearly have in mind the thesis you intend to argue. But you still have to organize the material, and, doubtless, even as you set about organizing it, you will find points that will require you to do some additional research and much additional thinking.

Divide your notes into clusters, each devoted to one theme or point (for instance, one cluster on the extent of use of steroids, another on evidence that steroids are harmful, yet another on arguments that even if harmful they should be permitted). If your notes are in a computer file, use your word processor's Cut and Paste features to rearrange the notes into appropriate clusters. If you use index cards, simply sort them into packets. If you take notes in a notebook, either mark each note with a number or name indicating the cluster to which it belongs, or cut the notes apart and arrange them as you would cards. Put aside all notes that—however interesting—you now see are irrelevant to your paper.

Next, arrange the clusters or packets into a tentative sequence. In effect, you are preparing a **working outline.** At its simplest, say, you will give three arguments on behalf of X and then three counterarguments. (Or you might decide that it is better to alternate material from the two sets of three clusters each, following each argument with an objection. At this stage, you can't be sure of the organization you will finally use, but make a tentative decision.)

The First Draft

Draft the essay, without worrying much about an elegant opening paragraph. Just write some sort of adequate opening that states the topic and your thesis. When you revise the whole later, you can put some effort into developing an effective opening. (Most experienced writers find that the opening paragraph in the final version is almost the last thing they write.)

If your notes are on cards or notebook paper, carefully copy into the draft all quotations that you plan to use. If your notes are in a computer, you may simply cut and paste them from one file to another. Do keep in mind, however, that rewriting or retyping quotations will make you think carefully about them and may result in a more focused and thoughtful paper. (In the next section of this chapter we will talk briefly about leading into quotations and about the form of quotations.) Be sure to include citations in your drafts so that if you must check a reference later it will be easy to do so.

Later Drafts

Give the draft, and yourself, a rest—perhaps for a day or two—and then go back to it. Read it over, make necessary revisions, and then **outline** it. That is, on a sheet of paper chart the organization and development, perhaps by jotting down a sentence summarizing each paragraph or each group of closely related paragraphs. Your outline or map may now show you that the paper obviously suffers from poor organization. For instance, it may reveal that you neglected to respond to one argument or that one point is needlessly treated in two places. It may also help you to see that if you gave three arguments and then three counterarguments, you probably should instead have followed each argument with its rebuttal. On the other hand, if you alternated arguments and objections, it may now seem better to use two main groups, all the arguments and then all the criticisms.

No one formula is always right. Much will depend on the complexity of the material. If the arguments are highly complex, it is better to respond to them one by one than to expect a reader to hold three complex arguments in mind before you get around to responding. If, however, the arguments can be stated briefly and clearly, it is effective to state all three and then to go on to the responses. If you write on a word processor, you will find it easy, even fun, to move passages of text around. Even so, you will probably want to print out a hard copy from time to time to review the structure of your paper. Allow enough time to produce several drafts.

A few more words about organization: There is a difference between

- A paper that *has* an organization and
- A paper that helpfully lets the reader know what the organization is.

Write papers of the second sort, but (there is always a "but") take care not to belabor the obvious. Inexperienced writers sometimes either hide the organization so thoroughly that a reader cannot find it, or they so ploddingly lay out the structure ("Eighth, I will show . . .") that the reader becomes impatient. Yet it is better to be overly explicit than to be obscure.

The ideal, of course, is the middle route. Make the overall strategy of your organization evident by occasional explicit signs at the beginning of a paragraph ("We have seen . . . ," "It is time to consider the objections . . . ," "By far the most important . . ."); elsewhere make certain that the implicit structure is evident to the reader. When you reread your draft, if you try to imagine that you are one of your classmates, you will probably be able to sense exactly where explicit signs are needed and where they are not needed. Better still, exchange drafts with a classmate in order to exchange (tactful) advice.

Choosing a Tentative Title

By now a couple of tentative titles for your essay should have crossed your mind. If possible, choose a title that is both interesting and informative. Consider these three titles:

Are Steroids Harmful?
The Fuss over Steroids
Steroids: A Dangerous Game

"Are Steroids Harmful?" is faintly interesting, and it lets the reader know the gist of the subject, but it gives no clue about the writer's thesis, the writer's contention or argument. "The Fuss over Steroids" is somewhat better, for it gives information about the writer's position. "Steroids: A Dangerous Game" is still better; it announces the subject ("steroids") and the thesis ("dangerous"), and it also displays a touch of wit because "game" glances at the world of athletics.

Don't try too hard, however; better a simple, direct, informative title than a strained, puzzling, or overly cute one. And remember to make sure that everything in your essay is relevant to your title. In fact, your title should help you to organize the essay and to delete irrelevant material.

The Final Draft

When at last you have a draft that is for the most part satisfactory, check to make sure that **transitions** from sentence to sentence and from paragraph to paragraph are clear ("Further evidence," "On the other hand," "A weakness, however, is apparent"), and then worry about your opening and your closing paragraphs. Your **opening paragraph** should be clear, interesting, and focused; if neither the title nor the first paragraph announces your thesis, the second paragraph probably should do so.

The **final paragraph** need not say, "In conclusion, I have shown that. . . ." It should effectively end the essay, but it need not summarize your conclusions. We have already offered a few words about final paragraphs (pp. 236–37), but the best way to learn how to write such paragraphs is to study the endings of some of the essays in this book and to adopt the strategies that appeal to you.

Be sure that all indebtedness is properly acknowledged. We have talked about plagiarism; now we will turn to the business of introducing quotations effectively.

QUOTING FROM SOURCES

The Use and Abuse of Quotations

When is it necessary, or appropriate, to quote? Sometimes the reader must see the exact words of your source; the gist won't do. If you are arguing that Z's definition of *rights* is too inclusive, your readers have to know exactly how Z defined *rights*. Your brief summary of the definition may be unfair to Z; in fact, you want to convince your readers that you are being fair, and so you quote Z's definition, word for word. Moreover, if the passage is only a sentence or two long, or even if it runs to a paragraph, it may be so compactly stated that it defies summary. And to attempt to paraphrase it—substituting *natural* for *inalienable*, and so forth—saves no space and only introduces imprecision. There is nothing to do but to quote it, word for word.

Second, you may want to quote a passage that could be summarized but that is so effectively stated that you want your readers to have the pleasure of reading the original. Of course, readers will not give you credit for writing these words, but they will give you credit for your taste and for your effort to make especially pleasant the business of reading your paper.

In short, use (but don't overuse) quotations. Speaking roughly, quotations should occupy no more than 10 or 15 percent of your paper, and they may occupy much less. Most of your paper should set forth your ideas, not other people's ideas.

How to Quote

Long and Short Quotations   Long quotations (five or more lines of typed prose or three or more lines of poetry) are set off from your text. To set off material, start on a new line, indent one inch from the left margin, and type the quotation double-spaced. Do not enclose quotations within quotation marks if you are setting them off.

Short quotations are treated differently. They are embedded within the text; they are enclosed within quotation marks, but otherwise they do not stand out.

All quotations, whether set off or embedded, must be exact. If you omit any words, you must indicate the ellipsis by substituting three spaced periods for the omission; if you insert any words or punctuation, you must indicate the addition by enclosing it within square brackets, not to be confused with parentheses.

Leading into a Quotation   Now for a less mechanical matter, the way in which a quotation is introduced. To say that it is "introduced" implies that one leads into it, though on rare occasions a quotation appears without an introduction, perhaps immediately after the title. Normally one leads into a quotation by giving the name of the author and (no less important) clues about the content of the quotation and the purpose it serves in the present essay. For example:

> William James provides a clear answer to Huxley when he says
> that ". . ."

The writer has been writing about Huxley and now is signaling readers that they will be getting James's reply. The writer is also signaling (in "a clear answer") that the reply is satisfactory. If the writer believed that James's answer was not really acceptable, the lead-in might have run thus:

> William James attempts to answer Huxley, but his response does
> not really meet the difficulty Huxley calls attention to. James
> writes, ". . ."

or thus:

> William James provided what he took to be an answer to Huxley when
> he said that ". . ."

In this last example, clearly the words "what he took to be an answer" imply that the essayist will show, after the quotation from James, that the answer is in some degree inadequate. Or the essayist may wish to suggest the inadequacy even more strongly:

> William James provided what he took to be an answer to Huxley, but
> he used the word <u>religion</u> in a way that Huxley would not have
> allowed. James argues that ". . ."

If after reading something by Huxley the writer had merely given us "William James says . . . ," we wouldn't know whether we were getting confirmation, refutation, or something else. The essayist would have put a needless burden on the readers. Generally speaking, the more difficult the quotation, the more important is the introductory or explanatory lead-in, but even the simplest quotation profits from some sort of brief lead-in, such as "James reaffirms this point when he says. . . ."

DOCUMENTATION

In the course of your essay, you will probably quote or summarize material derived from a source. You must give credit, and although there is no one form of documentation to which all scholarly fields subscribe, you will probably be asked to use one of two. One, established by the

Modern Language Association (MLA), is used chiefly in the humanities; the other, established by the American Psychological Association (APA), is used chiefly in the social sciences.

We include two papers that use sources. "Why Trials Should Not Be Televised" (p. 195) uses the MLA format. "The Role of Spirituality and Religion in Mental Health" (p. 211) follows the APA format. (You may notice that various styles are illustrated in other selections we have included.)

A Note on Footnotes (and Endnotes)

Before we discuss these two formats, a few words about footnotes are in order. Before the MLA and the APA developed their rules of style, citations commonly were given in footnotes. Although today footnotes are not so frequently used to give citations, they still may be useful for another purpose. (The MLA suggests endnotes rather than footnotes, but all readers know that, in fact, footnotes are preferable to endnotes. After all, who wants to keep shifting from a page of text to a page of notes at the rear?) If you want to include some material that may seem intrusive in the body of the paper, you may relegate it to a footnote. For example, in a footnote you might translate a quotation given in a foreign language, or you might demote from text to footnote a paragraph explaining why you are not taking account of such-and-such a point. By putting the matter in a footnote you are signaling the reader that it is dispensable; it is something relevant but not essential, something extra that you are, so to speak, tossing in. Don't make a habit of writing this sort of note, but there are times when it is appropriate.

MLA Format:
Citations within the Text

Brief citations within the body of the essay give credit, in a highly abbreviated way, to the sources for material you quote, summarize, or make use of in any other way. These *in-text citations* are made clear by a list of sources, titled Works Cited, appended to the essay. Thus, in your essay you may say something like this:

> Commenting on the relative costs of capital punishment and life imprisonment, Ernest van den Haag says that he doubts "that capital punishment really is more expensive" (33).

The **citation,** the number 33 in parentheses, means that the quoted words come from page 33 of a source (listed in the Works Cited) written by van den Haag. Without a Works Cited, a reader would have no way of knowing that you are quoting from page 33 of an article that appeared in the February 8, 1985, issue of the *National Review.*

Usually the parenthetic citation appears at the end of a sentence, as in the example just given, but it can appear elsewhere; its position will depend chiefly on your ear, your eye, and the context. You might, for example, write the sentence thus:

> Ernest van den Haag doubts that "capital punishment really is more expensive" than life imprisonment (33), but other writers have presented figures that contradict him.

Five points must be made about these examples:

1. **Quotation marks** The closing quotation mark appears after the last word of the quotation, *not* after the parenthetic citation. Since the citation is not part of the quotation, the citation is not included within the quotation marks.

2. **Omission of words (ellipsis)** If you are quoting a complete sentence or only a phrase, as in the examples given, you do not need to indicate (by three spaced periods) that you are omitting material before or after the quotation. But if for some reason you want to omit an interior part of the quotation, you must indicate the omission by inserting an *ellipsis,* the three spaced dots. To take a simple example, if you omit the word "really" from van den Haag's phrase, you must alert the reader to the omission:

> Ernest van den Haag doubts that "capital punishment . . . is more expensive" than life imprisonment (33).

Suppose you are quoting a sentence but wish to omit material from the end of the sentence. Suppose, also, that the quotation forms the end of your sentence. Write a lead-in phrase, quote what you need from your source, then type the bracketed ellipses for the omission, close the quotation, give the parenthetic citation, and finally type a fourth period to indicate the end of your sentence.

Here's an example. Suppose you want to quote the first part of a sentence that runs, "We could insist that the cost of capital punishment be reduced so as to diminish the differences." Your sentence would incorporate the desired extract as follows:

> Van den Haag says, "We could insist that the cost of capital punishment be reduced . . ." (33).

3. **Punctuation with parenthetic citations**   In the preceding examples, the punctuation (a period or a comma in the examples) *follows* the citation. If, however, the quotation ends with a question mark, include the question mark *within* the quotation, since it is part of the quotation, and put a period *after* the citation:

> Van den Haag asks, "Isn't it better—more just and more useful—that criminals, if they do not have the certainty of punishment, at least run the risk of suffering it?" (35).

But if the question mark is your own and not in the source, put it after the citation, thus:

> What answer can be given to van den Haag's doubt that "capital punishment really is more expensive" (33)?

4. **Two or more works by an author**   If your list of Works Cited includes two or more works by an author, you cannot, in your essay, simply cite a page number because the reader will not know which of the works you are referring to. You must give additional information. You can give it in your lead-in, thus:

> In "New Arguments against Capital Punishment," van den Haag expresses doubt "that capital punishment really is more expensive" than life imprisonment (33).

Or you can give the title, in a shortened form, within the citation:

> Van den Haag expresses doubt that "capital punishment really is more expensive" than life imprisonment ("New Arguments" 33).

5. **Citing even when you do not quote**   Even if you don't quote a source directly, but use its point in a paraphrase or a summary, you will give a citation:

> Van den Haag thinks that life imprisonment costs more than capital punishment (33).

Note that in all of the previous examples, the author's name is given in the text (rather than within the parenthetic citation). But there are several other ways of giving the citation, and we shall look at them now. (We have already seen, in the example given under paragraph 4, that the title and the page number can be given within the citation.)

AUTHOR AND PAGE NUMBER IN PARENTHESES

It has been argued that life imprisonment is more costly than capital punishment (van den Haag 33).

AUTHOR, TITLE, AND PAGE NUMBER IN PARENTHESES

We have seen that if the Works Cited list includes two or more works by an author, you will have to give the title of the work on which you are drawing, either in your lead-in phrase or within the parenthetic citation. Similarly, if you are citing someone who is listed more than once in the Works Cited, and for some reason you do not mention the name of the author or the work in your lead-in, you must add the information in your citation:

Doubt has been expressed that capital punishment is as costly as life imprisonment (van den Haag, "New Arguments" 33).

A GOVERNMENT DOCUMENT OR A WORK
OF CORPORATE AUTHORSHIP

Treat the issuing body as the author. Thus, you will write something like this:

The Commission on Food Control, in Food Resources Today, concludes that there is no danger (37–38).

A WORK BY TWO OR MORE AUTHORS

If a work is by *two or three authors,* give the names of all authors, either in the parenthetic citation (the first example below) or in a lead-in (the second example below):

There is not a single example of the phenomenon (Smith, Dale, and Jones 182–83).

Smith, Dale, and Jones insist there is not a single example of the phenomenon (182–83).

If there are *more than three authors,* give the last name of the first author, followed by *et al.* (an abbreviation for *et alii,* Latin for "and others"), thus:

Gittleman et al. argue (43) that . . .

or

On average, the cost is even higher (Gittleman et al. 43).

PARENTHETIC CITATION OF AN INDIRECT SOURCE (CITATION OF MATERIAL THAT ITSELF WAS QUOTED OR SUMMARIZED IN YOUR SOURCE)

Suppose you are reading a book by Jones in which she quotes Smith and you wish to use Smith's material. Your citation must refer the reader to Jones—the source you are using—but of course, you cannot attribute the words to Jones. You will have to make it clear that you are quoting Smith, and so after a lead-in phrase like "Smith says," followed by the quotation, you will give a parenthetic citation along these lines:

(qtd. in Jones 324–25).

PARENTHETIC CITATION OF TWO OR MORE WORKS

The costs are simply too high (Smith 301; Jones 28).

Notice that a semicolon, followed by a space, separates the two sources.

A WORK IN MORE THAN ONE VOLUME

This is a bit tricky. If you have used only one volume, in the Works Cited you will specify the volume, and so in the parenthetic in-text citation you will not need to specify the volume. All that you need to include in the citation is a page number, as illustrated by most of the examples that we have given.

If you have used more than one volume, your parenthetic citation will have to specify the volume as well as the page, thus:

Jackson points out that fewer than one hundred fifty people fit this description (2: 351).

The reference is to page 351 in volume 2 of a work by Jackson.

If, however, you are citing not a page but an entire volume—let's say volume 2—your parenthetic citation will look like this:

Jackson exhaustively studies this problem (vol. 2).

or

Jackson (vol. 2) exhaustively studies this problem.

Notice the following points:

- In citing a volume and page, the volume number, like the page number, is given in arabic (not roman) numerals, even if the original used roman numerals to indicate the volume number.
- The volume number is followed by a colon, then a space, then the page number.
- If you cite a volume number without a page number, as in the last example quoted, the abbreviation is *vol.* Otherwise do *not* use such abbreviations as *vol.* and *p.* and *pg.*

AN ANONYMOUS WORK

For an anonymous work, give the title in your lead-in, or give it in a shortened form in your parenthetic citation:

A Prisoner's View of Killing includes a poll taken of the inmates on death row (32).

or

A poll is available (Prisoner's View 32).

AN INTERVIEW

Probably you won't need a parenthetic citation because you'll say something like

Vivian Berger, in an interview, said . . .

or

According to Vivian Berger, in an interview . . .

and when your reader turns to the Works Cited, he or she will see that Berger is listed, along with the date of the interview. But if you do not mention the source's name in the lead-in, you will have to give it in the parentheses, thus:

Contrary to popular belief, the death penalty is not reserved for serial killers and depraved murderers (Berger).

AN ELECTRONIC SOURCE

Electronic sources, such as those found on CD-ROMs or the Internet, are generally not divided into pages. Therefore, the in-text citation for such sources cite the author's name (or, if a work is anonymous, the title) only:

> According to the World Wide Web site for the American Civil Liberties Union . . .

If the source does use pages or breaks down further into paragraphs or screens, insert the appropriate identifier or abbreviation (*p.* or *pp.* for page or pages; *par.* or *pars.* for paragraph or paragraphs; *screen* or *screens*) before the relevant number:

> The growth of day care has been called "a crime against posterity" by a spokesman for the Institute for the American Family (Terwilliger, screens 1–2).

MLA Format: The List of Works Cited

As the previous pages explain, parenthetic documentation consists of references that become clear when the reader consults the list titled Works Cited given at the end of an essay.

The list of Works Cited continues the pagination of the essay; if the last page of text is 10, then the Works Cited begins on its own page, in this case page 11. Type the page number in the upper right corner, a half inch from the top of the sheet and flush with the right margin. Next, type the heading Works Cited (*not* enclosed within quotation marks and not italic), centered, one inch from the top, and then double-space and type the first entry.

An Overview Here are some general guidelines.

FORM ON THE PAGE
- Begin each entry flush with the left margin, but if an entry runs to more than one line, indent a half inch, for each succeeding line of the entry. This is known as a hanging indent, and most word processing programs can achieve this effect easily.
- Double-space each entry, and double-space between entries.
- Underline titles of works published independently—for instance, books, pamphlets, and journals. Enclose within quotation marks a work not published independently—for instance, an article in a journal, or a short story.
- If you are citing a book that includes the title of another book, underline the main title, but do *not* underline the title mentioned. Example:

A Study of Mill's On Liberty

- In the sample entries below, pay attention to the use of commas, colons, and the space after punctuation.

ALPHABETIC ORDER
- Arrange the list alphabetically by author, with the author's last name first.
- For information about anonymous works, works with more than one author, and two or more works by one author, see below.

A Closer Look   Here is more detailed advice.

THE AUTHOR'S NAME
Notice that the last name is given first, but otherwise the name is given as on the title page. Do not substitute initials for names written out on the title page.

If your list includes two or more works by an author, do not repeat the author's name for the second title but represent it by three hyphens followed by a period. The sequence of the works is determined by the alphabetic order of the titles. Thus, Smith's book titled *Poverty* would be listed ahead of her book *Welfare*. See the example on page 179, listing two works by Roger Brown.

Anonymous works are listed under the first word of the title or the second word if the first is *A, An,* or *The* or a foreign equivalent. We discuss books by more than one author, government documents, and works of corporate authorship on page 180.

THE TITLE
After the period following the author's name, allow one space and then give the title. Take the title from the title page, not from the cover or the spine, but disregard any unusual typography such as the use of all capital letters or the use of the ampersand (&) for *and*. Underline the title and subtitle (separate them by a colon) with one continuous underline to indicate italics, but do not underline the period that concludes this part of the entry.

- Capitalize the first word and the last word.
- Capitalize all nouns, pronouns, verbs, adjectives, adverbs, and subordinating conjunctions (for example, *although, if, because*).
- Do not capitalize (unless it's the first or last word of the title or the first word of the subtitle) articles (*a, an, the*), prepositions (for instance, *in, on, toward, under*), coordinating conjunctions (for instance, *and, but, or, for*), or the *to* in infinitives.

Examples:

The Death Penalty: A New View

On the Death Penalty: Toward a New View

On the Penalty of Death in a Democracy

PLACE OF PUBLICATION, PUBLISHER, AND DATE

For the place of publication, provide the name of the city; you can usually find it either on the title page or on the reverse of the title page. If a number of cities are listed, provide only the first. If the city is not likely to be known, or if it may be confused with another city of the same name (as is Oxford, Mississippi, with Oxford, England), add the name of the state, abbreviated using the two-letter postal code.

The name of the publisher is abbreviated. Usually the first word is enough (*Random House* becomes *Random*), but if the first word is a first name, such as in *Alfred A. Knopf,* the surname (*Knopf*) is used instead. University presses are abbreviated thus: *Yale UP, U of Chicago P, State U of New York P.*

The date of publication of a book is given when known; if no date appears on the book, write *n.d.* to indicate "no date."

SAMPLE ENTRIES   Here are some examples, illustrating the points we have covered thus far:

Brown, Roger. Social Psychology. New York: Free, 1965.

——. Words and Things Glencoe, IL: Free, 1958.

Douglas, Ann. The Feminization of American Culture. New
     York: Knopf, 1977.

Hartman, Chester. The Transformation of San Francisco. Totowa:
     Rowman, 1984.

Kellerman, Barbara. The Political Presidency: Practice of Leadership
     from Kennedy through Reagan. New York: Oxford UP, 1984.

Notice that a period follows the author's name and another period follows the title. If a subtitle is given, as it is for Kellerman's book, it is separated from the title by a colon and a space. A colon follows the place of publication, a comma follows the publisher, and a period follows the date.

A BOOK BY MORE THAN ONE AUTHOR

The book is alphabetized under the last name of the first author named on the title page. If there are *two or three authors,* the names of these are given (after the first author's name) in the normal order, *first name first:*

> Gilbert, Sandra M., and Susan Gubar. The Madwoman in the Attic: The Woman Writer and the Nineteenth-Century Literary Imagination. New Haven: Yale UP, 1979.

Notice, again, that although the first author's name is given *last name first,* the second author's name is given in the normal order, first name first. Notice, too, that a comma is put after the first name of the first author, separating the authors.

If there are *more than three authors,* give the name only of the first and then add (but *not* enclosed within quotation marks and not italic) *et al.* (Latin for "and others").

> Altshuler, Alan, et al. The Future of the Automobile. Cambridge: MIT P, 1984.

GOVERNMENT DOCUMENTS

If the writer is not known, treat the government and the agency as the author. Most federal documents are issued by the Government Printing Office (abbreviated to *GPO*) in Washington, D.C.

> United States. Cong. Office of Technology Assessment. Computerized Manufacturing Automation:Employment, Education, and the Workplace. Washington: GPO, 1984.

WORKS OF CORPORATE AUTHORSHIP

Begin the citation with the corporate author, even if the same body is also the publisher, as in the first example:

> American Psychiatric Association. Psychiatric Glossary. Washington: American Psychiatric Association, 1984.

> Carnegie Council on Policy Studies in Higher Education. Giving Youth a Better Chance: Options for Education, Work, and Service. San Francisco: Jossey, 1980.

A REPRINT (FOR INSTANCE, A PAPERBACK VERSION OF AN OLDER CLOTHBOUND BOOK)

After the title, give the date of original publication (it can usually be found on the reverse of the title page of the reprint you are using), then a period, and then the place, publisher, and date of the edition you are using. The example indicates that Gray's book was originally published in 1970 and that the student is using the Vintage reprint of 1971.

> Gray, Francine du Plessix. Divine Disobedience: Profiles in Catholic Radicalism. 1970. New York: Vintage, 1971.

A BOOK IN SEVERAL VOLUMES

If you have used more than one volume, in a citation within your essay you will (as explained on p. 175) indicate a reference to, say, page 250 of volume 3 thus: (3: 250).

If, however, you have used only one volume of the set—let's say volume 3—in your entry in the Works Cited, specify which volume you used, as in the next example:

> Friedel, Frank. Franklin D. Roosevelt. Vol. 3. Boston: Little, 1973. 4 vols.

With such an entry in the Works Cited, the parenthetic citation within your essay would be to the page only, not to the volume and page, because a reader who consults the Works Cited will understand that you used only volume 3. In the Works Cited, you may specify volume 3 and not give the total number of volumes, or you may add the total number of volumes, as in the example above.

ONE BOOK WITH A SEPARATE TITLE IN A SET OF VOLUMES

Sometimes a set with a title makes use also of a separate title for each book in the set. If you are listing such a book, use the following form:

> Churchill, Winston. The Age of Revolution. New York: Dodd, 1957. Vol. 3 of History of the English-Speaking Peoples. 4 vols. 1956–58.

A BOOK WITH AN AUTHOR AND AN EDITOR

Churchill, Winston, and Franklin D. Roosevelt. The Complete
   Correspondence. Ed. Warren F. Kimball. 3 vols. Princeton:
   Princeton UP, 1985.

Kant, Immanuel. The Philosophy of Kant: Immanuel Kant's Moral and
   Political Writings. Ed. Carl J. Friedrich. New York: Modern,
   1949.

If you are making use of the editor's introduction or other editorial
material rather than of the author's work, list the book under the name
of the editor rather than of the author, as shown below under An
Introduction, Foreword, or Afterword.

A REVISED EDITION OF A BOOK

Arendt, Hannah. Eichmann in Jerusalem. Rev. and enlarged ed. New
   York: Viking, 1965.

Honour, Hugh, and John Fleming. The Visual Arts: A History. 2nd ed.
   Englewood Cliffs: Prentice, 1986.

A TRANSLATED BOOK

Franqui, Carlos. Family Portrait with Fidel: A Memoir. Trans. Alfred
   MacAdam. New York: Random, 1984.

AN INTRODUCTION, FOREWORD, OR AFTERWORD

Goldberg, Arthur J. Foreword. An Eye for an Eye? The Morality of
   Punishing by Death. By Stephen Nathanson. Totowa: Rowman,
   1987. v-vi.

Usually an introduction or comparable material is listed under the name
of the author of the book (here Nathanson) rather than under the name
of the writer of the foreword (here Goldberg), but if you are referring to
the apparatus rather than to the book itself, use the form just given. The
words *Introduction, Preface, Foreword,* and *Afterword* are neither
enclosed within quotation marks nor underlined.

A BOOK WITH AN EDITOR BUT NO AUTHOR

Let's assume that you have used a book of essays written by various people but collected by an editor (or editors), whose name(s) appears on the collection.

LaValley, Albert J., ed. Focus on Hitchcock. Englewood Cliffs: Prentice, 1972.

If the book has one editor, the abbreviation is *ed.;* if two or more editors, *eds.*

A WORK WITHIN A VOLUME OF WORKS BY ONE AUTHOR

The following entry indicates that a short work by Susan Sontag, an essay called "The Aesthetics of Silence," appears in a book by Sontag titled *Styles of Radical Will.* Notice that the inclusive page numbers of the short work are cited, not merely page numbers that you may happen to refer to but the page numbers of the entire piece.

Sontag, Susan. "The Aesthetics of Silence." Styles of Radical Will. New York: Farrar, 1969. 3–34.

A BOOK REVIEW

Here is an example, citing Gerstein's review of Walker's book. Gerstein's review was published in a journal called *Ethics.*

Gerstein, Robert S. Rev. of Punishment, Danger and Stigma: The Morality of Criminal Justice, by Nigel Walker. Ethics 93 (1983): 408–10.

If the review has a title, give the title between the period following the reviewer's name and *Rev.*

If a review is anonymous, list it under the first word of the title, or under the second word if the first is *A, An,* or *The.* If an anonymous review has no title, begin the entry with *Rev. of,* and then give the title of the work reviewed; alphabetize the entry under the title of the work reviewed.

AN ARTICLE OR ESSAY (NOT A REPRINT) IN A COLLECTION

A book may consist of a collection (edited by one or more persons) of new essays by several authors. Here is a reference to one essay in such a book. (The essay by Balmforth occupies pages 19 to 35 in a collection edited by Bevan.)

Balmforth, Henry. "Science and Religion." Steps to Christian
Understanding. Ed. R. J. W. Bevan. London: Oxford UP, 1958.
19–35.

AN ARTICLE OR ESSAY REPRINTED IN A COLLECTION

The previous example (Balmforth's essay in Bevan's collection) was
for an essay written for a collection. But some collections reprint earlier
material, such as essays from journals or chapters from books. The following example cites an essay that was originally printed in a book
called *The Cinema of Alfred Hitchcock*. This essay has been reprinted in
a later collection of essays on Hitchcock, edited by Albert J. LaValley,
and it was LaValley's collection that the student used.

Bogdanovich, Peter. "Interviews with Alfred Hitchcock." The Cinema
of Alfred Hitchcock. New York: Museum of Modern Art, 1963.
15–18. Rpt. in Focus on Hitchcock. Ed. Albert J. LaValley.
Englewood Cliffs: Prentice, 1972. 28–31.

The student has read Bogdanovich's essay or chapter, but not in
Bogdanovich's book, where it occupied pages 15 to 18. The material was
actually read on pages 28 to 31 in a collection of writings on Hitchcock,
edited by LaValley. Details of the original publication—title, date, page
numbers, and so forth—were found in LaValley's collection. Almost all
editors will include this information, either on the copyright page or at
the foot of the reprinted essay, but sometimes they do not give the original page numbers. In such a case, you need not include the original
numbers in your entry.

Notice that the entry begins with the author and the title of the work
you are citing (here, Bogdanovich's interviews), not with the name of the
editor of the collection or the title of the collection.

AN ENCYCLOPEDIA OR OTHER ALPHABETICALLY
ARRANGED REFERENCE WORK

The publisher, place of publication, volume number, and page number do *not* have to be given. For such works, list only the edition (if it is
given) and the date.

For a *signed* article, begin with the author's last name. (If the article
is signed with initials, check elsewhere in the volume for a list of abbreviations, which will inform you who the initials stand for, and use the
following form.)

Williams, Donald C. "Free Will and Determinism." Encyclopedia
Americana. 1987 ed.

For an *unsigned article,* begin with the title of the article:

"Automation." The Business Reference Book. 1977 ed.

"Tobacco." Encyclopaedia Britannica: Macropaedia. 1988 ed.

A TELEVISION OR RADIO PROGRAM
Be sure to include the title of the episode or segment (in quotation
marks), the title of the show (underlined), the network, the call letters
and city of the station, and the date of broadcast. Other information,
such as performers, narrator, and so forth, may be included if
pertinent.

"Back to My Lai." Narr. Mike Wallace. 60 Minutes. CBS. 29 Mar. 1998.

"Juvenile Justice." Narr. Ray Suarez. Talk of the Nation. Natl. Public
Radio. WBUR, Boston. 15 Apr. 1998.

AN ARTICLE IN A SCHOLARLY JOURNAL   The title of the article
is enclosed within quotation marks, and the title of the journal is underlined to indicate italics.

Some journals are paginated consecutively; the pagination of the
second issue begins where the first issue leaves off. Other journals begin
each issue with page 1. The forms of the citations differ slightly.

A JOURNAL THAT IS PAGINATED CONSECUTIVELY

Vilas, Carlos M. "Popular Insurgency and Social Revolution in Central
America." Latin American Perspectives 15 (1988): 55–77.

Vilas's article occupies pages 55 to 77 in volume 15, which was published in 1988. (Notice that the volume number is followed by a space,
then by the year in parentheses, and then by a colon, a space, and the
page numbers of the entire article.) Because the journal is paginated
consecutively, the issue number does *not* need to be specified.

A JOURNAL THAT BEGINS EACH ISSUE WITH PAGE 1
If the journal is, for instance, a quarterly, there will be four page 1's
each year, so the issue number must be given. After the volume number,

type a period and (without hitting the space bar) the issue number, as in the next example:

> Greenberg, Jack. "Civil Rights Enforcement Activity of the Department
>   of Justice." Black Law Journal 8.1 (1983): 60–67.

Greenberg's article appeared in the first issue of volume 8 of the *Black Law Journal.*

AN ARTICLE IN A WEEKLY, BIWEEKLY, MONTHLY, OR BIMONTHLY PUBLICATION

Do not include volume or issue numbers, even if given.

> Lamar, Jacob V. "The Immigration Mess." Time 27 Feb. 1989: 14–15.

> Markowitz, Laura. "A Different Kind of Queer Marriage." Utne Reader
>   Sept.-Oct. 2000: 24–26.

AN ARTICLE IN A NEWSPAPER

Because a newspaper usually consists of several sections, a section number or a capital letter may precede the page number. The example indicates that an article begins on page 1 of section 2 and is continued on a later page.

> Chu, Harry. "Art Thief Defends Action." New York Times 8 Feb. 1989,
>   sec. 2: 1+.

AN UNSIGNED EDITORIAL

> "The Religious Tyranny Amendment." Editorial. New York Times 15
>   Mar. 1998, sec. 4: 16.

A LETTER TO THE EDITOR

> Lasken, Douglas. "Teachers Reject Bilingual Education." Letter. New
>   York Times 15 Mar. 1998, sec. 4: 16.

A PUBLISHED OR BROADCAST INTERVIEW

Give the name of the interview subject and the interviewer, followed by the relevant publication or broadcast information, in the following format:

Green, Al. Interview with Terry Gross. Fresh Air.
>   Natl. Public Radio. WFCR, Amherst, MA. 16 Oct. 2000.

AN INTERVIEW YOU CONDUCT

Jevgrafovs, Alexandre L. Personal [or Telephone] interview. 14 Dec.
>   2003.

PERSONAL CORRESPONDENCE

Raso, Robert. Letter [or E-mail] to the author. 6 Jan. 2004.

CD-ROM
CD-ROMs are cited very much like their printed counterparts. To
the usual print citation information, add (1) the title of the database,
underlined; (2) the medium (*CD-ROM*); (3) the vendor's name; and (4)
the date of electronic publication.

Louisberg, Margaret. Charlie Brown Meets Godzilla: What Are Our
>   Children Watching? Urbana: ERIC Clearinghouse on Elementary
>   and Early Childhood Education, 1990. ERIC. CD-ROM.
>   SilverPlatter. May 1997.

"Pornography." The Oxford English Dictionary. 2nd ed. CD-ROM.
>   Oxford: Oxford UP, 1992.

A PERSONAL OR PROFESSIONAL WEB SITE
Include the following elements, separated by periods: the name of
the person who created the site (omit if not given, as in the example
below), site title (underlined), name of any sponsoring institution or
organization, date of access, and electronic address.

School for Marine Science and Technology. U of Massachusetts
>   Dartmouth. 10 Oct. 2000 <http://www.cmast.umassd.edu/>.

AN ARTICLE IN AN ONLINE PERIODICAL
Give the same information as you would for a print article, plus the
date of access and electronic address.

Trammell, George W. "Cirque du O. J." Court Technology Bulletin.
>   July-Aug. 1995. 12 Sept. 1996 <http://www.ncsc.dni.us/ncsc/
>   bulletin/v07n04.htm>.

AN ONLINE POSTING

Citation includes the author's name, subject line of posting, description *(Online posting)*, date material was posted, name of the forum, date of access, and address.

> Ricci, Paul. "Global Warming." Online posting. 10 June 1996. Global Electronic Science Conference. 22 Sept. 1997 <http://www .science.envir/earth>.

A DATABASE SOURCE

Treat material obtained from a computer service, such as Bibliographies Retrieval Service (BRS), like other printed material, but at the end of the entry add (if available) the title of the database (underlined), publication medium *(Online)*, name of the computer service, and date of access.

> Jackson, Morton. "A Look at Profits." Harvard Business Review 40 (1962): 106–13. Online. BRS. 23 Dec. 1995.

Caution: Although we have covered the most usual kinds of sources, it is entirely possible that you will come across a source that does not fit any of the categories that we have discussed. For approximately two hundred pages of explanations of these matters, covering the proper way to cite all sorts of troublesome and unbelievable (but real) sources, see Joseph Gibaldi, *MLA Handbook for Writers of Research Papers*, Sixth Edition (New York: Modern Language Association of America, 2003).

APA Format: Citations within the Text

Your paper will conclude with a separate page headed References, in which you list all of your sources. If the last page of your essay is numbered 10, number the first page of the References 11.

The APA style emphasizes the date of publication; the date appears not only in the list of references at the end of the paper but also in the paper itself, when you give a brief parenthetic citation of a source that you have quoted or summarized or in any other way used. Here is an example:

> Statistics are readily available (Smith, 1989, p. 20).

The title of Smith's book or article will be given at the end of your paper, in the list titled References. We discuss the form of the material listed in

the References after we look at some typical citations within the text of
a student's essay.

A SUMMARY OF AN ENTIRE WORK

Smith (1988) holds the same view.

or

Similar views are held widely (Smith, 1988; Jones & Metz, 1990).

A REFERENCE TO A PAGE OR TO PAGES

Smith (1988) argues that "the death penalty is a lottery, and blacks
usually are the losers" (p. 17).

A REFERENCE TO AN AUTHOR WHO HAS MORE THAN ONE
WORK IN THE LIST OF REFERENCES

If in the References you list two or more works that an author published in the same year, the works are listed in alphabetic order, by the
first letter of the title. The first work is labeled *a*, the second *b*, and so
on. Here is a reference to the second work that Smith published in 1989:

Florida presents "a fair example" of how the death penalty is administered (Smith, 1989b, p. 18).

APA Format: The List of References

Your brief parenthetic citations are made clear when the reader
consults the list you give in the References. Type this list on a separate
page, continuing the pagination of your essay.

An Overview   Here are some general guidelines.

FORM ON THE PAGE

- Begin each entry flush with the left margin, but if an entry runs to
  more than one line, indent five spaces for each succeeding line of
  the entry.
- Double-space each entry, and double-space between entries.

ALPHABETIC ORDER

- Arrange the list alphabetically by author.
- Give the author's last name first and then the initial of the first
  name and of the middle name (if any).

- If there is more than one author, name all of the authors, again inverting the name (last name first) and giving only initials for first and middle names. (But do not invert the editor's name when the entry begins with the name of an author who has written an article in an edited book.) When there are two or more authors, use an ampersand (&) before the name of the last author. Example (here, of an article in the tenth volume of a journal called *Developmental Psychology*):

Drabman, R. S., & Thomas, M. H. (1974). Does media violence
    increase children's tolerance of real-life aggression?
    Developmental Psychology, 10, 418–421.

- If you list more than one work by an author, do so in the order of publication, the earliest first. If two works by an author were published in the same year, give them in alphabetic order by the first letter of the title, disregarding *A, An,* or *The,* and their foreign equivalent. Designate the first work as *a,* the second as *b.* Repeat the author's name at the start of each entry.

Donnerstein, E. (1980a). Aggressive erotica and violence against
    women. Journal of Personality and Social Psychology, 39,
    269–277.

Donnerstein, E. (1980b). Pornography and violence against women.
    Annals of the New York Academy of Sciences, 347, 227–288.

Donnerstein, E. (1983). Erotica and human aggression. In R. Green
    and E. Donnerstein (Eds.), Aggression: Theoretical and empiri-
    cal reviews (pp. 87–103). New York: Academic Press.

FORM OF TITLE

- In references to books, capitalize only the first letter of the first word of the title (and of the subtitle, if any) and capitalize proper nouns. Underline the complete title.
- In references to articles in periodicals or in edited books, capitalize only the first letter of the first word of the article's title (and subtitle, if any) and all proper nouns. Do not put the title within quotation marks. Type a period after the title of the article. For the

title of the journal and the volume and page numbers, see the next instruction.

- In references to periodicals, give the volume number in arabic numerals, and underline it. Do *not* use *vol.* before the number, and do not use *p.* or *pg.* before the page numbers.

Sample References Here are some samples to follow.

A BOOK BY ONE AUTHOR

Pavlov, I. P. (1927). Conditioned reflexes (G. V. Anrep, Trans.). London: Oxford University Press.

A BOOK BY MORE THAN ONE AUTHOR

Belenky, M. F., Clinchy, B. M., Goldberger, N. R., & Torule, J. M. (1986). Women's ways of knowing: The development of self, voice, and mind. New York: Basic Books.

A COLLECTION OF ESSAYS

Christ, C. P., & Plaskow, J. (Eds.). (1979). Womanspirit rising: A feminist reader in religion. New York: Harper & Row.

A WORK IN A COLLECTION OF ESSAYS

Fiorenza, E. (1979). Women in the early Christian movement. In C. P. Christ & J. Plaskow (Eds.), Woman-spirit rising: A feminist reader in religion (pp. 84–92). New York: Harper & Row.

GOVERNMENT DOCUMENTS

If the writer is not known, treat the government and the agency as the author. Most federal documents are issued by the U.S. Government Printing Office in Washington, D.C. If a document number has been assigned, insert that number in parentheses between the title and the following period.

United States Congress. Office of Technology Assessment. (1984). Computerized manufacturing automation: Employment, education, and the workplace. Washington, D.C.: U.S. Government Printing Office.

AN ARTICLE IN A JOURNAL WITH CONTINUOUS PAGINATION

Tversky, A., & Kahneman, D. (1981). The framing of decisions and the
    psychology of choice. Science, 211, 453–458.

**AN ARTICLE IN A JOURNAL THAT PAGINATES
EACH ISSUE SEPARATELY**

Foot, R. J. (1988–89). Nuclear coercion and the ending of the Korean
    conflict. International Security, 13(4), 92–112.

The reference informs us that the article appeared in issue number 4 of
volume 13.

AN ARTICLE FROM A MONTHLY OR WEEKLY MAGAZINE

Greenwald, J. (1989, February 27). Gimme shelter. Time, 133, 50–51.

Maran, S. P. (1988, April). In our backyard, a star explodes.
    Smithsonian, 19, 46–57.

AN ARTICLE IN A NEWSPAPER

Connell, R. (1989, February 6). Career concerns at heart of 1980s'
    campus protests. Los Angeles Times, pp. 1, 3.

(*Note:* If no author is given, simply begin with the title followed by the
date in parentheses.)

A BOOK REVIEW

Daniels, N. (1984). Understanding physician power [Review of the
    book The social transformation of American medicine].
    Philosophy and Public Affairs, 13, 347–356.

Daniels is the reviewer, not the author of the book. The book under
review is called *The Social Transformation of American Medicine,* but the
review, published in volume 13 of *Philosophy and Public Affairs,* had its
own title, "Understanding Physician Power."
    If the review does not have a title, retain the square brackets, and
use the material within as the title. Proceed as in the example just
given.

A WEB SITE

American Psychological Association. (1995). Lesbian and gay parent-
ing. Retrieved June 12, 2000, from the World Wide Web:
http://www.apa.org/pi/parent/html

A CHECKLIST FOR PAPERS USING SOURCES

☐ All borrowed words and ideas credited?

☐ Quotations and summaries not too long?

☐ Quotations accurate?

☐ Quotations provided with helpful lead-ins?

☐ Documentation in proper form?

And of course, you will also ask yourself the questions that you
would ask of a paper that did not use sources, such as:

☐ Topic sufficiently narrowed?

☐ Thesis (to be advanced or refuted) stated early and clearly, perhaps even in title?

☐ Audience kept in mind? Opposing views stated fairly and as
sympathetically as possible? Controversial terms defined?

☐ Assumptions likely to be shared by readers? If not, are they
argued rather than merely asserted?

☐ Focus clear (evaluation, recommendation of policy)?

☐ Evidence (examples, testimony, statistics) adequate and sound?

☐ Inferences valid?

☐ Organization clear (effective opening, coherent sequence of
arguments, unpretentious ending)?

☐ All worthy opposition faced?

☐ Tone appropriate?

☐ Has the paper been carefully proofread?

☐ Is the title effective?

☐ Is the opening paragraph effective?

☐ Is the structure reader-friendly?

☐ Is the closing paragraph effective?

AN ARTICLE IN AN ONLINE PERIODICAL

Carpenter, S. (2000, October). Biology and social environments jointly
    influence gender development. <u>Monitor on Psychology 31.</u>
    Retrieved September 20, 2000, from http://www.apa.org/moni-
    tor/oct00/maccoby.html

For a full account of the APA method of dealing with all sorts of
unusual citations, see the fifth edition (2001) of the APA manual,
Publication Manual of the American Psychological Association.

AN ANNOTATED STUDENT
RESEARCH PAPER IN MLA FORMAT

The following argument makes good use of sources. Early in the semes-
ter the students were asked to choose one topic from a list of ten, and to
write a documented argument of 750 to 1,250 words (three to five pages
of double-spaced typing). The completed paper was due two weeks after
the topics were distributed. The assignment, a prelude to working on a
research paper of 2,500 to 3,000 words, was in part designed to give students practice in finding and in using sources. Citations are given in the
MLA form.

The MLA Handbook does not insist on a title page and outline, but many instructors prefer them.

Why Trials Should Not Be Televised
By
Theresa Washington

Title one-third down page

Professor Wilson
English 102
December 12, 2003

All lines centered

Small roman numerals for page with outline

Outline

Thesis: The televising of trials is a bad idea because it has
several negative effects on the First Amendment: it
gives viewers a deceptive view of particular trials and
of the judicial system in general, and it degrades the
quality of media reporting outside the courtroom.

Roman numerals for chief units (I, II, etc.); capital letters for chief units within these largest units; for smaller and smaller units, arabic numerals and lowercase letters

I. Introduction

   A. Trend toward increasing trial coverage

   B. First Amendment versus Sixth Amendment

II. Effect of televising trials on First Amendment

   A. Provides deceptive version of truth

      1. Confidence in verdicts misplaced

         a. William Smith trial

         b. Rodney King trial

      2. Nature of TV as a medium

         a. Distortion in sound bites

         b. Stereotyping trial participants

         c. Misleading camera angles

         d. Commentators and commercials

   B. Confuses viewers about judicial system

      1. Contradicts basic concept "innocent until proven
guilty"

      2. Can't explain legal complexities

   C. Contributes to media circus outside of court

      1. Blurs truth and fiction

      2. Affects print media in negative ways

      3. Media makes itself the story

      4. Distracts viewers from other issues

III. Conclusion

Washington 1

Why Trials Should Not Be Televised

Although trials have been televised on and off since the 1950s,[1] in the last few years the availability of trials for a national audience has increased dramatically.[2] Media critics, legal scholars, social scientists, and journalists continue to debate the merits of this trend.

Proponents of cameras in the courtroom argue, falsely, I believe, that confidence in the fairness of our institutions, including the judicial system, depends on a free press, guaranteed by the First Amendment. Keeping trials off television is a form of censorship, they say. It limits the public's ability to understand (1) what is happening in particular trials and (2) how the judicial system operates, which is often confusing to laypeople. Opponents claim that televising trials threatens the defendant's Sixth Amendment rights to a fair trial because it can alter the behavior of the trial participants, including the jury ("Tale"; Thaler).

Regardless of its impact on due process of law,[3] TV in court does not serve the First Amendment well. Consider the first claim, that particular trials are easier to understand when televised. But does watching trials on television really allow the viewer to "see it like it is," to get the full scope and breadth of a trial? Steven Brill, founder of Court TV, would like us to believe so. He points out that most high-profile defendants in televised trials have been acquitted; he names William Kennedy Smith, Jimmy Hoffa, John Connally, and John Delorean as examples (Clark 821). "Imagine if [Smith's trial] had not been shown and he got off. Millions of people would have said the Kennedys fixed the case"

Title is focused and announces the thesis.

Double-space between title and first paragraph — and throughout the essay.

1" margin on each side and at bottom

Summary of opposing positions

Parenthetic reference to an anonymous source and also to a source with a named author

Superscript numerals indicate endnotes.

Parenthetic reference to author and page

Parenthetic reference to an indirect source (a borrowed quotation)

(Brill qtd. in "Tale" 29). Polls taken after the trial seem to confirm this claim, since they showed the public by and large agreed with the jury's decision to acquit (Quindlen).

However, Thaler points out that the public can just as easily disagree with the verdict as agree, and when this happens, the effects can be catastrophic. One example is the Rodney King case. Four white Los Angeles police officers were charged in 1991 with severely beating African American Rodney King, who, according to the officers, had been resisting arrest. At their first trial, all four officers were acquitted. This verdict outraged many African Americans throughout the country; they felt the evidence from watching the trial overwhelmingly showed the defendants to be guilty. The black community of south-central Los Angeles expressed its feelings by rioting for days (Thaler 50–51).

Clearly the black community did not experience the trial the same way the white community and the white jury did. Why? Marty Rosenbaum, an attorney with the New York State Defenders Association, points out that viewers cannot experience a trial the same way trial participants do. "What you see at home 'is not what jurors see'" (qtd. in Thaler 70).

Although no words are quoted, the idea is borrowed, and so the source is cited.

he trial process is slow, linear, and methodical, as the defense and prosecution each builds its case, one piece of information at a time (Thaler 11). The process is intended to be thoughtful and reflective, with the jury weighing all the evidence in light of the whole trial (Altheide 299–301). And it emphasizes words—both spoken and written—rather than images (Thaler 11).

Washington 3

In contrast, TV's general strength is in handling visual
images that entertain or that provoke strong feelings. News
editors and reporters choose footage for its assumed visual
and emotional impact on viewers. Words are made to fit the
images, not the other way around, and they tend to be short
catchy phrases, easy to understand (Thaler 4, 7). As a result,
the fifteen- to thirty-second "sound bites" in nightly news-
casts often present trial events out of context, emphasizing
moments of drama rather than of legal importance (Thaler 7;
Zoglin 62).

Clear transition ("In contrast")

Parenthetic citation of two sources

Furthermore, this emphasis on emotional visuals leads
to stereotyping the participants, making larger-than-life sym-
bols out of them, especially regarding social issues (Thaler 9):
abused children (the Menendez brothers), the battered wife
(Hedda Nussbaum), the abusing husband (Joel Steinberg,
O. J. Simpson), the jealous lover (Amy Fisher), the serial killer
(Jeffrey Dahmer), and date rapist (William Smith). It becomes
difficult for viewers to see defendants as ordinary human
beings.

One can argue, as Brill has done, that gavel-to-gavel
coverage of trials counteracts the distortions in sound-bite
journalism (Clark 821). Yet even here a number of editorial
assumptions and decisions affect what viewers see. Camera
angles and movements reinforce in the viewer differing
degrees of intimacy with the trial participant; close-ups are
often used for sympathetic witnesses, three-quarter shots for
lawyers, and profile shots for defendants (Entner 73–75).[4]

Summary of an opposing view countered with a clear transition ("Yet")

On-air commentators also shape the viewers' experience. Several media critics have noted how much commentators' remarks often have the play-by-play tone of sportscasters

Washington 4

informing viewers of what each side (the defense and the
prosecution) needs to win (Cole 245; Thaler 71, 151).
Continual interruptions for commercials add to the impression
of watching a spectacle. "The CNN coverage [of the Smith
trial] isn't so much gavel-to-gavel, actually, as gavel-to-com-
mercial-to-gavel, with former CNN Gulf War correspondent
Charles Jaco acting more as ringleader than reporter"
(Bianculli 60). This encourages a sensationalistic tone
to the proceedings that the jury does not experience. In addition, breaking for ads frequently occurs at important points in
the trial (Thaler 48).

    In-court proponents also believe that watching tele-
vised trials will help viewers understand the legal aspects of
the judicial system. In June 1991, a month before Court TV
went on the air, Vincent Blasi, a law professor at Columbia
University, told Time magazine, "Today most of us learn about
judicial proceedings from lawyers' sound bites and artists'
sketches. . . . Televised proceedings [such as Court TV] ought
to dispel some of the myth and mystery that shroud our legal
system" (qtd. in Zoglin 62).

    But after several years of Court TV and CNN, we can
now see this is not so. As a medium, TV is not good at educating the general public, either about concepts fundamental
to our judicial system or about the complexities in particular
cases.

    For example, one basic concept—"innocent until
proven guilty"—is contradicted in televised trials in numerous subtle ways: Commentators sometimes make remarks
about (or omit comment on) actions of the defense or prosecution that show a bias against the defendant.

---

*Author lets
reader hear the
opposition by
means of a
brief quotation*

*Omitted mate-
rial indicated
by three peri-
ods, with a
fourth to mark
the end of a
sentence*

Media critic Lewis Cole, watching the trial of Lorena
Bobbitt on Court TV in 1994, observed:

> Court TV commentators rarely challenged the
> state's characterization of what it was doing,
> repeating without comment, for instance, the
> prosecution's claims about protecting the reputa-
> tion of Lorena Bobbitt and concentrating on the
> prosecution decision to pursue both cases as a
> tactical matter, rather than inquiring how the
> prosecution's view of the incident as a "barroom
> brawl" had limited its approach to and under-
> standing of the case. (245)

Quotation of more than four lines, indented 1" from left margin (ten spaces), double-spaced, parenthetic reference set off from quotation

Camera angles play a role also: Watching the defendant day after day in profile, which makes him or her seem
either vulnerable or remote, tends to reinforce his or her guilt
(Entner 158).

Thaler points out that these editorial effects arise
because the goals of the media (print as well as electronic)
differ from the goals of the judicial system. His argument runs
as follows: The court is interested in determining only
whether the defendant broke the law. The media (especially
TV) focus on acts to reinforce social values, whether they're
codified into law or not. This can lead viewers to conclude
that a defendant is guilty because pretrial publicity or courtroom testimony reveals he or she has transgressed against the
community's moral code, even when the legal system later
acquits. This happened in the case of Claus von Bulow, who
between 1982 and 1985 was tried and acquitted twice for
attempting to murder his wife and who clearly had behaved in

Argument supported by specific examples

reprehensible ways in the eyes of the public (35). It also happened in the case of Joel Steinberg, who was charged with
murdering his daughter. Extended televised testimony by his
former partner, Hedda Nussbaum, helped paint a portrait of "a
monster" in the eyes of the public (140–42). Yet the jury
chose to convict him on the lesser charge of manslaughter.
When many viewers wrote to the prosecutor, Peter
Casolaro, asking why the verdict was not first-degree murder,
he had to conclude that TV does not effectively teach about
due process of law (176).

In addition to being poor at handling basic judicial
concepts, television has difficulty conveying more complex
and technical aspects of the law. Sometimes the legal nature
of the case makes for a poor translation to the screen. Brill
admitted that, despite attempts at hourly summaries, Court TV
was unable to convey to its viewers any meaningful understanding of the case of Manuel Noriega (Thaler 61), the
Panamanian leader who was convicted by the United States in
1992 of drug trafficking and money laundering ("Former"). In
other cases, like the Smith trial, the "civics lesson" gets
swamped by its sensational aspects (Thaler 45). In most cases
print media are better at exploring and explaining legal issues
than is TV (Thaler 4).

*Transition
briefly summa-
rizes and then
moves to
a new point.*
    In addition to shaping the viewer's perceptions of trial
reality directly, in-court TV also negatively affects the quality
of trial coverage outside of court, which in turn limits the
public's "right to know." Brill likes to claim that Court TV
helps to counteract the sensationalism of such tabloid TV
shows as A Current Affair and Hard Copy, which pay trial

participants to tell their stories and publish leaks from the prosecution and defense. "I think cameras in the courtroom is [sic] the best antidote to that garbage" (Brill qtd. in Clark 821). However, as founder and editor of Court TV, he obviously has a vested interest in affirming his network's social and legal worth. There are several ways that in-court TV, rather than supplying a sobering contrast, helps to feed the media circus surrounding high-profile trials (Thaler 43).

The author uses "[sic]" (Latin for "thus") to indicate that the oddity is in the source and is not by the author of the paper.

One way is by helping to blur the line between reality and fiction. This is an increasing trend among all media but is especially true of TV, whose footage can be combined and recombined in so many ways. An excellent example of this is the trial of Amy Fisher, who pleaded guilty in September 1992 to shooting her lover's wife and whose sentencing was televised by Court TV (Thaler 83). Three TV movies about this love triangle appeared on network TV in the same week, just one month after she had been sentenced to five to fifteen years of jail (Thaler 82). Then Geraldo Rivera, the syndicated TV talk-show host, held a mock grand jury trial of her lover, Joey Buttafuoco; even though Buttafuoco had not at that point been charged with a crime, Geraldo felt many viewers thought he ought to have been (Thaler 83). Then A Current Affair had a series that "tried" Fisher for events and behaviors that never got resolved in the actual trial. The announcer on the program said, "When Ms. Fisher copped a plea and went to jail, she robbed the public of a trial, leaving behind many unanswered questions. Tonight we will try to . . . complete the unwritten chapter" ("Trial"). Buttafuoco's lawyer from the trial served as a consultant on this program (Thaler 84). This is also a good

Useful analysis of effect of TV

example of how tabloid TV reinforces people's beliefs and plays on people's feelings. Had her trial not been televised, the excitement surrounding her case would not have been so high. Tabloid TV played off the audience's expectation for what a televised trial should and could reveal. Thus in-court television becomes one more ingredient in the mix of docu-dramas, mock trials, talk shows, and tabloid journalism. This limits the public's "right to know" by making it difficult to keep fact separate from storytelling.

Square brackets indicate that the author has altered text from a capital to a lowercase letter.

In-court TV also affects the quality of print journalism. Proponents like to claim that "[f]rom the standpoint of the public's right to know, there is no good reason why TV journalists should be barred from trials while print reporters are not" (Zoglin 62). But when TV is present, there is no level playing field among the media. Because it provides images, sound, movement, and a greater sense of speed and immediacy, TV can easily outcompete other media for audience attention and thus for advertising dollars. In attempts to keep pace, newspapers and magazines offer more and more of the kinds of stories that once were beneath their standards, such as elaborate focus both on sensational aspects of the case and on "personalities, analysis, and prediction" rather than news (Thaler 45). While these attributes have always been part of TV and the tabloid print press, this trend is increasingly apparent in supposedly reputable papers like the New York Times. During the Smith trial, for example, the Times violated previously accepted boundaries of propriety by not only identifying the rape victim but also giving lots of intimate details about her past (Thaler 45).

Because the media are, for the most part, commercial, slow periods—and all trials have them—must always be filled with some "story." One such story is increasingly the media self-consciously watching and analyzing itself, to see how it is handling (or mishandling) coverage of the trial (Thaler 43). At the Smith trial, for example, one group of reporters was covering the trial while another group covered the other reporters (Thaler 44).[5] As bizarre as this "media watching" is, there would be no "story" if the trial itself had not been televised.

No citation is needed for a point that can be considered common knowledge, but the second sentence is documented.

Last but not least, televising trials distracts viewers from other important issues. Some of these are abstract and thus hard to understand (like the savings-and-loan scandal in the mid-1980s or the causes of lingering unemployment in the 1990s), while others are painful to contemplate (like overseas wars and famines). Yet we have to stay aware of these issues if we are to function as active citizens in a democracy.

Altogether, televising trials is a bad idea. Not only does it provide deceptive impressions about what's happening in particular trials; it also doesn't reveal much about our judicial system. In addition, televising trials helps to lower the quality of trial coverage outside of court, thus increasingly depriving the public of neutral, fact-based reporting. A healthy free press depends on balance and knowing when to accept limits. Saturating viewers with extended media coverage of sensational trials oversteps those limits. In this case, more is not better.

Useful summary of main points

*Realistic
appraisal
of the current
situation and a
suggestion of
what the
reader can do*

Yet it is unlikely that TV coverage will be legally removed from the courtroom, now that it is here. Only one state (New York) has ever legislated a return to nontelevised trials (in 1991), and even it changed its mind in 1992 (Thaler 78). Perhaps the best we can do is to educate ourselves about the pitfalls of televising the judicial system, as we struggle to do so with the televised electoral process.

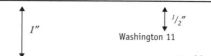

Washington 11

Notes

[1] Useful discussions of this history can be found in Clark (829–32) and Thaler (19–31).

[2] Cable networks have been showing trial footage to national audiences since at least 1982, when Cable News Network (CNN) covered the trial of Claus von Bulow (Thaler 33). It continues to show trials. In the first week of February 1995, four to five million homes accounted for the top fifteen most-watched shows on cable TV; all were CNN segments of the O. J. Simpson trial ("Cable TV"). In July 1991, Steven Brill founded the Courtroom Television Network, or "Court TV" (Clark 821). Like CNN, it broadcasts around the clock, showing gavel-to-gavel coverage. It now claims over fourteen million cable subscribers (Clark 821) and, as of January 1994, had televised over 280 trials ("In Camera" 27).

[3] Thaler's study The Watchful Eye is a thoughtful examination of the subtle ways in which TV in court can affect trial participants, inhibiting witnesses from coming forward, provoking grandstanding in attorneys and judges, and pressuring juries to come up with verdicts acceptable to a national audience.

[4] Sometimes legal restrictions determine camera angles. For example, in the Steinberg trial (1988), the audience and the jury were not allowed to be televised by New York state law. This required placing the camera so that the judge and witnesses were seen in "full frontal view" (generally a more neutral or positive stance). The lawyers could be seen only from the rear when questioning witnesses, and the defendant was shot in profile (Thaler 110–11). These camera

Double-space between heading and notes and throughout notes.

Superscript number followed by one space

Each note begins with ½" indent (five typewriter spaces), but subsequent lines of each note are flush left.

angles, though not chosen for dramatic effect, still resulted in emotionally laden viewpoints not experienced by the jury. George W. Trammell, a Los Angeles Superior Court Judge, has written on how technology can interfere with the fairness of the trial system. He claims that "Technology, well managed, can be a great benefit. Technology poorly managed benefits no one."

5 At the Smith trial a journalist from one German newspaper inadvertently filmed another German reporter from a competing newspaper watching the Smith trial in the press-room outside the courtroom (Thaler 44).

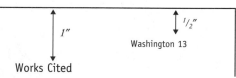

Washington 13

Works Cited

Altheide, David. "TV News and the Social Construction of
   Justice." Justice and the Media: Issues and Research.
   Ed. Ray Surette. Springfield, IL: Thomas, 1984.
   292–304.

Alphabetical by author's last name

Bianculli, David. "Shame on You, CNN." New York Post 11 Dec.
   1992: 60.

Hanging indent ½"

"Cable TV Squeezes High Numbers and Aces Competition." All
   Things Considered. Natl. Public Radio. 9 Feb. 1994.
   Unedited transcript. Segment 12. NPR Audience
   Services. Washington.

Transcript of radio program

Clark, Charles S. "Courts and the Media." CQ Researcher 23
   Sept. 1994: 817–40.

Cole, Lewis. "Court TV." Nation 21 Feb. 1994: 243–45.

Entner, Roberta. "Encoding the Image of the American
   Judiciary Institution: A Semiotic Analysis of Broadcast
   Trials to Ascertain Its Definition of the Court System."
   Diss. New York U, 1993.

The title of an unpublished work is not italicized but is enclosed within quotation marks.

"Former Panamanian Leader Noriega Sentenced." Facts on File
   16 July 1992: 526. InfoTrac: Magazine Index Plus
   1992–Feb. 1995. CD-ROM. Information Access. Feb.
   1995.

CD-ROM source

"In Camera with Court TV." New Yorker 24 Jan. 1994: 27–28.

Quindlen, Anna. "The Glass Eye." New York Times 18 Dec.
   1991: A29.

"A Tale of a Rug." Economist 15 Jan. 1994: 28–29.

Anonymous source alphabetized under first word (or second if first is A, An, or The)

Washington 14

Thaler, Paul. <u>The Watchful Eye: American Justice in the Age</u>
     <u>of the Television Trial</u>. Westport: Praeger, 1994.

Television program

"The Trial That Had to Happen: The People versus Amy
     Fisher." <u>A Current Affair</u>. Fox. WFXT, Boston. 1–4 Feb.
     1993.

No page reference for this in-text Internet citation

Trammell, George W. "Cirque du O. J." <u>Court Technology</u>
     <u>Bulletin</u> July/Aug. 1995. World Wide Web. 12 Sept.
     1995 <http:// www.ncsc.dni.us/ncsc/bulletin/
     v07n04.htm>.

Zoglin, Richard. "Justice Faces a Screen Test." <u>Time</u> 17 June
     1991: 62.

AN ANNOTATED
STUDENT RESEARCH PAPER
IN APA FORMAT

The following paper is an example of a student paper that uses APA format.

The Role of Spirituality and Religion
in Mental Health

*The APA-style
cover page gives
title, author,
and course
information.*

Laura DeVeau

English 102
Professor Gardner
April 12, 2004

The Role of Spirituality and Religion

in Mental Health

Short form of title and page number as running head

It has been called "a vestige of the childhood of mankind," "the feeling of something true, total and absolute," "an other-worldly answer as regards the meaning of life" (Jones, 1991, p. 1; Amaro, 2000; Kristeva, 1987, p. 27). It has been compared to medicine, described as a psychological cure for mental illness, and also referred to as the cause of a dangerous fanaticism. With so many differing opinions on the impact of religion in people's lives, where would one begin a search for the truth? Who has the answer: Christians, humanists, objectivists, atheists, psychoanalysts, Buddhists, philosophers, cults? This was my dilemma at the advent of my research into how religion and spirituality affect the mental health of society as a whole.

Citation of multiple works from references

In this paper, I explore the claims, widely accepted by professionals in the field of psychology, that religious and spiritual practices have a negative impact on mental health. In addition, though, I cannot help but reflect on how this exploration has changed my beliefs as well. Religion is such a personal experience that one cannot be dispassionate in reporting it. One can, however, subject the evidence provided by those who have studied the issue to critical scrutiny. Having done so, I find myself in disagreement with those who claim religious feelings are incompatible with sound mental health. There is a nearly limitless number of beliefs regarding spirituality. Some are organized and involve rituals like mass or worship. Many are centered around the existence of a higher being, while others focus on the self. I have attempted

Acknowledgment of opposing viewpoints

to uncover the perfect set of values that lead to a better lifestyle, but my research has pointed me in an entirely different direction, where no single belief seems to be adequate but where spiritual belief in general should be valued more highly than it is currently in mental health circles.

Thesis explicitly introduced

   I grew up in a moderately devout Catholic family. Like many young people raised in a household where one religion is practiced by both parents, it never occurred to me to question those beliefs. I went through a spiritual cycle, which I believe much of Western society also experiences. I attended religious services because I had to. I possessed a blind, unquestioning acceptance of what I was being taught because the adults I trusted said it was so. Like many adolescents and young adults, though, I stopped going to church when I was old enough to decide because I thought I had better things to do. At this stage, we reach a point when we begin searching for a meaning to our existence. For some, this search is brought on by a major crisis or a feeling of emptiness in their daily lives, while for others it is simply a part of growing up. This is where we begin to make personal choices, but with the barrage of options, where do we turn?

   Beginning with the holistic health movement in the eighties, there has been a mass shift from traditional religions to less structured spiritual practice such as meditation, yoga, the Cabala, and mysticism (Beyerman, 1989). They venture beyond the realm of conventional dogmatism and into the new wave of spirituality. Many of these practices are based on the notion that health of the mind and spirit equals health of the body. Associated with this movement is a proliferation of

Author and date cited for summary or paraphrase

retreats offering a chance to get in touch with the beauty and silence of nature and seminars where we can take "a break from our everyday environment where our brains are bustling and our bodies are exhausting themselves" ("Psychological benefits," 1999). A major concept of the spiritual new wave is that it focuses inward toward the individual psyche, rather than outward toward another being like a god. Practitioners do not deny the existence of this being, but they believe that to fully love another, we must first understand ourselves. Many find this a preferable alternative to religions where the individual is seen as a walking dispenser of sin who is very fortunate to have a forgiving creator. It is also a relief from the scare tactics like damnation used by traditional religions to make people behave. Many, therefore, praise the potential psychological benefits of such spirituality.

Anonymous source cited by title and date

While I believe strongly in the benefits of the new wave, I am not willing to do away with structured religion, for I found that it also has its benefits. Without the existence of churches and temples, it would be harder to expose the public to values beneficial to mental stability. It is much more diffi-cult to hand a child a copy of the Cabala and say "Read this, and then get back to me on it" than it is to bring a child to a service where the ideas are represented with concrete ex-amples. My religious upbringing presented me with a set of useful morals and values, and it does the same for millions of others who are brought up in this manner. Many people, including some followers of the new wave, are bitter toward Christianity because of events in history like the Crusades, the Inquisition, the Salem witch trials, and countless other

Clear transition refers to previ-ous paragraph

Religion in Mental Health 4

horrific acts supposedly committed in the name of God. But these events were not based on biblical teachings but on purely human greed and lust for power. We should not reject the benevolent possibilities of organized religion on the basis of historical atrocities any more than we should abandon public education because a few teachers are known to mistreat children.

Another factor contributing to the reluctance concerning religion is the existence of cults that seduce people into following their extreme teachings. The victims are often at vulnerable times in their lives, and the leaders are usually very charming, charismatic, and sometimes also psychotic or otherwise mentally unstable. Many argue that if we acknowledge these groups as dangerous cults, then we must do the same for traditional religions such as Christianity and Islam, which are likewise founded on the teachings of charismatic leaders. Again, though, critics are too quick to conflate all religious and spiritual practice; we must distinguish between those who pray and attend services and those who commit group suicide because they think that aliens are coming to take over the world. Cults have provided many psychologists, who are eager to discount religion as a factor in improving mental health, with an easy target. Ellis (1993), the founder of rational-emotive therapy, cites many extreme examples of religious commitment, such as cults and antiabortion killings, to show that commitment is hazardous to one's sanity. Anomalies like these should not be used to speak of religion as a whole, though. Religion is clearly the least of these people's mental problems.

When the author's name appears in text, only the date is cited in parentheses.

Besides Ellis, there are many others in the field of psychology who do not recognize religion as a potential aid for improving the condition of the psyche. Actually, fewer than 45 percent of the members of the American Psychiatric Association even believe in God. The general American public has more than twice that percentage of religious devotees (Larson, 1998). Going back to the days of Freud, many psychologists have held atheist views. The father of psychoanalysis himself called religion a "universal obsessional neurosis." Psychologists have long rejected research that demonstrates the benefits of spirituality by saying that this research is biased. They claim that such studies are out to prove that religion helps because the conductors are religious people who need to justify their beliefs.

While this may be true in some instances, there is also some quite empirical research available to support the claims of those who promote religion and spirituality. The Journal for the Scientific Study of Religion has conducted many studies examining the effects of religion on individuals and groups. In one example, the relationship between religious coping methods and positive recovery after major stressful events was observed. The results indicated not only that spirituality was not harmful to the mind but that "the positive religious coping pattern was tied to benevolent outcomes, including fewer symptoms of psychological distress, [and] reports of psychological and spiritual growth as a result of the stressor" (Pargament et al., 1998, p. 721). Clearly, the benefits of piety can, in fact, be examined empirically, and in some cases the results point to a positive correlation between religion and mental health.

Bracketed word in quotation not in original source

Author, date, and page number are cited for a direct quotation.

But let us get away from statistics and studies. If religion is both useless and dangerous, as so many psychologists claim, we must ask why has it remained so vital a part of humanity for so long. Even if it can be reduced to a mere coping method that humans use to justify their existence and explain incomprehensible events, is it futile? I would suggest that this alone represents a clear benefit to society. Should religion, if it cannot be proven as "true," be eliminated and life based on scientific fact alone? Surely many would find this a pointless existence. With all the conflicting knowledge I have gained about spirituality during my personal journey and my research, one idea is clear. It is not the depth of devotion, the time of life when one turns to religion, or even the particular beliefs or combination of beliefs one chooses to adopt that will improve the quality of life. There is no right or wrong answer when it comes to self-fulfillment. It is whatever works for the individual, even if that means holding no religious or spiritual beliefs at all. But clearly there are benefits to be gained, at least for some individuals, and mental health professionals need to begin acknowledging this fact in their daily practice.

Conclusion restates and strengthens thesis

Religion in Mental Health 7

References begin on a new page.

References

Amaro, J. (2000). Psychology, psychoanalysis and religious faith. Nielsen's psychology of religion pages. Retrieved March 6, 2000, from the World Wide Web: http://www.psywww.com/psyrelig/amaro.html

A World Wide Web source

Beyerman A. K. (1989). The holistic health movement. Tuscaloosa: Alabama University Press.

A book

Ellis, A. (1993). Dogmatic devotion doesn't help, it hurts. In B. Slife (Ed.), Taking sides: Clashing views on controversial psychological issues (pp. 297–301). New York: Scribner.

An article or chapter in a book

Jones, J. W. (1991). Contemporary psychoanalysis and religion: Transference and transcendence. New Haven: Yale University Press.

Kristeva, J. (1987). In the beginning was love: Psychoanalysis and faith. New York: Columbia University Press.

Larson, D. (1998). Does religious commitment improve mental health? In B. Slife (Ed.), Taking sides: Clashing views on controversial psychological issues (pp. 292–296). New York: Scribner.

Pargament, K. I., Smith, B. W., Koening, H. G., & Perez, L. (1998). Patterns of positive and negative religious coping with major life stressors. Journal for the Scientific Study of Religion, 37, 710–724.

An article in a journal

"Psychological benefits." (1999). Walking the labyrinth. Retrieved April 3, 2000, from the World Wide Web: http://www.labyrinthway.com/html/benefits.html

Anonymous source alphabetized by title

Further Views on Argument

8

A Philosopher's View: The Toulmin Model

In Chapter 3, we explained the contrast between *deductive* and *inductive* arguments to focus on the two main ways in which we reason, either

- Making explicit something concealed in what we already accept (**deduction**) or
- Using what we have observed as a basis for asserting or proposing something new (**induction**).

Both types of reasoning share some structural features, as we also noticed. Thus, all reasoning is aimed at establishing some **thesis** (or conclusion) and does so by means of some **reasons.** These are two basic characteristics that any argument contains.

After a little scrutiny we can in fact point to several features shared by all arguments, deductive and inductive, good and bad alike. We use the vocabulary popularized by Stephen Toulmin, Richard Rieke, and Allan Janik in their book *An Introduction to Reasoning* (1979; second edition 1984) to explore the various elements of argument.

THE CLAIM

Every argument has a purpose, goal, or aim—namely, to establish a **claim** (*conclusion* or *thesis*). Suppose you were arguing in favor of equal rights for women. You might state your thesis or claim as follows:

Men and women ought to have equal rights.

A more precise formulation of the claim might be

Men and women ought to have equal legal rights.

A still more precise formulation might be

Equal legal rights for men and women ought to be protected by our Constitution.

The third version of this claim states what the controversy in the 1970s over the Equal Rights Amendment was all about.

Consequently, in reading or analyzing someone else's argument, your first question should naturally be: What is the argument intended to prove or establish? *What claim is it making?* Has this claim been clearly and precisely formulated, so that it unambiguously asserts what its advocate wants to assert?

GROUNDS

Once we have the argument's purpose or point clearly in mind and thus know what the arguer is claiming to establish, then we can ask for the evidence, reasons, support—in short, for the **grounds**—on which that claim is based. In a deductive argument these grounds are the premises from which the claim is deduced; in an inductive argument the grounds are the evidence—a sample, an observation, or an experiment—that makes the claim plausible or probable.

Not every kind of claim can be supported by every kind of ground, and conversely, not every kind of ground gives equally good support for every kind of claim. Suppose I claim that half the students in the class-room are women. I can ground this claim in any of several ways.

1. I can count all the women and all the men. Suppose the total equals fifty. If the number of women is twenty-five and the number of men is twenty-five, I have vindicated my claim.

2. I can count a sample of, say, ten students and find that in the sample five of the students are women. I thus have induc-tive—plausible but not conclusive—grounds for my claim.

3. I can point out that the students in the college divide equally into men and women and claim that this class is a representative sample of the whole college.

Obviously, ground 1 is stronger than ground 2, and 2 is far stronger than ground 3.

So far we have merely restated points about premises and conclusions covered in Chapter 3. But now we want to consider four additional features of arguments.

WARRANTS

Once we have the claim or the point of an argument fixed in mind and the evidence or reasons offered in its support, the next question to ask is *why* these reasons support this conclusion. What is the **warrant,** or guarantee, that the reasons proffered do support the claim or lead to the conclusion? In simple deductive arguments, the warrant takes different forms, as we shall see. In the simplest cases, we can point to the way in which the *meanings* of the key terms are really equivalent. Thus, if John is taller than Bill, then Bill must be shorter than John because of the meaning in English of "is shorter than" and "is taller than." In this case, the warrant is something we can state quite literally and explicitly.

In other cases, we may need to be more resourceful. A reliable tactic is to think up a simple *parallel argument* — that is, an argument exactly parallel in form and structure to the argument we are trying to defend. We then point out that if we are ready to accept the simpler argument, then we must accept the more complex argument because both arguments have exactly the same structure. For example, in her much-discussed 1972 essay on the abortion controversy, "A Defense of Abortion," philosopher Judith Thomson argues that a pregnant woman has the right to an abortion to save her life, even if it involves the death of her unborn child. She anticipates that some readers may balk at her reasoning, and so she offers this parallel argument: Suppose you are locked in a tiny room with another human being, which through no fault of its own is growing uncontrollably, with the result that it is slowly crushing you to death. Of course, it would be morally permissible to kill the other person to save your own life. With the reader's presumed agreement on that conclusion, the parallel argument concerning the abortion situation — so Thomson hopes — is obvious and convincing.

In simple inductive arguments, we are likely to point to the way in which observations or sets of data constitute a *representative sample* of a whole (unexamined) population. Here, the warrant is the representativeness of the sample. For instance, in projecting a line on a graph through a set of points, we defend one projection over alternatives on the grounds that it makes the smoothest fit through most of the points. In this case, the warrant is *simplicity* and *inclusiveness*. Or in defending one explanation against competing explanations of a phenomenon, we appeal to the way in which the preferred explanation can be seen as a *special case* of generally accepted physical laws. Examples of such warrants for inductive reasoning will be offered in following pages (see Chapter 9, A Logician's View: Deduction, Induction, Fallacies, pp. 230–63).

Establishing the warrants for our reasoning—that is, explaining why our grounds really support our claims—can quickly become a highly technical and exacting procedure that goes far beyond what we can hope to explain in this book. Only a solid course or two in formal deductive logic and statistical methods can do justice to our current state of knowledge about these warrants. Developing a "feel" for why reasons or grounds are or are not relevant to what they are alleged to support is the most we can hope to do here without recourse to more rigorous techniques.

Even without formal training, however, one can sense that something is wrong with many bad arguments. Here is an example. British professor C. E. M. Joad found himself standing on a station platform, annoyed because he had just missed his train, when another train, making an unscheduled stop, pulled up to the platform in front of him. He decided to jump aboard, only to hear the porter say "I'm afraid you'll have to get off, sir. This train doesn't stop here." "In that case," replied Joad, "don't worry. I'm not on it."

BACKING

The kinds of reasons appropriate to support an amendment to the Constitution are completely different from the kinds appropriate to settle the question of what caused the defeat of Napoleon's invasion of Russia. Arguments for the amendment might be rooted in an appeal to fairness, whereas arguments about the military defeat might be rooted in letters and other documents in the French and Russian archives. The canons of good argument in each case derive from the ways in which the scholarly communities in law and history, respectively, have developed over the years to support, defend, challenge, and undermine a given kind of argument. Thus, the support or **backing** appropriate for one kind of argument might be quite inappropriate for another kind of argument.

Another way of stating this point is to recognize that once you have given reasons for a claim, you are then likely to be challenged to explain why these reasons are good reasons—why, that is, one should believe these reasons rather than regard them skeptically. Why (a simple example) should we accept the testimony of Dr. *X* when Dr. *Y,* equally renowned, supports the opposite side? Or why is it safe to rest a prediction on a small though admittedly carefully selected sample? Or why is it legitimate to argue that (1) if I dream I am the King of France, then I must exist, whereas it is illegitimate to argue that (2) if I dream I am the King of France, then the King of France must exist? To answer these kinds of challenges is to *back up* one's reasoning, and no argument is any better than its backing.

MODAL QUALIFIERS

As we have seen, all arguments are made up of assertions or propositions, which can be sorted into four categories:

- The *claim* (conclusion, thesis to be established),
- The *grounds* (explicit reasons advanced),
- The *warrant* (the principle that connects the ground to the claim), and
- The *backing* (implicit assumptions).

All these kinds of propositions have an explicit or tacit **modality** in which they are asserted, indicating the scope and character with which they are believed to hold true. Is the claim, for instance, believed to be *necessary*—or only *probable*? Is the claim believed to be *plausible*—or only *possible*? Of two reasons for a claim, both may be *good*, but one may be *better* than the other. Indicating the modality with which an assertion is advanced is crucial to any argument for or against it.

Empirical generalizations are typically *contingent* on various factors, and it is important to indicate such contingencies to protect the generalization against obvious counterexamples. Thus, consider this empirical generalization:

Students do best on final examinations if they study hard for them.

Are we really to believe that students who study regularly throughout the whole course and so do not need to cram for the final will do less well than students who neglect regular work in favor of several all-nighters at the last minute? Probably not; what is really meant is that *all other things being equal* (in Latin, *ceteris paribus*), concentrated study just before an exam will yield good results. Alluding to the contingencies in this way shows that the writer is aware of possible exceptions and that they are conceded right from the start.

Assertions also have varying **scope,** and indicating their scope is equally crucial to the role that an assertion plays in argument. Thus, suppose you are arguing against smoking, and the ground for your claim is this:

Heavy smokers cut short their life span.

Such an assertion will be clearer, as well as more likely to be true, if it is explicitly **quantified.** Here, there are three obvious alternative quantifications to choose among: *all* smokers cut short their life span, *most* do, or only *some* do. Until the assertion is quantified in one of these ways, we really do not know what is being asserted—and so we do not know what degree and kind of evidence and counterevidence is relevant. Other quantifiers include *few, rarely, many, often, sometimes, perhaps, usually, more or less, regularly, occasionally.*

In sum, sensitivity to the quantifiers and qualifiers appropriate for each of our assertions, whatever their role in an argument, will help prevent you from asserting exaggerations and other misguided generalizations.

REBUTTALS

Very few arguments of any interest are beyond dispute, conclusively knockdown affairs in which the claim of the argument is so rigidly tied to its grounds, warrants, and backing and its quantifiers and qualifiers so precisely orchestrated that it really proves its conclusion beyond any possibility of doubt. On the contrary, most arguments have many counterarguments, and sometimes one of these counterarguments is the most convincing.

Suppose one has taken a sample that appears to be random: An interviewer on your campus accosts the first ten students she encounters, and seven of them happen to be fraternity or sorority members. She is now ready to argue that seven-tenths of enrolled students belong to Greek organizations.

You believe, however, that the Greeks are in the minority and point out that she happens to have conducted her interview around the corner from the Panhellenic Society's office just off Sorority Row. Her random sample is anything but. The ball is now back in her court as you await her response to your rebuttal.

As this example illustrates, it is safe to say that we do not understand our own arguments very well until we have tried to get a grip on the places in which they are vulnerable to criticism, counterattack, or refutation. Edmund Burke (quoted in Chapter 3 but worth repeating) said, "He that wrestles with us strengthens our nerves, and sharpens our skill. Our antagonist is our helper." Therefore, cultivating alertness to such weak spots, girding one's loins to defend at these places, always helps strengthen one's position.

A MODEL ANALYSIS USING
THE TOULMIN METHOD

To see how the Toulmin method can be used, let's apply it to an argument in this book, Susan Jacoby's "A First Amendment Junkie" (p. 35).

The Claim   Jacoby's central thesis or claim is this: Any form of *censorship* — including feminist censorship of pornography in particular — *is wrong.*

Grounds   Jacoby offers six main reasons or grounds for her claim, roughly in this sequence (but arguably not in this order of importance).

First, feminists exaggerate the harm caused by pornography because they confuse expression of offensive ideas with harmful conduct.

Second, letting the government censor the expression of ideas and attitudes is the wrong response to the failure of parents to control the printed materials that get into the hands of their children.

Third, there is no unanimity even among feminists over what is pornography and what isn't.

Fourth, permitting censorship of pornography to please feminists could well lead to censorship on many issues of concern to feminists ("rape, abortion, menstruation, contraception, lesbianism").

Fifth, censorship under law shows a lack of confidence in the democratic process.

Finally, censorship of words and pictures is suppression of self-expression, and that violates the First Amendment.

Warrants   Each of these six grounds needs its own warrant, and the warrants vary considerably in their complexity. Jacoby (like most writers) is not so didactic as to make these warrants explicit. Taking them in order, this is what they look like.

First, since the First Amendment protects speech in the broadest sense, the censorship that the feminist attack on pornography advocates is *inconsistent* with the First Amendment.

Second, if feminists want to be consistent, then they must advocate censorship of *all* offensive self-expression, but such a radical interference with free speech (amounting virtually to repeal of the First Amendment) is indefensible.

Third, if feminists can't agree over what is pornographic, the censorship of pornography they propose is bound to be arbitrary.

Fourth, feminists ought to see that *they risk losing more than they can hope to gain* if they succeed in censoring pornography.

Fifth, the democratic process can be trusted to weed out harmful utterances.

Sixth, if feminists have a legal right to censor pornography, anti-feminists will claim the same right on other issues.

Backing   Why should the reader agree with Jacoby's grounds? She does not appeal to expert authority, the results of experimental tests or other statistical data, or the support of popular opinion. Instead, she relies principally on two things—but without saying so explicitly.

First, she assumes that the reader accepts the propositions that *freedom of self-expression is valuable* and that *censoring self-expression requires the strongest of reasons*. If there is no fundamental agreement on these propositions, several of her reasons cease to support her claim.

Second, she relies on the reader's open-mindedness and willingness to evaluate common sense (untechnical, ordinary, familiar) considerations at each step of the way. She relies also on the reader having had some personal experience with erotica, pornography, and art. Without that open-mindedness and experience, a reader is not likely to be persuaded by her rejection of the feminist demand for censorship.

Modal Qualifiers   Jacoby defends what she calls an "absolute interpretation" of the First Amendment—that is, the view that *all* censorship of words, pictures, and ideas is not only inconsistent with the First Amendment but is also politically unwise and morally objectionable. She allows that *some* pornography is highly offensive (it offends her, she insists); she allows that *some* pornography ("kiddie porn") may even be harmful to *some* viewers. But she also insists that *more* harm than good would result from the censorship of pornography. She points out that *some* paintings of nude women are art, not pornography; she implies that it is *impossible* to draw a sharp line between permissible erotic pornography and impermissible offensive pornography. She clearly believes that *all* Americans ought to understand and defend the First Amendment under the "absolute interpretation" she favors.

Rebuttals   Jacoby mentions several objections to her views, and perhaps the most effective aspect of her entire argument is her skill in identifying possible objections and meeting them effectively. (Notice the diversity of the objections and the various ways in which she replies.)

Objection: Some of her women friends tell her she is wrong.

Rebuttal: She admits she's a "First Amendment junkie," and she doesn't apologize for it.

Objection: "Kiddie porn" is harmful and deserves censorship.

Rebuttal: Such material is *not* protected by the First Amendment because it is an "abuse of power" of adults over children.

Objection: Pornography is a form of violence against women, and therefore it is especially harmful.

Rebuttal: (1) No, it really isn't harmful, but it is disgusting and offensive. (2) In any case, it's surely not as harmful as allowing American neo-Nazis to parade in Jewish neighborhoods. (Jacoby is referring to the march in Skokie, Illinois, in 1977, upheld by the courts as permissible political expression under the First Amendment despite its offensiveness to survivors of the Nazi concentration camps.)

Objection: Censoring pornography advances public respect for women.

Rebuttal: Censoring *Ms.* magazine, which antifeminists have already done, undermines women's freedom and self-expression.

Objection: Reasonable people can tell pornography when they see it, so censoring it poses no problems.

Rebuttal: Yes, there are clear cases of gross pornography; but there are lots of borderline cases, as women themselves prove when they disagree over whether a photo in *Penthouse* is offensively erotic or "lovely" and "sensuous."

A CHECKLIST FOR USING THE TOULMIN METHOD

☐ What claim does the argument make?

☐ What grounds are offered for the claim?

☐ What warrants the inferences from the grounds to the claim?

☐ What backing supports the claim?

☐ With what modalities are the claim and grounds asserted?

☐ To what rebuttals are the claim, grounds, and backing vulnerable?

See the companion Web site **bedfordstmartins.com/barnetbedau** for links related to the Toulmin model.

9

A Logician's View:
Deduction, Induction,
Fallacies

In Chapter 3 we introduced these terms. Here we discuss them in greater detail.

DEDUCTION

The basic aim of deductive reasoning is to start with some assumption or premise and extract from it a conclusion—a logical consequence— that is concealed but implicit in it. Thus, taking the simplest case, if I assert as a premise

    1a. Nuclear power poses more risks of harm to the environment than fossil fuels.

then it is a matter of simple deduction to infer the conclusion that

    1b. Fossil fuels pose fewer risks of harm to the environment than nuclear power.

Anyone who understands English would grant that 1b follows 1a—or equivalently, that 1b can be validly deduced from 1a—because whatever two objects, *A* and *B*, you choose, if *A* does *more things than B*, then *B* must do *fewer things than A*.

    Thus, in this and all other cases of valid deductive reasoning, we can say not only that we are entitled to *infer* the conclusion from the premise—in this case, infer 1b from 1a—but that the premise *implies* the conclusion. Remember, too, the conclusion (1b) that fossil fuels pose fewer risks than nuclear power—inferred or deduced from the statement (1a) that nuclear power poses more risks—does not depend on the truth of the statement that nuclear power poses more risks. If the speaker (falsely) asserts that nuclear power poses more risks, then the hearer validly (that is to say, logically) concludes that fossil fuels pose fewer risks. Thus, 1b follows from 1a whether or not 1a is true; consequently, if 1a is true then so is 1b; but if 1a is false then 1b must be false also.

Let's take another example—more interesting but comparably simple:

2a. President Truman was underrated by his critics.

Given 2a, a claim amply verified by events of the 1950s, one is entitled to infer

2b. His critics underrated President Truman.

On what basis can we argue that 2a implies 2b? The two propositions are equivalent because a rule of English grammar assures us that we can convert the position of subject and predicate phrases in a sentence by shifting from the passive to the active voice (or vice versa) without any change in the conditions that make the proposition true (or false).

Both pairs of examples illustrate that in deductive reasoning, our aim is to transform, reformulate, or restate in our conclusion some (or, as in the two examples above, all) of the information contained in our premises.

Remember, even though a proposition or statement follows from a previous proposition or statement, the statements need not be true. We can see why if we consider another example. Suppose someone asserts or claims that

3a. The Gettysburg Address is longer than the Declaration of Independence.

As every student of American history knows, 3a is false. But false or not, we can validly deduce from it that

3b. The Declaration of Independence is shorter than the Gettysburg Address.

This inference is valid (even though the conclusion is untrue) because the conclusion follows logically (more precisely, deductively) from 3a: In English, as we know, the meaning of "*A* is shorter than *B*," which appears in 3b, is simply the converse of "*B* is longer than *A*," which appears in 3a.

The deductive relation between 3a and 3b reminds us again that the idea of *validity*, which is so crucial to deduction, is not the same as the idea of *truth*. False propositions have implications—logical consequences—too, just as true propositions do.

In the three pairs of examples so far, what can we point to as the *warrant* for our claims? Well, look at the reasoning in each case; the arguments rely on rules of ordinary English, on the accepted meanings of words like *on, under,* and *underrated*.

In many cases, of course, the deductive inference or pattern of reasoning is much more complex than that which we have seen in the examples so far. When we introduced the idea of deduction in Chapter 3, we gave as our primary example the *syllogism*. Here is another example:

4. Texas is larger than California; California is larger than Arizona; therefore, Texas is larger than Arizona.

The conclusion in this syllogism is derivable from the two premises; that is, anyone who asserts the two premises is committed to accepting the conclusion as well, whether or not one thinks of it.

Notice again that the *truth* of the conclusion is not established merely by validity of the inference. The conclusion in this syllogism happens to be true. And the premises of this syllogism imply the conclusion. But the argument establishes the conclusion only because both of the premises on which the conclusion depends are true. Even a Californian admits that Texas is larger than California, which in turn is larger than Arizona. In other words, argument 4 is a *sound* argument because (as we explained in Chapter 3) it is valid and all its premises are true. All—and only—arguments that *prove* their conclusions have these two traits.

How might we present the warrant for the argument in 4? Short of a crash course in formal logic, either of two strategies might suffice. One is to argue from the fact that the validity of the inference depends on the meaning of a key concept, *being larger than*. This concept has the property of *transitivity*, a property that many concepts share (for example, *is equal to, is to the right of, is smarter than*—all are transitive concepts). Consequently, whatever *A, B,* and *C* are, if *A* is larger than *B*, and *B* is larger than *C*, then *A* will be larger than *C*. The final step is to substitute "Texas," "California," and "Arizona" for *A, B,* and *C*, respectively.

A second strategy, less abstract and more graphic, is to think of representing Texas, California, and Arizona by nested circles. Thus, the first premise in argument 4 would look like this:

The second premise would look like this:

The conclusion would look like this:

We can see that this conclusion follows from the premises because it amounts to nothing more than what one gets by superimposing the two premises on each other. Thus, the whole argument can be represented like this:

The so-called middle term in the argument—California—disappears from the conclusion; its role is confined to be the link between the other two terms, Texas and Arizona, in the premises. (This is an adaptation of the technique used in elementary formal logic known as Venn diagrams.) In this manner one can give graphic display to the important fact that the conclusion follows from the premises because one can literally *see* the conclusion represented by nothing more than a representation of the premises.

Both of these strategies bring out the fact that validity of deductive inference is a purely *formal* property of argument. Each strategy abstracts the form from the content of the propositions involved to show how the concepts in the premises are related to the concepts in the conclusion.

For the sake of illustration, here is another syllogistic argument with the same logical features as argument 4. (A nice exercise is to re-state argument 5 using diagrams in the manner of argument 4.)

5. African American slaves were treated worse than white inden-tured servants. Indentured white servants were treated worse than free white labor. Therefore, African American slaves were treated worse than free white labor.

Not all deductive reasoning occurs in syllogisms, however, or at least not in syllogisms like the ones in 4 and 5. (The term *syllogism* is sometimes used to refer to any deductive argument of whatever form, provided only that it has two premises.) In fact, syllogisms such as 4 are not the commonest form of our deductive reasoning at all. Nor are they the simplest (and of course, not the most complex). For an argument that is even simpler, consider this:

6. If a youth is an African American slave, he is probably treated worse than a youth in indentured service. This youth is an African American slave. Therefore, he is probably treated worse than if he had been an indentured servant.

Here the pattern of reasoning has the form: If *A*, then *B; A;* there-fore, *B*. Notice that the content of the assertions represented by *A* and *B* do not matter; any set of expressions having the same form or structure will do equally well, including assertions built out of meaningless terms, as in this example:

7. If the slithy toves, then the gyres gimble. The slithy toves. Therefore, the gyres gimble.

Argument 7 has the form: If *A*, then *B; A;* therefore *B*. As a piece of de-ductive inference it is every bit as good. Unlike 6, however, 7 is of no in-terest to us because none of its assertions make any sense (unless you are a reader of Lewis Carroll's "Jabberwocky," and even then the sense of 7 is doubtful). You cannot, in short, use a valid deductive argument to prove anything unless the premises and the conclusion are *true*, but they can't be true unless they *mean* something in the first place.

This parallel between arguments 6 and 7 shows once again that de-ductive validity in an argument rests on the *form* or structure of the ar-gument, and not on its content or meaning. If all one can say about an argument is that it is valid—that is, its conclusion follows from the premises—one has not given a sufficient reason for accepting the argu-ment's conclusion. It has been said that the Devil can quote Scripture; similarly, an argument can be deductively valid and of no further interest or value whatever because valid (but false) conclusions can be drawn from false or even meaningless assumptions. For example,

8. New York's Metropolitan Museum of Art has the finest collection of abstract impressionist painting in the world. The finest collection of abstract impressionist paintings includes dozens of canvases by Winslow Homer. Therefore, the Metropolitan Museum of Art has dozens of paintings by Winslow Homer.

Here, the conclusion follows validly from the premises, even though all three propositions are false. Nevertheless, although validity by itself is not enough, it is a necessary condition of any deductive argument that purports to establish its conclusion.

Now let us consider another argument with the same form as 8, only more interesting.

9. If President Truman knew the Japanese were about to surrender, then it was immoral of him to order that atom bombs be dropped on Hiroshima and Nagasaki. Truman knew the Japanese were about to surrender. Therefore, it was immoral of him to order dropping those bombs.

As in the two previous examples, anyone who assents to the premises in argument 9 must assent to the conclusion; the form of arguments 8 and 9 is identical. But do the premises of argument 9 *prove* the conclusion? That depends on whether both premises are true. Well, are they? This turns on a number of considerations, and it is worthwhile pausing to examine this argument closely to illustrate the kinds of things that are involved in answering this question.

Let us begin by examining the second (minor) premise. Its truth is controversial even to this day. Autobiography, memoranda, other documentary evidence—all are needed to assemble the evidence to back up the grounds for the thesis or claim made in the conclusion of this valid argument. Evaluating this material effectively will probably involve not only further deductions, but inductive reasoning as well.

Now consider the first (major) premise in argument 9. Its truth doesn't depend on what history shows but on the moral principles one accepts. The major premise has the form of a hypothetical proposition ("if . . . then . . .") and asserts a connection between two very different kinds of things. The antecedent of the hypothetical (the clause following "if") mentions facts about Truman's *knowledge,* and the consequent of the hypothetical (the clause following "then") mentions facts about the *morality* of his conduct in light of such knowledge. The major premise as a whole can thus be seen as expressing *a principle of moral responsibility.*

Such principles can, of course, be controversial. In this case, for instance, is the principle peculiarly relevant to the knowledge and conduct of a president of the United States? Probably not; it is far more likely that this principle is merely a special case of a more general proposition about anyone's moral responsibility. (After all, we know a great deal more about the conditions of our own moral responsibility than we do about those of high government officials.) We might express this more general principle in this way: If we have knowledge that would make our violent conduct unnecessary, then we are immoral if we deliberately act violently anyway. Thus, accepting this general principle can serve as a basis for defending the major premise of argument 9.

We have examined this argument in some detail because it illustrates the kinds of considerations needed to test whether a given argument is not only valid but whether its premises are true—that is, whether its premises really prove the conclusion.

The great value of the form of argument known as hypothetical syllogism, exemplified by arguments 6 and 7, is that the structure of the argument is so simple and so universally applicable in reasoning that it is often both easy and worthwhile to formulate one's claims so that they can be grounded by an argument of this sort.

Before leaving the subject of deductive inference, consider three other forms of argument, each of which can be found in actual use elsewhere in the readings in this volume. The simplest of these is **disjunctive syllogism,** so called because its major premise is a **disjunction.** For example,

10. Either censorship of television shows is overdue, or our society is indifferent to the education of its youth. Our society is not indifferent to the education of its youth. Therefore, censorship of television is overdue.

Notice, by the way, that the validity of an argument, as in this case, does not turn on pedantic repetition of every word or phrase as the argument moves along; nonessential elements can be dropped, or equivalent expressions substituted for variety without adverse effect on the reasoning. Thus, in conversation or in writing, the argument in 10 might actually be presented like this:

11. Either censorship of television is overdue, or our society is indifferent to the education of its youth. But, of course, we aren't indifferent; it's censorship that's overdue.

The key feature of disjunctive syllogism, as example 11 suggests, is that the conclusion is whichever of the disjuncts is left over after the others have been negated in the minor premise. Thus, we could easily have a very complex disjunctive syllogism, with a dozen disjuncts in the major premise, and seven of them denied in the minor premise, leaving a conclusion of the remaining five. Usually, however, a disjunctive argument is formulated in this manner: Assert a disjunction with two or more disjuncts in the major premise; then *deny all but one* in the minor premise; and infer validly the remaining disjunct as the conclusion. That was the form of argument 11.

Another type of argument, especially favored by orators and rhetoricians, is the **dilemma.** Ordinarily we use the term *dilemma* in the sense of an awkward predicament, as when we say, "His dilemma was that he didn't have enough money to pay the waiter." But when logicians refer to a dilemma, they mean a forced choice between two or more equally unattractive alternatives. For example, the predicament of the U.S. government during the mid-1980s as it faced the crisis brought on by terrorist attacks on American civilian targets, which were believed, during that time, to be inspired and supported by the Libyan government, can be formulated in a dilemma:

12. If the United States bombs targets in Libya, innocent people will be killed, and the Arab world will be angered. If the United States doesn't bomb Libyan targets, then terrorists will go unpunished, and the United States will lose respect among other governments. Either the United States bombs Libyan targets, or it doesn't. Therefore, in either case unattractive consequences will follow: The innocent will be killed, or terrorists will go unpunished.

Notice first the structure of the argument: two conditional propositions asserted as premises, followed by another premise that states a **necessary truth.** (The premise, "Either we bomb the Libyans, or we don't," is a disjunction; since its two alternatives are exhaustive, one of the two alternatives must be true. Such a statement is often called analytically true, or a *tautology*.) No doubt the conclusion of this dilemma follows from its premises.

But does the argument prove, as it purports to do, that whatever the U.S. government does, it will suffer "unattractive consequences"? It is customary to speak of "the horns of the dilemma," as though the challenge posed by the dilemma were like a bull ready to gore you whichever direction you turn. But if the two conditional premises failed to exhaust the possibilities, then one can escape from the dilemma by going "between the horns"; that is, by finding a third alternative. If (as in this case) that is not possible, one can still ask whether both of the main premises are true. (In this argument, it should be clear that neither of these main premises spells out all or even most of the consequences that could be foreseen.) Even so, in cases where both these conditional premises are true, it may be that the consequences of one alternative are nowhere nearly so bad as those of the other. If that is true, but our reasoning stops before evaluating that fact, we may be guilty of failing to distinguish between the greater and the lesser of two admitted evils. The logic of the dilemma itself cannot decide this choice for us. Instead, we must bring to bear empirical inquiry and imagination to the evaluation of the grounds of the dilemma itself.

Writers commonly use the term *dilemma* without explicitly formulating the dilemma to which they refer, leaving it for the readers to do. And sometimes, what is called a dilemma really isn't one. (Remember the dog's tail? Calling it a leg doesn't make it one.) As an example, consider the plight of Seaman Holmes in the case of *United States v. Holmes*. Either Holmes decides to throw some passengers overboard to keep the rowboat afloat, or he doesn't. If he does throw some overboard, he may be guilty of murder. If he doesn't throw them overboard, the rowboat may sink and all the passengers and crew in it drown. Neither the defense, the prosecuting attorney, nor the judge actually formulates Holmes's predicament in the language of a dilemma, as we have, but this is exactly how we ought to view Holmes's problem: Which of the horns of the dilemma should he embrace, and why? Or is there a third way for him to act, allowing him to go between those horns?

Finally, one of the most powerful and dramatic forms of argument is **reductio ad absurdum** (from the Latin, meaning "reduction to absurdity"). The idea of a reductio argument is to disprove a proposition by showing the absurdity of its inevitable conclusion. It is used, of course, to refute your opponent's position and prove your own. For example, in Plato's *Republic*, Socrates asks an old gentleman, Cephalus, to define what right conduct is. Cephalus says that it consists of paying your debts and keeping your word. Socrates rejects this answer by showing that it leads to a contradiction. He argues that Cephalus cannot have given the correct answer because if we believe that he did, we will be quickly led into contradictions; in some cases when you keep your word you will nonetheless be doing the wrong thing. For suppose, says Socrates, that you borrowed a weapon from a man, promising to return it when he asks for it. One day he comes to your door, demanding his weapon and swearing angrily that he intends to murder a neighbor. Keeping your word under those circumstances is absurd, Socrates implies, and the reader of the dialogue is left to infer that Cephalus's definition, which led to this result, is refuted.

Let's take a closer look at another example. Suppose you are opposed to any form of gun control, whereas I am in favor of gun control.

I might try to refute your position by attacking it with a reductio argument. To do that, I start out by assuming the very opposite of what I believe or favor and try to establish a contradiction that results from following out the consequences of this initial assumption. My argument might look like this:

13. Let's assume your position—namely, that there ought to be no legal restrictions whatever on the sale and ownership of guns. That means that you'd permit having every neighborhood hardware store sell pistols and rifles to whoever walks in the door. But that's not all. You apparently also would permit selling machine guns to children, antitank weapons to lunatics, small-bore cannons to the near-sighted, as well as guns and the ammunition to go with them to anyone with a criminal record. But this is utterly preposterous. No one could favor such a dangerous policy. So the only question worth debating is what kind of gun control is necessary.

Now in this example, my reductio of your position on gun control is not based on claiming to show that you have strictly contradicted yourself, for there is no purely logical contradiction in opposing all forms of gun control. Instead, what I have tried to do is to show that there is a contradiction between what you profess—no gun controls whatever—and what you probably really believe, if only you will stop to think about it—no lunatic should be allowed to buy a loaded machine gun.

My refutation of your position rests on whether I succeed in establishing an inconsistency among your own beliefs. If it turns out that you really believe lunatics should be free to purchase guns and ammunition, then my attempted refutation fails.

In explaining reductio ad absurdum, we have had to rely on another idea fundamental to logic, that of **contradiction,** or inconsistency. (We used this idea, remember, to define validity in Chapter 3. A deductive argument is valid if and only if affirming the premises and denying the conclusion results in a contradiction.) The opposite of contradiction is **consistency,** a notion of hardly less importance to good reasoning than validity. These concepts deserve a few words of further explanation and illustration. Consider this pair of assertions:

14. Abortion is homicide.
15. Racism is unfair.

No one would plausibly claim that we can infer or deduce 15 from 14, or, for that matter, 14 from 15. This almost goes without saying, because there is no evident connection between these two assertions. They are unrelated assertions; logically speaking, they are *independent* of each other. In such cases the two assertions are mutually *consistent;* that is, both could be true—or both could be false. But now consider another proposition:

16. Euthanasia is not murder.

Could a person assert 14 (*Abortion is homicide*) and also assert 16 (*Euthanasia is not murder*) and be consistent? This question is equivalent to asking whether one could assert the **conjunction** of these two propositions—namely,

17. Abortion is homicide, and euthanasia is not murder.

It is not so easy to say whether 17 is consistent or inconsistent. The kinds of moral scruples that might lead a person to assert one of these conjuncts (that is, one of the two initial propositions, *Abortion is homicide* and *Euthanasia is not murder*) might lead to the belief that the other one must be false and thus to the conclusion that 17 is inconsistent. (Notice that if 14 were the assertion that *Abortion is murder,* instead of *Abortion is homicide,* the problem of asserting consistently both 14 and 15 would be more acute.) Yet if we think again, we might imagine someone being convinced that there is no inconsistency in asserting that *Abortion is homicide,* say, and that *Euthanasia is not murder,* or even the reverse. (For instance, suppose you believed that the unborn deserve a chance to live and that putting elderly persons to death in a painless manner and with their consent confers a benefit on them.)

Let us generalize: We can say of any set of propositions that they are *consistent* if and only if *all could be true together.* (Notice that it follows from this definition that propositions that mutually imply each other, as do *Seabiscuit was America's's fastest racehorse* and *America's fastest racehorse was Seabiscuit.* Remember that, once again, the truth of the assertions in question does not matter. Two propositions can be consistent or not, quite apart from whether they are true. Not so with falsehood: It follows from our definition of consistency that an *inconsistent* proposition must be *false.* (We have relied on this idea in explaining how a reductio ad absurdum works.)

Assertions or claims that are not consistent can take either of two forms. Suppose you assert proposition 14, that abortion is homicide, early in an essay you are writing, but later you assert that

18. Abortion is harmless.

You have now asserted a position on abortion that is strictly contrary to the one with which you began; contrary in the sense that both assertions 14 and 18 cannot be true. It is simply not true that if an abortion involves killing a human being (which is what *homicide* strictly means), then it causes no one any harm (killing a person always causes harm— even if it is excusable, justifiable, not wrong, the best thing to do in the circumstances, and so on). Notice that although 14 and 18 cannot both be true, they can both be false. In fact, many people who are perplexed about the morality of abortion believe precisely this. They concede that abortion does harm the fetus, so 18 must be false; but they also believe that abortion doesn't kill a person, so 14 must also be false.

Or consider another, simpler case. If you describe the glass as half empty and I describe it as half full, both of us can be right; the two assertions are consistent, even though they sound vaguely incompatible. (This is the reason that disputing over whether the glass is half full or half empty has become the popular paradigm of a futile, purely *verbal disagreement.*) But if I describe the glass as half empty whereas you insist that it is two-thirds empty, then we have a real disagreement; your description and mine are strictly contrary, in that both cannot be true—although both can be false. (Both are false if the glass is only one-quarter full.)

This, by the way, enables us to define the difference between a pair of **contradictory** propositions and a pair of **contrary** propositions. Two propositions are contrary if and only if both cannot be true (though both can be false); two propositions are contradictory if and only if they are such that if one is true the other must be false, and vice versa. Thus, if Jack says that Alice Walker's *The Color Purple* is a better novel than Mark Twain's *Huckleberry Finn*, and Jill says, "No, *Huckleberry Finn* is better than *The Color Purple*," she is contradicting Jack. If what either one of them says is true, then what the other says must be false.

A more subtle case of contradiction arises when two or more of one's own beliefs implicitly contradict each other. We may find ourselves saying "Travel is broadening," and saying an hour later, "People don't really change." Just beneath the surface of these two beliefs lies a self-contradiction: How can travel broaden us unless it influences—and changes—our beliefs, values, and outlook? But if we can't really change ourselves, then traveling to new places won't change us, either. (Indeed, there is a Roman saying to the effect that travelers change the skies above them, not their hearts.) "Travel is broadening" and "People don't change" collide with each other; something has to give.

Our point, of course, is not that you must never say today something that contradicts something you said yesterday. Far from it; if you think you were mistaken yesterday, of course you will take a different position today. But what you want to avoid is what George Orwell called *doublethink* in his novel *1984*: "*Doublethink* means the power of holding two contradictory beliefs in one's mind simultaneously, and accepting them both."

Genuine contradiction, and not merely contrary assertion, is the situation we should expect to find in some disputes. Someone advances a thesis—such as the assertion in 14, *Abortion is homicide*—and someone else flatly contradicts it by the simple expedient of negating it, thus:

19. Abortion is not homicide.

If we can trust public opinion polls, many of us are not sure whether to agree with 14 or with 19. But we should agree that whichever is true, *both* cannot be true, and *both* cannot be false. The two assertions, between them, exclude all other possibilities; they pose a forced choice for our belief. (Again, we have met this idea, too, in a reductio ad absurdum.)

Now it is one thing for Jack and Jill in a dispute or argument to contradict each other. It is quite another matter for Jack to contradict himself. One wants (or should want) to avoid self-contradiction because of the embarrassing position in which one then finds oneself. Once I have contradicted myself, what are others to believe I really believe? What, indeed, *do* I believe, for that matter?

It may be, as Emerson observed, that a "foolish consistency is the hobgoblin of little minds"—that is, it may be shortsighted to purchase a consistency in one's beliefs at the expense of flying in the face of common sense. But making an effort to avoid a foolish inconsistency is the hallmark of serious thinking.

While we are speaking of inconsistency, we should spend a moment on **paradox.** The word refers to two different things:

- An assertion that is essentially self-contradictory and therefore cannot be true and
- A seemingly contradictory assertion that nevertheless may be true.

An example of the first might be, "Evaluations concerning quality in literature are all a matter of personal judgment, but Shakespeare is the world's greatest writer." It is hard to make any sense out of this assertion. Contrast it with a paradox of the second sort, a *seeming* contradiction that may make sense, such as "The longest way round is the shortest way home," or "Work is more fun than fun," or "The best way to find happiness is not to look for it." Here we have assertions that are striking because as soon as we hear them we realize that although they seem inconsistent and self-defeating, they contain (or may contain) profound truths. Paradoxes of this second sort are especially common in religious texts, where they may imply a mysterious reality concealed by a world of contradictory appearances. Examples are "Some who are last shall be first, and some who are first shall be last" (Jesus, quoted in Luke

13:30), and "Death, thou shalt die" (the poet John Donne, alluding to the idea that the person who has faith in Jesus dies to this world but lives eternally). If you use the word *paradox* in your own writing—for instance, to characterize an argument that you are reading—be sure that your reader will understand in which sense you are using the word. (And, of course, you will not want to write paradoxes of the first, self-contradictory sort.)

INDUCTION

Deduction involves logical thinking that applies to any assertion or claim whatever—because every possible statement, true or false, has its deductive logical consequences. Induction is relevant to one kind of assertion only; namely, to **empirical** or *factual* claims. Other kinds of assertions (such as definitions, mathematical equations, and moral or legal norms) simply are not the product of inductive reasoning and cannot serve as a basis for further inductive thinking.

And so, in studying the methods of induction, we are exploring tactics and strategies useful in gathering and then using **evidence**—empirical, observational, experimental—in support of a belief as its ground. Modern scientific knowledge is the product of these methods, and they differ somewhat from one science to another because they depend on the theories and technology appropriate to each of the sciences. Here, all we can do is discuss generally the more abstract features common to inductive inquiry generally. For fuller details, you must eventually consult your local physicist, chemist, geologist, or their colleagues and counterparts in other scientific fields.

Observation and Inference

Let us begin with a simple example. Suppose we have evidence (actually we don't, but that will not matter for our purposes) in support of the claim that

1. In a sample of 500 smokers, 230 persons observed have cardiovascular disease.

The basis for asserting 1—the evidence or ground—would be, presumably, straightforward physical examination of the 500 persons in the sample, one by one.

With this claim in hand, we can think of the purpose and methods of induction as being pointed in both of two opposite directions: toward establishing the basis or ground of the very empirical proposition with which we start (in this example the observation stated in 1) or toward understanding what that observation indicates or suggests as a more general, inclusive, or fundamental fact of nature.

In each case, we start from something we *do* know (or take for granted and treat as a sound starting point)—some fact of nature, perhaps a striking or commonplace event that we have observed and recorded—and then go on to something we do *not* fully know and perhaps cannot directly observe. In example 1, only the second of these two orientations is of any interest, and so let us concentrate exclusively on it. Let us also generously treat as a *method* of induction any regular pattern or style of nondeductive reasoning that we could use to support a claim such as that in 1.

Anyone truly interested in the observed fact that *230 of 500 smokers have cardiovascular disease* is likely to start speculating about, and thus be interested in finding out, whether any or all of several other propositions are also true. For example, one might wonder whether

2. *All* smokers have cardiovascular disease or will develop it during their lifetimes.

This claim is a straightforward generalization of the original observation as reported in claim 1. When we think inductively about the linkage between 1 and 2, we are reasoning from an observed sample (some smokers—that is, 230 of the 500 *observed*) to the entire membership of a more inclusive class (*all* smokers, whether observed or not). The fundamental question raised by reasoning from the narrower claim 1 to the broader claim 2 is whether we have any ground for believing that what is true of *some* members of a class is true of them *all*. So the difference between 1 and 2 is that of *quantity* or scope.

We can also think inductively about the *relation* between the factors mentioned in 1. Having observed data as reported in 1, we may be tempted to assert a different and profounder kind of claim:

3. Smoking *causes* cardiovascular disease.

Here our interest is not merely in generalizing from a sample to a whole class; it is the far more important one of *explaining* the observation with which we began in claim 1. Certainly the preferred, even if not the only, mode of explanation for a natural phenomenon is a *causal* explanation. In proposition 3, we propose to explain the presence of one phenomenon (cardiovascular disease) by the prior occurrence of an independent phenomenon (smoking). The observation reported in 1 is now being used as evidence or support for this new conjecture stated in 3.

Our original claim in 1 asserted no causal relation between anything and anything else; whatever the cause of cardiovascular disease may be, that cause is not observed, mentioned, or assumed in assertion 1. Similarly, the observation asserted in claim 1 is consistent with many explanations. For example, the explanation of 1 might not be 3, but some other, undetected, carcinogenic factor unrelated to smoking—for instance, exposure to high levels of radon. The question one now faces is what can be added to 1, or teased out of it, to produce an adequate ground for claiming 3. (We shall return to this example for closer scrutiny.)

But there is a third way to go beyond 1. Instead of a straightforward generalization, as we had in 2, or a pronouncement on the cause of a phenomenon, as in 3, we might have a somewhat more complex and cautious further claim in mind, such as this:

4. Smoking is a factor in the causation of cardiovascular disease in some persons.

This proposition, like 3, advances a claim about causation. But 4 is obviously a weaker claim than 3. That is, other observations, theories, or evidence that would require us to reject 3 might be consistent with 4; evidence that would support 4 could easily fail to be enough to support 3. Consequently, it is even possible that 4 is true although 3 is false, because 4 allows for other (unmentioned) factors in the causation of cardiovascular disease (genetic or dietary factors, for example) which may not be found in all smokers.

Propositions 2, 3, and 4 differ from proposition 1 in an important respect. We began by assuming that 1 states an empirical fact based on direct observation, whereas these others do not. Instead, they state empirical *hypotheses* or conjectures—tentative generalizations not fully confirmed—each of which goes beyond the observed facts asserted in 1. Each of 2, 3, and 4 can be regarded as an *inductive inference* from 1. We can also say that 2, 3, and 4 are hypotheses relative to 1, even if relative to some other starting point (such as all the information that scientists today really have about smoking and cardiovascular disease) they are not.

Probability

Another way of formulating the last point is to say that whereas proposition 1, a statement of observed fact (*230 out of 500 smokers have cardiovascular disease*), has a **probability** of 1.0—that is, it is absolutely certain—the probability of each of the hypotheses stated in 2, 3, and 4, *relative* to 1 is smaller than 1.0. (We need not worry here about how much smaller than 1.0 the probabilities are, nor about how to calculate these probabilities precisely.) Relative to some starting point other than 1, however, the probability of these same three hypotheses might be quite different. Of course, it still would not be 1.0, absolute certainty. But it takes only a moment's reflection to realize that, whatever may be the probability of 2 or 3 or 4 relative to 1, those probabilities in each case will be quite different relative to different information, such as this:

5. Ten persons observed in a sample of 500 smokers have cardio-vascular disease.

The idea that a *given proposition can have different probabilities* relative to different bases is fundamental to all inductive reasoning. It can be convincingly illustrated by the following example. Suppose we want to consider the probability of this proposition being true:

6. Susanne Smith will live to be eighty.

Taken as an abstract question of fact, we cannot even guess what the probability is with any assurance. But we can do better than guess; we can in fact even calculate the answer, if we are given some further information. Thus, suppose we are told that

7. Susanne Smith is seventy-nine.

Our original question then becomes one of determining the probability that 6 is true given 7; that is, relative to the evidence contained in proposition 7. No doubt, if Susanne Smith really is seventy-nine, then the probability that she will live to be eighty is greater than if we know only that

8. Susanne Smith is more than nine years old.

Obviously, a lot can happen to Susanne in the seventy years between nine and seventy-nine that is not very likely to happen to her in the one year between seventy-nine and eighty. And so, proposition 6 is more probable relative to proposition 7 than it is relative to proposition 8.

Let us disregard 7 and instead further suppose for the sake of the argument that the following is true:

9. Ninety percent of the women alive at seventy-nine live to be eighty.

Given this additional information, we now have a basis for answering our original question about proposition 6 with some precision. But suppose, in addition to 8, we are also told that

10. Susanne Smith is suffering from inoperable cancer.

and also that

11. The survival rate for women suffering from inoperable cancer is 0.6 years (that is, the average life span for women after a diagnosis of inoperable cancer is about seven months).

With this new information, the probability that 6 will be true has dropped significantly, all because we can now estimate the probability in relation to a new body of evidence.

The probability of an event, thus, is not a fixed number but one that varies because it is always relative to some evidence—and given different evidence, one and the same event can have different probabilities. In other words, the probability of any event is always relative to how much is known (assumed, believed), and because different persons may know different things about a given event, or the same person may know different things at different times, one and the same event can have two or more probabilities. This conclusion is not a paradox but a logical consequence of the concept of what it is for an event to have (that is, to be assigned) a probability.

If we shift to the *calculation* of probabilities, we find that generally we have two ways to calculate them. One way to proceed is by the method of **a priori** or **equal probabilities**—that is, by reference to the relevant possibilities taken abstractly and apart from any other information. Thus, in an election contest with only two candidates, Smith and Jones, each of the candidates has a fifty-fifty chance of winning (whereas in a three-candidate race, each candidate would have one chance in three of winning). Therefore, the probability that Smith will win is 0.5, and the probability that Jones will win is also 0.5. (The sum of the probabilities of all possible independent outcomes must always equal 1.0, which is obvious enough if you think about it.)

But in politics the probabilities are not reasonably calculated so abstractly. We know that many empirical factors affect the outcome of an election and that a calculation of probabilities in ignorance of those factors is likely to be drastically misleading. In our example of the two-candidate election, suppose Smith has strong party support and is the incumbent, whereas Jones represents a party long out of power and is further handicapped by being relatively unknown. No one who knows anything about electoral politics would give Jones the same chance of winning as Smith. The two events are not equiprobable in relation to all the information available.

Not only that, a given event can have more than one probability. This happens whenever we calculate a probability by relying on different bodies of data that report how often the event in question has been observed to happen. Probabilities calculated in this way are **relative frequencies.** Our earlier hypothetical example of Susanne Smith provides an illustration. If she is a smoker and we have observed that 100 out of a random set of 500 smokers are observed to have cardiovascular disease, we have a basis for claiming that she has a probability of 100 in 500, or 0.2 (one-fifth), of having this disease. However, if we had other data showing that 250 out of 500 women smokers aged eighty or older have cardiovascular disease, we have a basis for believing that there is a probability of 250 in 500, or 0.5 (one-half), that she has this disease. Notice, of course, that in both calculations we assume that Susanne Smith is not among the persons we have examined. In both cases we infer the probability with which she has this disease from observing its frequency in populations that exclude her.

Both methods of calculating probabilities are legitimate; in each case the calculation is relative to observed circumstances. But as the examples show, it is most reasonable to have recourse to the method of equiprobabilities only when few or no other factors affecting possible outcomes are known.

Mill's Methods

Let us return to our earlier discussion of smoking and cardiovascular disease and consider in greater detail the question of a causal connection between the two phenomena. We began thus:

1. In a sample of 500 smokers 230 persons observed have cardiovascular disease.

We regarded 1 as an observed fact, though in truth, of course, it is mere supposition. Our question now is, how might we augment this information so as to strengthen our confidence that

3. Smoking *causes* cardiovascular disease.

or at least

4. Smoking is a factor in the causation of cardiovascular disease in some persons.

Suppose further examination showed that

12. In the sample of 230 smokers with cardiovascular disease, no other suspected factor (such as genetic predisposition, lack of physical exercise, age over fifty) was also observed.

Such an observation would encourage us to believe 3 or 4 is true. Why? We are encouraged to believe it because we are inclined to believe also that whatever the cause of a phenomenon is, it must *always* be present when its effect is present. Thus, the inference from 1 to 3 or 4 is supported by 12, using **Mill's Method of Agreement,** named after the British philosopher, John Stuart Mill (1806–1873), who first formulated it. It is called a method of agreement because of the way in which the inference relies on *agreement* among the observed phenomena where a presumed cause is thought to be *present.*

Let us now suppose that in our search for evidence to support 3 or 4 we conduct additional research and discover that

13. In a sample of 500 nonsmokers, selected to be representative of both sexes, different ages, dietary habits, exercise patterns, and so on, none is observed to have cardiovascular disease.

This observation would further encourage us to believe that we had obtained significant additional confirmation of 3 or 4. Why? Because we now know that factors present (such as male sex, lack of exercise, family history of cardiovascular disease) in cases where the effect is absent (no cardiovascular disease observed) cannot be the cause. This is an example of **Mill's Method of Difference,** so called because the cause or causal factor of an effect must be *different* from whatever the factors are that are present when the effect is *absent.*

Suppose now that, increasingly confident we have found the cause of cardiovascular disease, we study our first sample of 230 smokers ill with the disease, and discover this:

14. Those who smoke two or more packs of cigarettes daily for ten or more years have cardiovascular disease either much younger or much more severely than those who smoke less.

This is an application of **Mill's Method of Concomitant Variation,** perhaps the most convincing of the three methods. Here we deal not merely with the presence of the conjectured cause (smoking) or the absence of the effect we are studying (cardiovascular disease), as we were previously, but with the more interesting and subtler matter of the *degree and regularity of the correlation* of the supposed cause and effect. According to the observations reported in 14, it strongly appears that the more we have of the "cause" (smoking), the sooner or the more intense the onset of the "effect" (cardiovascular disease).

Notice, however, what happens to our confirmation of 3 and 4 if, instead of the observation reported in 14, we had observed

15. In a representative sample of 500 nonsmokers, cardiovascular disease was observed in 34 cases.

(Let us not pause here to explain what makes a sample more or less representative of a population, although the representativeness of samples is vital to all statistical reasoning.) Such an observation would lead us almost immediately to suspect some other or additional causal factor: Smoking might indeed be *a* factor in causing cardiovascular disease, but it can hardly be *the* cause because (using Mill's Method of Difference) we cannot have the effect, as we do in the observed sample reported in 15, unless we also have the cause.

An observation such as the one in 15, however, is likely to lead us to think our hypothesis that *smoking causes cardiovascular disease* has been disconfirmed. But we have a fallback position ready; we can still defend a weaker hypothesis, namely 4, *Smoking is a factor in the causation of cardiovascular disease in some persons.* Even if 3 stumbles over the evidence in 15, 4 does not. It is still quite possible that smoking is a factor in causing this disease, even if it is not the *only* factor—and if it is, then 4 is true.

Confirmation, Mechanism, and Theory

Notice that in the discussion so far, we have spoken of the *confirmation* of a hypothesis, such as our causal claim in 4, but not of its *verification.* (Similarly, we have imagined very different evidence, such as that stated in 15, leading us to speak of the *dis*confirmation of 3, though not of its *falsi*fication.) Confirmation (getting some evidence for) is weaker than verification (getting sufficient evidence to regard as true); and our (imaginary) evidence so far in favor of 4 falls well short of conclusive support. Further research—the study of more representative or much larger samples, for example—might yield very different observations. It might lead us to conclude that although initial research had confirmed our hypothesis about smoking as the cause of cardiovascular disease, the additional information obtained subsequently disconfirmed the hypothesis. For most interesting hypotheses, both in detective stories and in modern science, there is both confirming and disconfirming evidence simultaneously. The challenge is to evaluate the hypothesis by considering such conflicting evidence.

As long as we confine our observations to *correlations* of the sort reported in our several (imaginary) observations, such as proposition 1, *230 smokers in a group of 500 have cardiovascular disease,* or 12, *230 smokers with the disease share no other suspected factors,* such as lack of exercise, any defense of a *causal* hypothesis such as claim 3, *Smoking causes cardiovascular disease,* or claim 4, *Smoking is a factor in causing the disease,* is not likely to convince the skeptic or lead those with beliefs alternative to 3 and 4 to abandon them and agree with us. Why is that?

It is because a causal hypothesis without any account of the *underlying mechanism* by means of which the (alleged) cause produces the effect will seem superficial. Only when we can specify in detail *how* the (alleged) cause produces the effect will the causal hypothesis be convincing.

In other cases, in which no mechanism can be found, we seek instead to embed the causal hypothesis in a larger *theory*, one that rules out as incompatible any causal hypothesis except the favored one. (That is, we appeal to the test of consistency and thereby bring deductive reasoning to bear on our problem.) Thus, perhaps we cannot specify any mechanism—any underlying structure that generates a regular sequence of events, one of which is the effect we are studying—to explain why, for example, the gravitational mass of a body causes it to attract other bodies. But we can embed this claim in a larger body of physical theory that rules out as inconsistent any alternative causal explanation. To do that convincingly in regard to any given causal hypothesis, as this example suggests, requires detailed knowledge of the current state of the relevant body of scientific theory, something far beyond our aim or need to consider in further detail here.

FALLACIES

The straight road on which sound reasoning proceeds gives little latitude for cruising about. Irrationality, carelessness, passionate attachment to one's unexamined beliefs, and the sheer complexity of some issues, not to mention original sin, occasionally spoil the reasoning of even the best of us. Although in this book we reprint many varied voices and arguments, we hope we have reprinted no readings that exhibit the most flagrant errors or commit the graver abuses against the canons of good reasoning. Nevertheless, an inventory of those abuses and their close examination can be an instructive (as well as an amusing) exercise—instructive because the diagnosis and repair of error helps to fix more clearly the principles of sound reasoning on which such remedial labors depend; amusing because we are so constituted that our perception of the nonsense of others can stimulate our mind, warm our heart, and give us comforting feelings of superiority.

The discussion that follows, then, is a quick tour through the twisting lanes, mudflats, forests, and quicksands of the faults that one sometimes encounters in reading arguments that stray from the highway of clear thinking.

We can and do apply the term *fallacy* to many types of errors, mistakes, and confusions in oral and written discourse, in which our reasoning has gone awry. For convenience, we can group the fallacies by referring to the six aspects of reasoning identified in the Toulmin Method, described earlier (p. 221). Let us take up first those fallacies that spoil our *claims* or our *grounds* for them. These are errors in the meaning, clarity, or sense of a sentence or of some word or phrase in a sentence being used in the role of a claim or ground. They are thus not so much errors of *reasoning* as they are errors in *reasons* or in the *claims* that our reasons are intended to support or criticize.

Many Questions

The old saw, "When did you stop beating your wife?" illustrates the **fallacy of many questions.** This question, as one can readily see, is unanswerable unless all three of its implicit presuppositions are true. The questioner presupposes that (1) the addressee has or had a wife, (2) he has beaten her, and (3) he has stopped beating her. If any of these presuppositions is false, then the question is pointless; it cannot be answered strictly and simply with a date.

Ambiguity

Near the center of the town of Concord, Massachusetts, is an empty field with a sign reading "Old Calf Pasture." Hmm. A pasture in former times in which calves grazed? A pasture now in use for old calves? An erstwhile pasture for old calves? These alternative readings arise because of **ambiguity;** brevity in the sign has produced a group of words that give rise to more than one possible interpretation, confusing the reader and (presumably) frustrating the sign writer's intentions.

Consider a more complex example. Suppose someone asserts *People have equal rights* and also *Everyone has a right to property.* Many people believe both these claims, but their combination involves an ambiguity. On one interpretation, the two claims entail that everyone has an *equal right* to property. (That is, you and I each have an equal right to whatever property we have.) But the two claims can also be interpreted to mean that everyone has a *right to equal property.* (That is, whatever property you have a right to, I have a right to the same, or at least equivalent, property.) The latter interpretation is radically revolutionary, whereas the former is not. Arguments over equal rights often involve this ambiguity.

Death by a Thousand Qualifications

In a letter of recommendation, sent in support of an applicant for a job on your newspaper, you find this sentence: "Young Smith was the best student I've ever taught in an English course." Pretty strong endorsement, you think, except that you do not know, because you have not been told, the letter writer is a very junior faculty member, has been teaching for only two years, is an instructor in the history department, taught a section of freshman English as a courtesy for a sick colleague, and had only eight students enrolled in the course. Thanks to these implicit qualifications, the letter writer did not lie or exaggerate in his praise; but the effect of his sentence on you, the unwitting reader, is quite misleading. The explicit claim in the letter, and its impact on you, is quite different from the tacitly qualified claim in the mind of the writer.

Death by a thousand qualifications gets its name from the ancient torture of death by a thousand small cuts. Thus, a bold assertion can be virtually killed, its true content reduced to nothing, bit by bit, as all the appropriate or necessary qualifications are added to it. Consider another example. Suppose you hear a politician describing another country (let's call it Ruritania so as not to offend anyone) as a "democracy" — except it turns out that Ruritania doesn't have regular elections, lacks a written constitution, has no independent judiciary, prohibits religious worship except of the state-designated deity, and so forth. So what is left of the original claim that Ruritania is a democracy is little or nothing. The qualifications have taken all the content out of the original description.

Oversimplification

"Poverty causes crime," "Taxation is unfair," "Truth is stranger than fiction" — these are examples of generalizations that exaggerate and therefore oversimplify the truth. Poverty as such can't be the sole cause of crime because many poor people do not break the law. Some taxes may be unfairly high, others unfairly low — but there is no reason to believe that *every* tax is unfair to all those who have to pay it. Some true stories do amaze us as much or more than some fictional stories, but the reverse is true, too. (In the language of the Toulmin Method, **oversimplification** is the result of a failure to use suitable modal qualifiers in formulating one's claims or grounds or backing.)

False Dichotomy

Sometimes oversimplification takes a more complex form, in which contrary possibilities are wrongly presented as though they were exhaustive and exclusive. "Either we get tough with drug users, or we must surrender and legalize all drugs." Really? What about doing neither and instead offering education and counseling, detoxification programs, and incentives to "Say no"? A favorite of debaters, **either/or** reasoning always runs the risk of ignoring a third (or fourth) possibility. Some disjunctions are indeed exhaustive: "Either we get tough with drug users, or we do not." This proposition, though vague (what does "get tough" really mean?), is a tautology; it cannot be false, and there is no third alternative. But most disjunctions do not express a pair of *contradictory* alternatives: They offer only a pair of *contrary* alternatives, and mere contraries do not exhaust the possibilities (recall our discussion of contraries versus contradictories on p. 241).

Hasty Generalization

From a logical point of view, **hasty generalization** is the precipitous move from true assertions about *one* or a *few* instances to dubious or even false assertions about *all*. For example, while it may be true, based on your personal experience, that the only native Hungarians you personally know do not speak English very well, that is no basis for asserting that Hungarians do not speak English very well. Or if the clothes you recently ordered by mail turn out not to fit very well, it doesn't follow that *all* mail-order clothes turn out to be too large or too small. A hasty generalization usually lies behind a **stereotype**—that is, a person or event treated as typical of a whole class. Thus, in 1914, after the German invasion of Belgium, during which some atrocities were committed by the invaders, the German troops were quickly stereotyped by the Allies as brutal savages who skewered helpless babies on their bayonets.

Equivocation

In a delightful passage in Lewis Carroll's *Through the Looking Glass*, the king asks his messenger, "Who did you pass on the road?" and the messenger replies, "Nobody." This prompts the king to observe, "Of course, Nobody walks slower than you," provoking the messenger's sullen response: "I do my best. I'm sure nobody walks much faster than I do." At this the king remarks with surprise, "He can't do that or else he'd have been here first!" (This, by the way, is the classic predecessor of the famous comic dialogue "Who's on First?" between the comedians Bud Abbott and Lou Costello.) The king and the messenger are equivocating on the term *nobody*. The messenger uses it in the normal way as an indefinite pronoun equivalent to "not anyone." But the king uses the word as though it were a proper noun, *Nobody,* the rather odd name of some person. No wonder the king and the messenger talk right past each other.

Equivocation (from the Latin for "equal voice"— that is, giving utterance to two meanings at the same time in one word or phrase) can ruin otherwise good reasoning, as in this example: *Euthanasia is a* *good death; one dies a good death when one dies peacefully in old age; therefore, euthanasia is dying peacefully in old age.* The etymology of *euthanasia* is literally "a good death," and so the first premise is true. And the second premise is certainly plausible. But the conclusion of this syllogism is false. Euthanasia cannot be defined as a peaceful death in one's old age, for two reasons. First, euthanasia requires the intervention of another person who kills someone (or lets the person die); second, even a very young person can be euthanized. The problem arises because "a good death" is used in the second premise in a manner that does not apply to euthanasia. Both meanings of "a good death" are legitimate, but when used together, they constitute an equivocation that spoils the argument.

The fallacy of equivocation takes us from the discussion of confusions in individual claims or grounds to the more troublesome fallacies that infect the linkages between the claims we make and the grounds (or reasons) for them. These are the fallacies that occur in statements that, following the vocabulary of the Toulmin Method, are called the *warrant* of reasoning. Each fallacy is an example of reasoning that involves a **non sequitur** (Latin for "It does not follow"). That is, the *claim* (the conclusion) does not follow from the *grounds* (the premises).

For a start, here is an obvious non sequitur: "He went to the movies on three consecutive nights, so he must love movies." Why doesn't the claim ("he must love movies") follow from the grounds ("He went to the movies on three consecutive nights")? Perhaps the person was just fulfilling an assignment in a film course (maybe he even hated movies so much that he had postponed three assignments to see films and now had to see them all in quick succession), or maybe he went with a girlfriend who was a movie buff, or maybe . . . —well, one can think of any number of other possible reasons.

Composition

Could an all-star team of professional basketball players beat the Boston Celtics in their heyday—say, the team of 1985 to 1986? Perhaps in one game or two, but probably not in seven out of a dozen games in a row. As students of the game know, teamwork is an indispensable part of outstanding performance, and the 1985 to 1986 Celtics were famous for their self-sacrificing style of play.

The **fallacy of composition** can be convincingly illustrated, therefore, in this argument: *A team of five NBA all-stars is the best team in basketball if each of the five players is the best at his position.* The fallacy is called composition because the reasoning commits the error of arguing from the true premise that each member of a group has a certain property to the not necessarily true conclusion that the group (the composition) itself has the property. (That is, because *A* is the best player at forward, *B* is the best center, and so on, therefore, the team of *A, B,* . . . is the best team.)

Division

In the Bible, we are told that the apostles of Jesus were twelve and that Matthew was an apostle. Does it follow that Matthew was twelve? No. To argue in this way from a property of a group to a property of a member of that group is to commit the **fallacy of division.** The example of the apostles may not be a very tempting instance of this error; here is a classic version that is a bit more interesting. If it is true that the average American family has 1.8 children, does it follow that your brother and sister-in-law are likely to have 1.8 children? If you think it does, you have committed the fallacy of division.

Poisoning the Well

During the 1970s some critics of the Equal Rights Amendment (ERA) argued against it by pointing out that Marx and Engels, in their *Communist Manifesto,* favored equality of women and men — and therefore the ERA was immoral, undesirable, and perhaps even a Communist plot. This kind of reasoning is an attempt to **poison the well;** that is, an attempt to shift attention from the merits of the argument — the validity of the reasoning, the truth of the claims — to the source or origin of the argument. Such criticism nicely deflects attention from the real issue; namely, whether the view in question is true and what the quality of evidence is in its support. The mere fact that Marx (or Hitler, for that matter) believed something does not show that the belief is false or immoral; just because some scoundrel believes the world is round, that is no reason for you to believe it is flat.

Ad Hominem

Closely allied to poisoning the well is another fallacy, **ad hominem** argument (from the Latin for "against the person"). A critic can easily yield to the temptation to attack an argument or theory by trying to impeach or undercut the credentials of its advocates.

Example: Jones is arguing that prayer should not be permitted in public schools, and Smith responds by pointing out that Jones has twice been convicted of assaulting members of the clergy. Jones's behavior doubtless is reprehensible, but the issue is not Jones, it is prayer in school, and what must be scrutinized is Jones's argument, not his police record or his character.

The Genetic Fallacy

Another member of the family of related fallacies that includes poisoning the well and ad hominem is the **genetic fallacy.** Here the error takes the form of arguing against some claim by pointing out that its origin (genesis) is tainted or that it was invented by someone deserving our contempt. Thus, one might attack the ideas of the Declaration of Independence by pointing out that its principal author, Thomas Jefferson, was a slaveholder. Assuming that it is not anachronistic and inappropriate to criticize a public figure of two centuries ago for practicing slavery, and conceding that slavery is morally outrageous, it is nonetheless fallacious to attack the ideas or even the sincerity of the Declaration by attempting to impeach the credentials of its author. Jefferson's moral faults do not by themselves falsify, make improbable, or constitute counterevidence to the truth or other merits of the claims made in his writings. At most, one's faults cast doubt on one's integrity or sincerity if one makes claims at odds with one's practice.

The genetic fallacy can take other forms less closely allied to ad hominem argument. For example, an opponent of the death penalty might argue,

> Capital punishment arose in barbarous times; but we claim to be civilized; therefore, we should discard this relic of the past.

Such reasoning shouldn't be persuasive because the question of the death penalty for our society must be decided by the degree to which it serves our purposes—justice and defense against crime, presumably—to which its historic origins are irrelevant. The practices of beer- and wine-making are as old as human civilization, but their origin in antiquity is no reason to outlaw them in our time. The curious circumstances in which something originates usually play no role whatever in its validity. Anyone who would argue that nothing good could possibly come from molds and fungi is refuted by Sir Alexander Fleming's discovery of penicillin in 1928.

Appeal to Authority

The example of Jefferson can be turned around to illustrate another fallacy. One might easily imagine someone from the South in 1860 defending the slave-owning society of that day by appealing to the fact that no less a person than Jefferson—a brilliant public figure, thinker, and leader by any measure—owned slaves. Or today one might defend capital punishment on the ground that Abraham Lincoln, surely one of the nation's greatest presidents, signed many death warrants during the Civil War, authorizing the execution of Union soldiers. No doubt the esteem in which such figures as Jefferson and Lincoln are deservedly held amounts to impressive endorsement for whatever acts and practices, policies and institutions, they supported. But the **authority** of these figures in itself is not *evidence* for the truth of their views, and so their authority cannot be a reason for anyone to agree with them. Obviously, Jefferson and Lincoln themselves could not support their beliefs by pointing to the fact that they held them. Because their own authority is no reason for them to believe what they believe, it is no reason for anyone else, either.

Sometimes the appeal to authority is fallacious because the authoritative person is not an expert on the issue in dispute. The fact that a high-energy physicist has won the Nobel Prize is no reason for attaching any special weight to her views on the causes of cancer, the reduction of traffic accidents, or the legalization of marijuana. On the other hand, one would be well advised to attend to her views on the advisability of ballistic missile-defense systems, for there may be a connection between the kind of research for which she received the prize and the defense research projects.

All of us depend heavily on the knowledge of various experts and authorities, and so we tend not to ignore their views. Conversely, we should resist the temptation to accord their views on diverse subjects the same respect that we grant them in the area of their expertise.

The Slippery Slope

One of the most familiar arguments against any type of government regulation is that if it is allowed, then it will be just the first step down the path that leads to ruinous interference, overregulation, and totalitarian control. Fairly often we encounter this mode of argument in the public debates over handgun control, the censorship of pornography, and physician-assisted suicide. The argument is called the **slippery slope argument** (or the **wedge argument,** from the way we use the thin end of a wedge to split solid things apart; it is also called, rather colorfully, "letting the camel's nose under the tent"). The fallacy here is in implying that the first step necessarily leads to the second, and so on down the slope to disaster, when in fact there is no necessary slide from the first step to the second. (Would handgun registration lead to a police state? Well, it hasn't in Switzerland.) Sometimes the argument takes the form of claiming that a seemingly innocent or even attractive principle that is being applied in a given case (censorship of pornography, to avoid promoting sexual violence) requires one for the sake of consistency to apply the same principle in other cases, only with absurd and catastrophic results (censorship of everything in print, to avoid hurting anyone's feelings).

Here's an extreme example of this fallacy in action:

Automobiles cause more deaths than handguns do. If you oppose handguns on the ground that doing so would save lives of the innocent, you'll soon find yourself wanting to outlaw the automobile.

Does opposition to handguns have this consequence? Not necessarily. Most people accept without dispute the right of society to regulate the operation of motor vehicles by requiring drivers to have a license, a greater restriction than many states impose on gun ownership. Besides, a gun is a lethal weapon designed to kill, whereas an automobile or truck is a vehicle designed for transportation. Private ownership and use in both cases entail risks of death to the innocent. But there is no inconsistency in a society's refusal to tolerate this risk in the case of guns and its willingness to do so in the case of automobiles.

Closely related to the slippery slope is what lawyers call a **parade of horrors,** an array of examples of terrible consequences that will or might follow if we travel down a certain path. A good example appears in Justice William Brennan's opinion for the Supreme Court in *Texas v. Johnson*, concerned with a Texas law against burning the American flag in political protest. If this law is allowed to stand, Brennan suggests, we may next find laws against burning the presidential seal, state flags, and the Constitution.

Appeal to Ignorance

In the controversy over the death penalty, the issues of deterrence and executing the innocent are bound to be raised. Because no one knows how many innocent persons have been convicted for murder and wrongfully executed, it is tempting for abolitionists to argue that the death penalty is too risky. It is equally tempting for the proponent of the death penalty to argue that since no one knows how many people have been deterred from murder by the threat of execution, we abolish it at our peril.

Each of these arguments suffers from the same flaw: the **fallacy of appeal to ignorance.** Each argument invites the audience to draw an inference from a premise that is unquestionably true—but what is that premise? It asserts that there is something "we don't know." But what we *don't* know cannot be *evidence* for (or against) anything. Our ignorance is no reason for believing anything, except perhaps that we ought to try to undertake an appropriate investigation in order to reduce our ignorance and replace it with reliable information.

Begging the Question

The argument we have just considered also illustrates another fallacy. From the fact that you live in a death-penalty state and were not murdered yesterday, we cannot infer that the death penalty was a deterrent. Yet it is tempting to make this inference, perhaps because—all unawares—we are relying on the **fallacy of begging the question.** If someone tacitly assumes from the start that the death penalty is an effective deterrent, then the fact that you weren't murdered yesterday certainly looks like evidence for the truth of that assumption. But it isn't, so long as there are competing but unexamined alternative explanations, as in this case. (The fallacy is called "begging the question," *petitio principii* in Latin, because the conclusion of the argument is hidden among its assumptions—and so the conclusion, not surprisingly, follows from the premises.)

Of course, the fact that you weren't murdered is *consistent* with the claim that the death penalty is an effective deterrent, just as someone else's being murdered is also consistent with that claim (for an effective deterrent need not be a *perfect* deterrent). In general, from the fact that two propositions are consistent with each other, we cannot infer that either is evidence for the other.

Note: The term "begging the question" is often wrongly used to mean "raises the question," as in "His action of burning the flag begs the question, What drove him to do such a thing?"

False Analogy

Argument by analogy, as we point out in Chapter 3 and as many of the selections in this book show, is a familiar and even indispensable mode of argument. But it can be treacherous because it runs the risk of the **fallacy of false analogy.** Unfortunately, we have no simple or foolproof way of distinguishing between the useful, legitimate analogies and the others. The key question to ask yourself is this: Do the two things put into analogy differ in any essential and relevant respect, or are they different only in unimportant and irrelevant aspects?

In a famous example from his discussion in support of suicide, philosopher David Hume rhetorically asked: "It would be no crime in me to divert the Nile or Danube from its course, were I able to effect such purposes. Where then is the crime of turning a few ounces of blood from their natural channel?" This is a striking analogy, except that it rests on a false assumption. No one has the right to divert the Nile or the Danube or any other major international watercourse; it would be a catastrophic crime to do so without the full consent of people living in the region, their government, and so forth. Therefore, arguing by analogy, one might well say that no one has the right to take his or her own life, either. Thus, Hume's own analogy can be used to argue against his thesis that suicide is no crime. But let us ignore the way in which his example can be turned against him. The analogy is a terrible one in any case. Isn't it obvious that the Nile, whatever its exact course, would continue to nourish Egypt and the Sudan, whereas the blood flowing out of someone's veins will soon leave that person dead? The fact that the blood is the same blood, whether in one's body or in a pool on the floor (just as the water of the Nile is the same body of water whatever path it follows to the sea) is, of course, irrelevant to the question of whether one has the right to commit suicide.

Let us look at a more complex example. During the 1960s, when the United States was convulsed over the purpose and scope of its military involvement in Southeast Asia, advocates of more vigorous U.S. military participation appealed to the so-called domino effect, supposedly inspired by a passing remark from President Eisenhower in the 1950s. The analogy refers to the way in which a row of standing dominoes will collapse, one after the other, if the first one is pushed. If Vietnam turns Communist, according to this analogy, so too will its neighbors, Laos and Cambodia, followed by Thailand and then Burma, until the whole region is as communist as China to the north. The domino analogy (or metaphor) provided, no doubt, a vivid illustration and effectively portrayed the worry of many anti-Communists. But did it really shed any light on the likely pattern of political and military developments in the region? The history of events there during the 1970s and 1980s did not bear out the domino analogy.

Post Hoc, Ergo Propter Hoc

One of the most tempting errors in reasoning is to ground a claim about causation on an observed temporal sequence; that is, to argue "after this, therefore because of this" (which is what the phrase **post hoc, ergo propter hoc** means in Latin). Nearly forty years ago, when the medical community first announced that smoking tobacco caused lung cancer, advocates for the tobacco industry replied that doctors were guilty of this fallacy.

These industry advocates argued that medical researchers had merely noticed that in some people, lung cancer developed *after* considerable smoking, indeed, years after; but (they insisted) this correlation was not at all the same as a causal relation between smoking and lung cancer. True enough. The claim that *A causes B* is not the same as the claim that *B* comes after *A*. After all, it was possible that smokers as a group had some other common trait and that this factor was the true cause of their cancer.

As the long controversy over the truth about the causation of lung cancer shows, to avoid the appearance of fallacious *post hoc* reasoning one needs to find some way to link the observed phenomena (the correlation of smoking and the onset of lung cancer). This step requires some further theory and preferably some experimental evidence for the exact sequence or physical mechanism, in full detail, of how ingestion of tobacco smoke is a crucial factor—and is not merely an accidental or happenstance prior event—in the subsequent development of the cancer.

Protecting the Hypothesis

In Chapter 3, we contrast *reasoning* and *rationalization* (or the finding of bad reasons for what one intends to believe anyway). Rationalization can take subtle forms, as the following example indicates. Suppose you're standing with a friend on the shore or on a pier, and you watch as a ship heads out to sea. As it reaches the horizon, it slowly disappears—first the hull, then the upper decks, and finally the tip of the mast. Because the ship (you both assume) isn't sinking, it occurs to you that you have in this sequence of observations convincing evidence that the earth's surface is curved. Nonsense, says your companion. Light waves sag, or bend down, over distances of a few miles, and so a flat surface (such as the ocean) can intercept them. Hence the ship, which appears to be going "over" the horizon, really isn't: It's just moving steadily farther and farther away in a straight line. Your friend, you discover to your amazement, is a card-carrying member of the Flat Earth Society (yes, there really is such an organization). Now most of us would regard the idea that light rays bend down in the manner required by the Flat Earther's argument as a rationalization whose sole purpose is to protect the flat-earth doctrine against counterevidence. We would be convinced it was a rationalization, and not a very good one at that, if the Flat Earther held to it despite a patient and thorough explanation from a physicist that showed modern optical theory to be quite incompatible with the view that light waves sag.

This example illustrates two important points about the *backing* of arguments. First, it is always possible to protect a hypothesis by abandoning adjacent or connected hypotheses; this is the tactic our Flat Earth friend has used. This maneuver is possible, however, only because—and this is the second point—whenever we test a hypothesis, we do so by taking for granted (usually quite unconsciously) many other hypotheses as well. So the evidence for the hypothesis we think we are confirming is impossible to separate entirely from the adequacy of the connected hypotheses. As long as we have no reason to doubt that light rays travel in straight lines (at least over distances of a few miles), our Flat Earth friend's argument is unconvincing. But once that hypothesis is itself put in doubt, the idea that looked at first to be a pathetic rationalization takes on an even more troublesome character.

There are, then, not one but two fallacies exposed by this example. The first and perhaps graver is in rigging your hypothesis so that *no matter what* observations are brought against it, you will count nothing as falsifying it. The second and subtler is in thinking that as you test one hypothesis, all of your other background beliefs are left safely to one side, immaculate and uninvolved. On the contrary, our beliefs form a corporate structure, intertwined and connected to each other with great complexity, and no one of them can ever be singled out for unique and isolated application, confirmation, or disconfirmation, to the world around us.

A CHECKLIST FOR EVALUATING AN ARGUMENT FROM A LOGICAL POINT OF VIEW

☐ Is the argument purely deductive, purely inductive, or a mixture of the two?

☐ If it is deductive, is it valid?

☐ If it is valid, are all its premises and assumptions true?

☐ If it is not valid, what fallacy does it commit?

☐ If it is not valid, are the claims at least consistent with each other?

☐ If it is not valid, can you think of additional plausible assumptions that would make it valid?

☐ If the argument is inductive, on what observations is it based?

☐ If the argument is inductive, how probable are its premises and its conclusion?

☐ In any case, can you think of evidence that would further confirm the conclusion? Disconfirm the conclusion?

See the companion Web site **bedfordstmartins.com/barnetbedau** for a series of brain teasers and links related to the logical point of view in argument.

10

A Psychologist's View:
Rogerian Argument

Carl R. Rogers (1902–1987), perhaps best known for his book entitled *On Becoming a Person* (1961), was a psychotherapist, not a teacher of writing. However, his short essay "Communication: Its Blocking and Facilitation" exerted much influence on instructors who teach argument. Written in the 1950s, this essay reflects the political climate of the cold war between the United States and the Soviet Union, which dominated headlines for more than forty years (1947–1989). Several of Rogers's examples of bias and frustrated communication allude to the tensions of that era.

On the surface, many arguments seem to show *A* arguing with *B*, presumably seeking to change *B*'s mind; but *A*'s argument is really directed not to *B* but to *C*. This attempt to persuade a nonparticipant is evident in the courtroom, where neither the prosecutor (*A*) nor the defense lawyer (*B*) is really trying to convince the opponent. Rather, both are trying to convince a third party, the jury (*C*). Prosecutors do not care whether they convince defense lawyers; they don't even mind infuriating defense lawyers because their only real goal is to convince the jury. Similarly, the writer of a letter to a newspaper, taking issue with an editorial, does not expect to change the paper's policy. Rather, the writer hopes to convince a third party, the reader of the newspaper.

But suppose *A* really does want to bring *B* around to *A*'s point of view. Suppose Mary really wants to persuade the teacher to allow her little lamb to stay in the classroom. Rogers points out that when we engage in an argument, if we feel our integrity or our identity is threatened, we will stiffen our position. (The teacher may feel that his or her dignity is compromised by the presence of the lamb and will scarcely attend to Mary's argument.) The sense of threat may be so great that we are unable to consider the alternative views being offered, and we therefore remain unpersuaded. Threatened, we may defend ourselves rather than our argument, and little communication takes place. Of course, a third party might say that we or our opponent presented the more convincing case, but we, and perhaps the opponent, have scarcely listened to each other, and so the two of us remain apart.

Rogers suggests, therefore, that a writer who wishes to communicate with someone (as opposed to convincing a third party) needs to reduce the threat. In a sense, the participants in the argument need to become partners rather than adversaries. Rogers writes, "Mutual communication tends to be pointed toward solving a problem rather than toward attacking a person or group." Thus, an essay on whether schools should test students for use of drugs, need not—and probably should not—see the issue as black or white, *either/or*. Such an essay might indicate that testing is undesirable because it may have bad effects, *but in some circumstances* it may be acceptable. This qualification does not mean that one must compromise. Thus, the essayist might argue that the potential danger to liberty is so great that no circumstances justify testing students for drugs. But even such an essayist should recognize the merit (however limited) of the opposition and should grant that the position being advanced itself entails great difficulties and dangers.

A writer who wishes to reduce the psychological threat to the opposition and thus facilitate the partnership in the study of some issue can do several things:

- One can show sympathetic understanding of the opposing argument,
- One can recognize what is valid in it, and
- One can recognize and demonstrate that those who take the other side are nonetheless persons of goodwill.

Advocates of Rogerian argument are likely to contrast it with Aristotelian argument, saying that the style of argument associated with Aristotle (384–322 B.C., Greek philosopher and rhetorician)

- Is adversarial, seeking to refute other views, and
- Sees the listener as wrong, someone who now must be overwhelmed by evidence.

In contrast to the confrontational Aristotelian style, which allegedly seeks to present an airtight case that compels belief, Rogerian argument (it is said)

- Is nonconfrontational, collegial, and friendly;
- Respects other views and allows for plural truths; and
- Seeks to achieve some degree of assent rather than convince utterly.

Thus a writer who takes Rogers seriously will, usually, in the first part of an argumentative essay

1. State the problem,
2. Give the opponent's position, and
3. Grant whatever validity the writer finds in that position — for instance, will recognize the circumstances in which the position would indeed be acceptable.

Next, the writer will, if possible,

4. Attempt to show how the opposing position will be improved if the writer's own position is accepted.

Sometimes, of course, the differing positions may be so far apart that no reconciliation can be proposed, in which case the writer will probably seek to show how the problem can best be solved by adopting the writer's own position.

A CHECKLIST FOR ANALYZING
ROGERIAN ARGUMENT

☐ Have I stated the problem and indicated that a dialogue is possible?

☐ Have I stated at least one other point of view in a way that would satisfy its proponents?

☐ Have I been courteous to those who hold views other than mine?

☐ Have I enlarged my own understanding to the extent that I can grant validity, at least in some circumstances, to at least some aspects of other positions?

☐ Have I stated my position and indicated the contexts in which I believe it is valid?

☐ Have I pointed out the ground that we share?

☐ Have I shown how other positions will be strengthened by accepting some aspects of my position?

See the companion Web site **bedfordstmartins.com/barnetbedau** for links related to Rogerian argument.

Index of Terms